Tricia Austin & Richard Doust

New Media
Design

Laurence King Publishing

Introduction

What is graphic design?   9
What is old media?   10
What is new media?   11
What is new-media graphic
   design?   21
The aim of this book   21
Summary   22

1

Starting Points

Historical overview   25
Graphic design and the impact
   of new media   33
Changing and emerging areas of
   practice   37
Summary   60

2

Designing for New Media

New-media design vocabularies
   and techniques   63
The design process   80
The creative process   85
Summary   89

3

The Internet Environment

From cyberspace to the real world   93
Routes into the labyrinth   100
Social space   102
Discovery and learning   107
e-learning   108
Intranets and extranets   110
Email   111
Digital broadcasting   112
Marketing and commerce online   113
Summary   116

4

Imaginary Worlds

Computer graphics: imaging real and unreal worlds   119
Simulation   123
The virtual graphic-design studio: the digital island   125
Multimedia   128
The digital effects industry   132
The computer games industry   137
Electronic and virtual worlds   145
Summary   146

5

Next Steps

Why choose new-media design?   149
The qualities you need to succeed   149
Working environments   151
Young, independent new-media design companies   153
Freelancing in new-media design   156
Workflow   159
Collaboration   160
Getting your first job   162
Telling the world about yourself and your work   164
What you need to know   169
Summary   178

• • •

Glossary 180
Further Reading 184
Websites 185
Index 187

LAURENCE KING

This book has been produced by
Central Saint Martins Book Creation
Southampton Row, London WC1B 4AP, UK

Laurence King Publishing Ltd
361–373 City Road, London EC1V 1LR
T +44 20 7841 6900
F +44 20 7841 6910
F enquiries@laurenceking.co.uk
www.laurenceking.co.uk

A catalogue record for this book is available from the
British Library.

ISBN-13:   978-1-85669-431-5
ISBN-10:   1-85669-431-3

Design by Richard Doust
Typeset in Bliss and Enigma
Editorial consultant: Alan Pipes

Printed in China

Introduction

Traditional Media

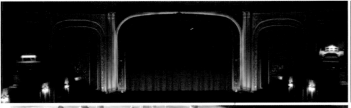

▲ *Top down:* Printed magazine display in a typical newsagent's shop. Traditionally printed books on a shelf. Cinema audience. Traditional chessboard game.

▶ *Top down: Vogue* magazine website, *Condé Nast*. Music download website, *Livewire*. Interactive TV controller, *Sky TV*. Computer game: *Black & White 2*. Computer-generated images at a theme park ride. Interactive museum installation by Rom and Son, Horniman Museum, London.

Introduction

What is graphic design?

Graphic design is the process by which textual and visual information – words and pictures – are arranged, given form and structure, to communicate a mood or a message in an aesthetically pleasing way. Graphic design is everywhere. How would you find your way around the subway system without signs and maps to orientate you? How would you be able to find what you are looking for on a website without a clear navigational system? How would you know which medicine to take without the labels on the bottles? How would you choose which book, CD or magazine to buy if there wasn't an attractive and informative cover that described what was inside? How would you recognize the beginning of your favourite TV programme if it weren't for the title sequence?

Graphic designers have made the numerous messages you encounter in the street, in the supermarket, in clubs or galleries, at home on television, on your computer, or in magazines, posters and books, more exciting and accessible. They use their skills and imagination in assembling text and images to communicate all the vital information you need in order to find your way around real and virtual space. Their work informs our decisions about what we buy, and even what we think we want. But it also goes deeper than that: graphic design enables us to imagine ourselves in stories, films and games. We even collect graphics: for example, the posters, CDs and old concert tickets that trigger some of our most cherished memories.

However, if you tell someone you are a graphic designer, more often than not they don't know what you mean. Graphic design is a booming profession globally, yet somehow it remains a mystery to many people. The reason why people might find graphic design unfathomable is that it takes so many different forms. The term includes typeface design (the design of letter forms); editorial design (the layout of books and magazines); the design of environmental signage (way-finding systems such as street signs); the design of posters; corporate-identity design (the design of logos, letterheads, websites, brochures that convey the brand values of a company); packaging design; information design (diagrams, charts, maps, manuals); advertisements; title sequences for television; music videos; characters and environments for computer games; interface design for websites and kiosks – stand-alone interactive touch-screen information displays found in museums, visitor centres, concert halls and theatres.

This book is about new media, but what exactly do we mean by old media?

▲ Without directions such as these road signs, we would find it very difficult to get around in unfamiliar and even in familiar locations.

▲ Some designers, such as Jeanne Verdoux who works in New York and France, combine illustration with typography.

What is old media?

While the focus of this book is on new media, it is useful to explore first what is meant by old media and its various characteristics. What we now call old media are those that were developed before computers and the Internet came into widespread use, namely print, film and television, with the allied skills of illustration, photography and graphic design. It is not a term widely used, except in contrast with so-called new media. Although computers are now ubiquitous and almost indispensable in all media, old and new, it is technically possible to create books, newspapers and magazines without them, although the skills and equipment needed are virtually obsolete. New media, as we shall see later, cannot exist without computers.

It is hard to believe when we hold an illustrated second-hand book from the 1960s in our hands that it was produced entirely with analogue technology, using either hot-metal or photographically produced type, cut-and-paste layout with designers employing scalpels and gum or wax, and printed by plates processed in baths of chemical solutions. It is also almost unbelievable now that early television went out live to air. For repeats, they got the actors in again and broadcast it live once more, just like a theatrical performance. When video recorders became available, tape was so expensive that many classic comedy and light entertainment programmes were quickly wiped and the tape reused.

The characteristics of old media

What are the fundamental differences between old and new media? Old media were analogue; new media are digital. Old media were sequential; new media are interactive. Old media were static; new media are dynamic.

What do we mean by analogue? On an old vinyl long-playing record, for example, the music is stored as a continuously variable spectrum of vibrations, as smooth waves cut into the grooves. On a digital CD, however, the music has been sampled into discrete chunks with each given a number. These are stored on the disc as bumps and pits, equivalent to the 1s and 0s of binary arithmetic, just like the bits (binary digits) that make a computer work. It may appear a crude method of representing the richness of sound, but the bumps are so tiny that our ears do not notice the transitions. And because the technology is digital, the numbers can be copied and manipulated endlessly with no loss of quality. Indeed, some early computers were analogue, adding together two voltages for example to create a sum, but digital won the day.

Old media mainly means print: books, newspapers, magazines, packaging, posters, and other publications, such as manuals, company brochures and point-of-sale displays. These are static linear media, meaning they impose a rigid pattern of reading – left to right, from top to bottom, start to finish. Of course, users can dip into a magazine, or consult an entry in a dictionary or encyclopedia, but by and large they perpetuate a narrative structure based on traditional storytelling techniques, i.e. with a beginning, middle and end. Traditional film, television, radio and animation also work the same way, presenting narratives in a linear fashion. The usefulness of old media is further limited by its physical size, need for storage and lack of portability.

What is new media?

By new media we mean: the Internet, computer games, CD-Roms and DVDs, interactive environments, in fact anything digital and moving; and in the future it will include things like electronic paper that can be updated automatically. It is the term used to describe the huge explosion of new entertainment and information systems developed in the past ten years, all made possible by developments in computing. In the early 1990s, you might have amused yourself by reading magazines, watching movies on video or playing computer games on your TV screen. Now the options have been vastly extended: for example, you can play games 'live' online with real people all over the world; create your own music by downloading samples and loops; use the remote control to change the camera angle of the picture on your interactive TV; take a ride in a virtual environment at a theme park or museum; tour representations of buildings that haven't yet been built; or fly through detailed 3D reconstructions of cities and even through immersive representations of the human body.

Interactivity is possibly the most novel and challenging aspect of new media. Compare fixed and static print, photography, radio, television or film to the dynamic responsive Internet or interactive exhibits, objects and environments.

▲ Interactive graphics in museums and visitor centres enable people to navigate their way around immense volumes of information, such as this interactive display from *Imagining the City*, Urbis, the museum of urban culture, Manchester, UK. The graphic designer no longer simply interprets the brief set by the client. The interactive possibilities within the digital medium itself have become the focus of interest. *Land Design Studio*

▼ *Imagining the City* is a sensory table interface that instantly transforms into an overhead projected city. *Image: Nick Wood*

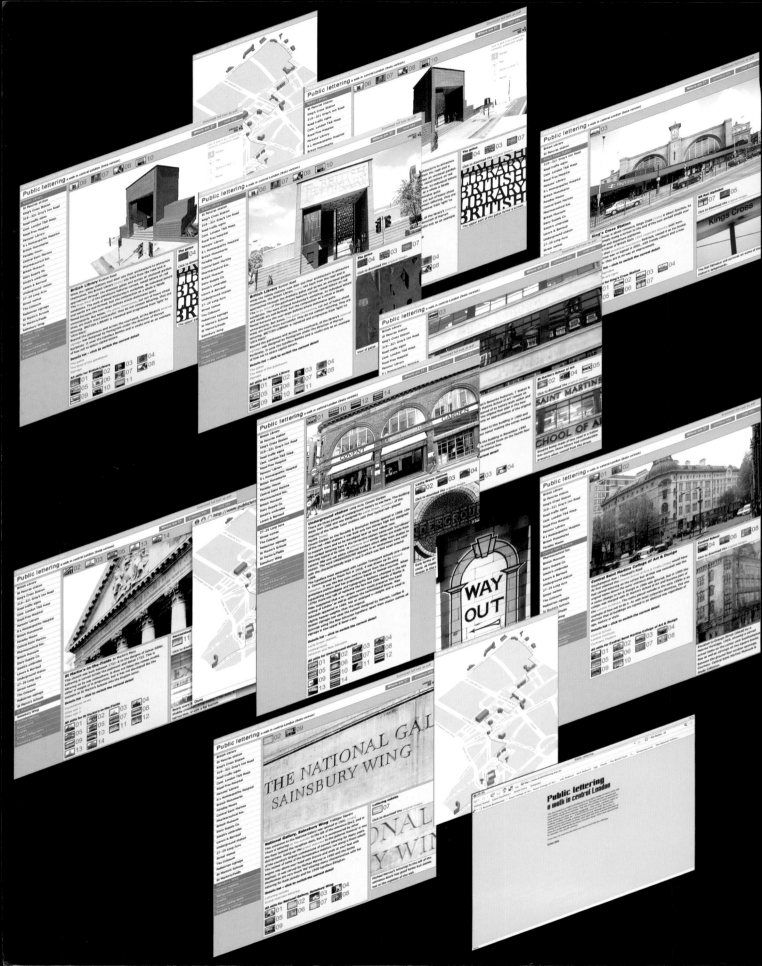

◄ *Public Lettering a walk in central London* was devised by Phil Baines for graphic design students at Central Saint Martin's School of Art and Design, London. The route maps the locations of interesting lettering on buildings and the webpages show details in close-up. Sample screens from the website show how hyperlinks allow virtual visitors to choose their own direction as they investigate the examples of public lettering with the click of a mouse. Some museums and galleries have websites and CDRoms that provide access to their collections for study, or to enhance a visit. *www.publiclettering.org.uk Content: Phil Baines and Catherine Dixon. Design and Development: Matt Hyde, Jack Schulze and George Agnelli.*© *Phil Baines.*

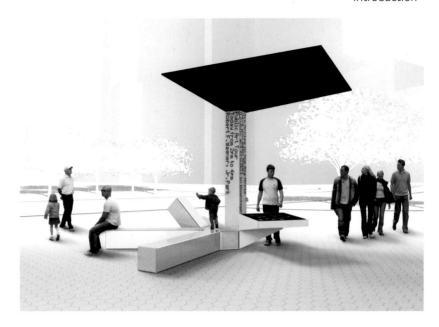

We, the audience, absorb and reflect on the content of traditional media as passive observers. Interactive environments, on the other hand, require that we choose, change and create our own journey through the images, films, texts and games. On the Internet you can input your own material and converse with the computer or, through the computer, with other people. This has brought about the most profound change in the way in which graphic designers must think if they are working in new media. They are now asked not only to make us notice, read, smile or remember a message; they also have to enable us to act. Interactivity has opened up new roles, new ways of thinking, new products and new business opportunities for graphic designers.

The media is constantly changing, as are the ways in which new media can be experienced. Digital TV has become more interactive with on-demand movies and a choice of sports to watch, say when athletics meetings are on. With ever-larger TV screens and projection systems, and their convergence with ever-cheaper desktop or portable computers and hard-disc PVRs (personal video recorders), it doesn't take a futurologist to predict that we will soon have millions of high-definition TV channels available to watch on either machine, in real time, or to watch again. Games machines too are becoming more versatile and portable with Sony's PlayStation Portable (PSP) joining Nintendo's Game Boy. Portable media players, such as Apple's iPod, not only play MP3s, but videos too. Cell phones take digital photos and short films. How long before we have all-in-one devices with constant access to the Internet and GPS (Global Positioning System) satellites?

In addition, the ways we communicate and interact with other people are also evolving: from SMS (Short Message Service) text, photo and video messaging by mobile phone to email, instant messenger, chatrooms, forums, video conferencing and photo sharing via a desktop or portable computer. You can see and talk to

▲ Antenna Design, Civic Exchange, Van Alen Institute, New York, 2005. Winning proposal for a public interactive information installation. Antenna used computer rendering and inserted photographic images of real people to create the look and feel of the installation in its setting.

family and friends more quickly or directly than before via webcam and Voice Over Internet Protocol (VoIP) telephony, at little or no cost. You can acquire and distribute information easily: for example, you can make your own homepage or weblog, create music and artwork and distribute it to your friends and family or across the globe, or you can search online for bargain flights or colleges where you might want to study.

The products of the computer revolution surround us: large screens on buildings and in stores, rows of desktop machines in offices, personal computers at home, laptops, hand-held PDAs (Personal Digital Assistants) and mobile phones with added functionality. These are just the visible periphery of a vast network of cables that run underground, overland and underwater, broadcasting through wireless hotspots, and extend around the planet via communications satellites. But new-media communications systems do not rely only on physical and broadcast networks; they also depend on the matrix of individuals, communities, businesses and government organizations that own, develop or use the systems. Graphic designers have a vital part to play in the success of new-media communications enterprises. They contribute to the content and also the design and usability of the interfaces we see on the screen.

The worlds of design, film, music, theatre, fine art, photography and architecture used to be considered as distinct and separate forms of communication or media until the computer enabled us to roll them into one. However, it should be stressed that 'new media' is not simply the old media combined in new ways, so-called multimedia: it has its own distinctive characteristics, and offers its own unique set of advantages and constraints.

The characteristics of new media

As stated earlier, new media could not exist without the computer. In a world without computers, we could happily produce books, magazines and newspapers, films and TV, but it wouldn't be easy. What defines new media is that it is digital, as opposed to the analogue technologies of old media. Digital technologies work by converting whatever you feed into them, for example, a sound, a string of text or a photo, into units of binary code (zeros and ones). Everything is stored in numerical form. So a photograph is stored as a series of bits and bytes in the computer memory. A bit (binary digit) is the basic unit (value 0 or 1); a byte is a bundle of bits, normally eight bits. When instructed, the computer reconstitutes the photograph on screen. Images, sounds, etc., are all stored as numbers or chains of numbers and are described as data.

Why is reducing all media to units in numerical form useful? Digital information stored as numbers can be replicated with no loss of quality, unlike analogue information that degrades each time it is copied. A copy of a digital photo will be identical to the original (unless some 'lossy' compression method such as JPEG is used where a degree of data and therefore quality may be lost). Furthermore, digital data can be changed or manipulated by numerical formulae called

▲ Times Square, New York City – a multimedia riot of display screens clamouring for the attention of locals and tourists by day and night.

The binary system: bits and bytes – how computers interpret text and images

"That's one small step for a man, one giant leap for mankind."

Neil Armstrong, Apollo 11 July 20th 1969

▲ The computer sees photographs in the same way that it sees any other information, as a series of 0s and 1s. Shown here: Buzz Aldrin on the Moon. © *NASA*

▲ The binary code representing the words broadcast to Earth by Neil Armstrong as he stepped onto the Moon's surface. Each string of instructions and letters is represented by eight 'bits' forming a 'byte'.

A photograph or piece of text is just another set of electronic code to the computer, which stores and manipulates all data and information – text, pictures, sounds – as numbers. Computers use the binary system, which contains only zeros and ones, each known as a 'bit', and represented in the computer by alternate 'off' or 'on' electrical states – 0 is off and 1 is on. By stringing both together, the computer can express any number as a sequence of electrical pulses that is sent to an interpreter which in turn instructs a computer programme to display the information in a readable form.

'Before new media the job of a graphic designer was contents of a book, a poster, a magazine spread, etc designer now has to create not only graphic identity and other structures which will be used by the clien becomes interface designer.' **Lev Manovich**. Lev Manovich is a new-media artist and University of California, San Diego.

'Users of real-time online interactive media are muc they access than in any other medium. Here, the rela defined in paper communications, turns into an imp content and contexts onto each other. Designers of their consumers hungry for guidance and substance and expertise in orchestrating human response, from commanders.' **Max Bruinsma**. Max Bruinsma is a critic and author of *Deep Sites: Intelligent Innovation in Cc*

'The advent of new media is a double-edged sword fe graphics, sound, music and interfaces has empowere we were previously denied access to. These new tool need in order to achieve excellence in such multi-dis work in areas that were traditionally our exclusive d has emerged, and everything is up for grabs; a fluid n partner of Airside, the award-winning London-based design group with a distinctive body of work in digital media and music.

'You can be a graphic designer without ever touching e-designer without knowing the language of graphic used to convey messages in both print and digital m but, so far, the ends, if not the means, are the same.

(Allworth Press, 2001). He is chair of the graduate design programme at the School of Visual Arts, New York, and art director *of the*

ind the best form for fixed information: the
h new media, design becomes "meta-design." The
also information architecture, navigation system,
put in any information. In short, graphic designer

of *The Language of New Media* (MIT Press, 2001). He is associate professor in the visual arts department,

ore active participants in establishing the content
ship between sender and receiver, so unilaterally
ed dialogue between two parties who project
media who fail to recognize this will leave
igners, in short, must deepen their knowledge of
understanding that they are participants, not

Vebdesign (Thames & Hudson, 2003).

e graphic designer. The ability to create motion
igners and enabled us to explore new mediums that
ve in turn expanded the range of skills that we now
ned projects, as well as giving others the tools to
n, such as type and layout. A creative melting pot
is the essential requirement!' **Fred Deakin**. Fred Deakin is founding

xel in virtual space. But you cannot be an
ign. In the final analysis, the fundamental tools
are type and image. The result is often different,
re they?' **Steven Heller**. Steven Heller is the author of *The Education of an E-Designer*

nes *Book Review*.

algorithms. You can alter colour, scale, position, quality of light, etc., without having to repeat lengthy photo shoots or spending hours in the darkroom. This saves time if you are a graphic designer, but computers can do more than save you time – they also offer you new ways of creating work. You can shift and modify the words and images endlessly in a page-layout program but, even more magically, you can also use other programs to make them move and enable the viewer, visitor or 'user' to interact with the material. Graphic designers in new media often work in close collaboration with software developers and programmers, and may perhaps learn some programming themselves, but most commercial programs make it simple to manipulate images, text, video and sound stored in the computer (and known as 'assets' in the industry) to create new and wonderful designs.

Storing everything in numerical or digitized form not only allows you to manipulate material, it also enables you to combine separate units of media together: for example, moving images, sound and text. Different elements may all appear together on the same screen to create a whole but, because they are stored separately, each element can be modified even after it has been combined with others. Applications, such as Adobe Photoshop, have been designed to place material on different virtual layers, like the acetate overlays in old media, which means you can change details in a particular layer without altering or destroying other layers in the process. This allows image and colour management in print and on screen. It also gives you an extraordinary flexibility, permitting you to combine image, text, movement and sound in a greater variety of ways than ever before, in order to get your message across. And if you lose your way, there is always an 'Undo' button to take you back to when things were working well.

Images, text, movements and sounds can be stored as data in categories or 'fields' within databases. The different fields are not stored in any particular order. Data is organized according to the rules you, or the programmer, define. For example, database-driven websites such as eBay or Amazon create new pages tailored to users' commands or questions. The images, text, video and sound are called up from the database on command and flow into an invisible grid or template on the screen to create a customized page. The page you see is not stored as a page; it is constructed 'on the fly' and will cease to exist as a page when you click away. This process would be impossible in old media print or film, but it is possible to imagine a future magazine, say, made from e-paper being compiled according to each user's stated preferences.

People use databases in all sorts of different ways. Databases enable individuals to perform practical tasks such as booking tickets, or buying and selling online. Businesses and governments use databases to store and access records, and analyse performance. Designers and art directors often use databases to trigger new ideas by, for example, browsing image banks to get concepts for magazine covers or film title sequences.

Computers also present new opportunities because of their capacity to store and retrieve information in greater quantities and at higher speeds than our human brains, so the potential for searching, selecting and combining information has expanded beyond our wildest dreams. The huge increase in the circulation of information through networked systems has created new challenges for graphic designers by inventing ways for people to search and navigate the sea of data and access information stored in databases. This means new-media designers have to organize and classify information into bundles of content that can be signposted in a clear and user-friendly way. Some designers specialize in information architecture, structuring information (knowledge or data) to map out the number of layers and links in a website for example; others work with specialists in interface design, designing icons, menu bars and navigation systems.

Designers have to take into account the kinds of anxieties people might have as they encounter and begin to search unknown networks and databases. People often fear getting lost or feel stupid because they can't find the information they think is there. Designers need to understand how to build users' confidence and enable them to achieve their goals. In his book *Emotional Design: Why We Love (or Hate) Everyday Things* (Basic Books, 2004), Donald A. Norman argues that the appearance of, the pleasure of use of and the way we think about objects and interfaces has a strong effect on our emotions. This in turn affects our ability to use objects and interfaces. This means that to be successful a design shouldn't just be functional, but also appealing and memorable.

Another very important and unique characteristic of new media is the hyperlink. The principle here is that data inside the computer network can be connected and accessed in any order at any time, as long as they have been tied together by a tag, which pinpoints exactly where every bit of information is held. You don't need to start at the beginning of a text and read to the end; you can jump from one website to another by clicking on linked words. This has made it possible to mimic on screen the way the brain works, by association and not necessarily 'logically', moving from one web page to another at the click of the mouse.

Hyperlinks also allow you to choose your own path through material, enabling you to cut through the mountains of information out there in a fast and effective way. This is a very different experience from reading novels. You cannot leap from one book to another at the press of a key. Although in the past some attempts have been made to design non-sequential books, with different outcomes and endings depending on the reader's choice, in print you are more subject to the sequence and structure determined by the author and designer. To some designers, hyperlinks can be a challenge – they don't want users to leave their site as soon as they arrive without looking at all the other content, so may confine all links on a 'Links' page, or make exterior links appear in a new window.

The computer screen is merely a window into the computer database. An architect, for example, using a computer-aided design program could work on a skyscraper at full size, something not possible manually. Computers can build scalable forms.

▲ Navigation should create flows through a website, allowing users to find their way to the information they need easily and naturally, and reducing the anxiety of getting lost. Finding one's way back can be just as important as finding one's way through.

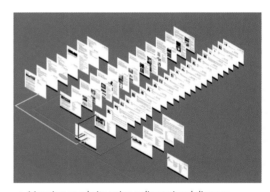

▲ Mapping a website using a dimensional diagram shows how 'pages' of information stack up like cards behind the 'homepage'. Such mapping makes it easier to see how the main navigation links, represented by coloured lines, connect the content in a logical order, and how deep each part of the site is.

IMAGE.jpg

▲ Computer images can be scaled, from the icons representing the files on your computer desktop and the small screen of a mobile phone, to computer displays and giant digital billboards. There are different formats in between and larger ones that conform to resolutions and standards for different devices.

So an image can be viewed as a small thumbnail, as a desktop image on different-sized screens, or it can be projected at the size of a cinema screen or even bigger. In addition, the computer enables you to make changes, add on elements and expand the original work. For example, you can build a simple text-based website and, at a later stage, incorporate additional pages, include video and add an interactive chatroom. As pioneering new media designer April Greiman says: 'The paint never dries', which means that new media (unless published as a DVD) can always be altered and improved, a fact that has implications in how new designers are paid, as we shall see later.

Websites, games, databases, interactive environments and software – are often described as 'dynamic' because of their ability to be extended or updated: in other words, to change. This gives rise to a novel characteristic. New-media entities are never finished. They are never complete in the way that a book is published and distributed as a finished object. This presents problems for the traditional ways of gathering, naming, identifying and authenticating new-media products, but it also presents new opportunities for exchange and distribution. These issues are further discussed in Chapter Three.

Computers allow you to sample, manipulate and combine material. They have other advantages too. The fact that computers can be linked together in networks, in particular the Internet, means you can communicate instantly in what is termed 'real time', which is in some ways similar to 'live' television broadcasts. In old media, the printing and distribution process means that newspapers and books are finally published anything from a few hours to a full year after they have been written. Now, with new media, there is a whole new, almost instantaneous time frame available to the designer.

What is new-media graphic design?

People often make one of two false assumptions about graphic design for new media. Some think of graphics as superficial and meaningless – flashy visuals added to the front end of a website to dazzle and distract you. Others think of graphic design for new media as simply the mechanistic process of cutting and pasting images and text into predetermined templates. Those in the business know that successful new-media graphic design is not about being flashy or conforming to templates. It's about understanding, organizing and interpreting content to find ways to make information accessible and meaningful to other people. It's about communicating and therefore requires an understanding of the audience, the technology and the goals of the organization you are working for. All these factors play a part in translating a message into a captivating experience, using an array of communication forms.

The variety of options and routes within the graphic design profession has been vastly expanded by the impact of new media. The widespread use of computers in the communications and entertainment industries has opened up new opportunities. For example, illustrators who might traditionally have created images for book jackets or magazine articles can now go into web animation, music videos or games design. They may work with sound design or post-production for film and television. Some argue that graphic or communication design, as it is sometimes called, is undergoing such a radical transformation that entirely new forms of communication are emerging which will need new definitions.

The aim of this book

This book is for those interested in a career in new-media graphic design – school-leavers, design students, practitioners in the industry wishing to broaden their practice and pursue new opportunities, and those who teach or advise people entering careers in new-media graphic design. It sets out to highlight the personal qualities and skills needed to enter this area of practice. It aims to capture the flavour and excitement of working in the field while also acting as a practical reference guide and learning resource.

This book does not set out to offer an exhaustive guide to new technologies or simply to present a series of snapshots of the latest websites and new-media installations. It provides a broad overview of the history, practice and debates of a profession in transition. It describes how traditional graphic design skills are being transformed and combined with other design disciplines through digital media. It explains how the graphic designer and the image-maker are taking advantage of digital media to create new design vocabularies, seeking new roles and new career opportunities. It is a guide to the spectrum of opportunities created by a young and inventive industry, using new technologies to communicate with audiences around the world in new ways.

Summary

Chapter One outlines the historical background of new media, from Gutenberg's invention of movable-type printing to the evolution of computers and the development of the World Wide Web. It defines new-media terms and Internet jargon and looks at changing and emerging areas of practice: web design, computer games, illustration and animation, motion graphics, information visualization, photography, experience design and music graphics.

Chapter Two addresses the key concepts and attributes behind new media that make it so compelling, including navigation, movement and narrative, and the crucial areas of accessibility and usability. Here we examine new-media design vocabularies and techniques and explore how the design process works, outlining the roles and processes involved in the design of commercial websites.

Chapter Three focuses on one specific but vitally important sector of new media – the Internet. It examines the Internet as an information space, a social space and a commercial space. It covers search engines, online communities, net art, weblogs, wikis, pornography, e-learning, and the astonishing growth of e-commerce and online shopping. It argues that the Internet demands a whole new approach to design thinking because it is a fluid, unstable and interactive medium, very different in nature from print.

Chapter Four takes us into the uncharted territory of virtual worlds and explores the work of the new-media designer in shaping imagined universes that exist only in virtual space. It starts with a history of the development of computer imaging, from simulation to the emergence of digital effects for film and television. It gives an overview of computer games, and considers the amazing domain of avatars, computer-generated cyberbeings who act as your representatives online, your friends or adversaries. Finally, it examines the concept of artificial life – imagined creatures or systems that exist only in cyberspace.

If all this excites you, how do you become part of the new-media workforce? **Chapter Five** describes the nitty-gritty of the work environment, how to find your first job, whether it be with a large corporation or a small practice, and embark on making a career in the field. It tells you what to expect in terms of workflow, collaboration and the working experience, and lists the personal qualities you need to succeed.

At the end of the book you will find a glossary of terms, a list of websites, and further reading as a spur to further investigation.

Starting Points 1

Print Graphics

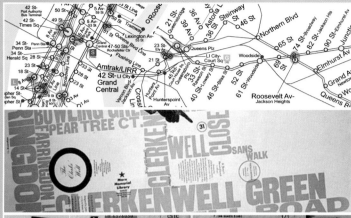

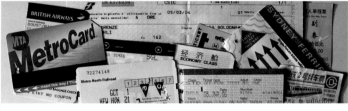

New-Media Graphics

▲ *Top down*: Manhattan Subway map, New York. Typographic map of Clerkenwell, London, *Alan Kitching*. Tickets for travel, events and purchases. Logotypes and symbols: Westinghouse, *Paul Rand*; Shell 1948; London Underground, *reproduced with kind permission of Transport for London*, and UPS, *Paul Rand © 2005 United Parcel Service*.

▶ *Top down*: eBay website, *eBay*. Television channel identity for BBC2, *BDH and BBC*. Animation, *Bunnies Studio Soi*. Video Jockeys in a music club environment, *The Light Surgeons*. Title sequence for a television drama, *BDH and BBC*. Scenes from *Myst*, the computer game, *Cyan Inc*.

This chapter sets out a historical context for new media and describes the fundamentals behind it: from Gutenberg's invention of movable-type printing in the Middle Ages, through the birth of photography and the camera-ready print revolution of the 1960s, to the proliferation of computers and development of the World Wide Web in the 1990s, without which web design, console games and virtual environments could not even be imagined. The opening up of the media, from the so-called 'old media' of print, film and television to the ever expanding applications of new media have provided enormous and exciting opportunities to the graphic designer, who can now not only add sound, movement and interactivity to their once static sequential designs, but are also facing fresh challenges as new technologies emerge and new possibilities for work present themselves. However, first we must travel back in time to find out how we got here and learn something about the sometimes mystifying terminology that is still in common use.

Historical overview

From the invention of movable type in the 1440s by Johann Gutenberg (1400–1468) until the mid-nineteenth century, the print process was dominated by text. There was a clear hierarchy of roles: the writer crystallized his or her thoughts; the printer/publisher gave the words form on the printed page through the layout and choice of typeface; and finally, the illustrator supplied images to shed light on the ideas expressed through the words.

Typefaces, the different styles of printed letter forms, evolved slowly from the fifteenth century until the early nineteenth century, when printers began producing a large variety by experimenting with proportion, geometry and symmetry. It was also during that era of rapid industrialization and invention that new print-based products emerged: for example, the magazine format, the poster and the design of packaging. Images were increasingly used with the printed word to inform or instruct readers, identify people and places, or to promote products and events.

Many of the words we use in new media have their origins in 'old media' print technology. 'Font', for example, a word we now use for different type designs (see box Type Terms), was once spelt 'fount' and makes reference to the foundry where hot-metal type was cast in moulds. The terms 'uppercase' and 'lowercase' come from the wooden cases loose type was kept in, with capitals on the upper level and small letters below. 'Leading', the spacing between lines, is named after the thin strips of

Type Terms

A **font** is a complete set in one size of all the letters of the alphabet, complete with associated ligatures (joined letters such as fi and fl), numerals, punctuation marks, and any other signs and symbols. In the days of hot metal, there were slightly different designs for different sizes; today they are usually scaled up and down from one master.

Typeface, often shortened to **face**, is the name given to the design of the alphabet and its associated marks and symbols. Every typeface has a name: after its designer, e.g. Garamond; the name of the publication it was originally designed for, e.g. Times New Roman; or a fanciful name intended to convey the 'feel' of the face, e.g. Futura.

A **type family** is a set of fonts related to the basic roman typeface that may include italic and bold plus a whole spectrum of different 'weights'. These range from ultra light to ultra bold. It includes different widths, ranging from ultra condensed to ultra expanded. It also includes typefaces that are related to one another. For example, the type family Century consists of typefaces such as Century Nova, Century Old Style and Century Schoolbook.

PostScript is a resolution-independent language, allowing type (and page layouts) to be output at the highest resolution possible from a PostScript-compatible printer. EPS (Encapsulated PostScript) is a vector image format, the usual output of Adobe Illustrator, for example.

Type anatomy
- Baseline: an imaginary line on which the capital and lowercase letters sit.
- Median: the imaginary line that defines the x-height.
- Cap height: the height of capital letterforms.
- x-height: the height of the lowercase 'x'.
- k-p distance: the distance from the top of a 'k' to the bottom of a 'p'.
- Uppercase: capital letterforms.
- Lowercase: small letterforms, not capitals.
- Small capitals: capitals the height of lowercase letters.
- Ascender characters: lowercase letterforms with ascenders (strokes rising above the main body of the letters).
- Descender characters: lowercase letterforms with descenders (strokes extending below the main body of the letters).
- Stroke: a line that defines the basic letterform.
- Sans serif: a typeface that does not have the small embellishments called 'serifs' at the end of strokes.

Typographic measurement
Letterforms were originally cast from lead, and the body of the type (the surface on which the letterform stood) was measured to determine the size. The unit used for the measurement of letterforms is the 'point'. The spacing between the lines of letters is referred to as leading (pronounced 'ledding'), because it was originally made by inserting strips of lead; it is also measured in points. A point is the equivalent of $1/72$ of an inch (0.35mm). Font size and leading are written as follows when specifying type: 10/12 Helvetica, meaning 10pt (point) Helvetica with 12pt leading.

apex
crossbar
serif

arm
beak

ascender
bowl

barb
spine

bracket
stem

cross stroke
finial

crotch
vertex

descender

dot

ear
link
loop

flag
terminal

leg

ligature

sans serif

shoulder

spur

stress

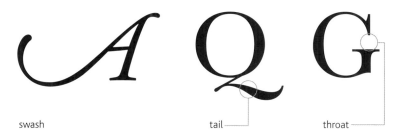

swash

tail

throat

counter

Type Design and Typography

Jeremy Tankard's passion is to create, manufacture and market high-quality digital type, designing new typefaces and offering a typographic design service tailored to meet clients' individual requirements.

Since graduating from Central Saint Martins and the Royal College of Art, he has gained a worldwide reputation for the high quality and unique character of his typefaces. He initially worked with major consultancies, advising on and creating some of the identities of the best-known international brand names before setting up Jeremy Tankard Typography in 1998.

Type Design

Digital type requires hours of careful attention in its design and construction. Some types are commissioned for specific purposes but most start with a spark of inspiration, which when developed with modern technology creates a product that is superior to pre-digital type.

Ideas are developed in a sketchbook, an approach that, although appearing dated, allows the designer greater freedom when modelling and focusing on the required image in the early stages.

Digitization

Digitization is a continuous process, which starts with putting the initial sketches onto the computer screen and then creating the correct form for each letter, by constantly making the required changes, right up to final typeface production. This method is far removed from the original hand-cut process, but it requires just as much attention to detail.

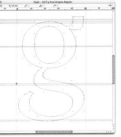

▶ Designing typefaces is a long process. Each character in a font set needs careful individual attention – a lot of work when you consider that there can be hundreds of glyphs in a single font. The number of glyphs increases with each addition to a font family. Illustrated here is the window in which the digital typographer constructs the individual characters that make up a font.

Hinting

Inconsistencies in the type image can occur at low resolutions. Hinting removes these visual errors by forcing the computer to restrict itself to a number of pixels at certain sizes, thus making the type look correct at low resolutions. If there was no hinting, type could look uneven and unbalanced to the eye.

Kerning

Kerning is the way in which the 'fit' of characters is controlled, especially those that are problematic. It is not only the letters that may require kerning – punctuation is often overlooked, as are accented characters. Careful kerning results in a more even colour to the overall type image which, in turn, improves readability.

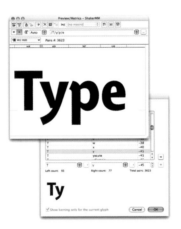

Testing

All elements of type design are continually tested. Attention is paid to consistency in weight and width as well as functionality. Exhaustive tests are also carried out to check that the fonts work across both Windows and Mac platforms.

Usage

It is reassuring for designers to know that the typeface they have purchased has been created not only to help them create fine work, but also that it has been manufactured to the very best standard possible with current technology.

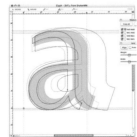

▲ Jeremy Tankard markets his typefaces online through an elegant website: www.typography.net. The entire transaction, including paying and downloading the font files, can be done remotely.

lead that were once used for that purpose. Type, whether in print or on websites, is still measured in 'points' (¹/₇₂ of an inch) and 'ems' (the width of a capital M). A new media designer may not need to know about old media print production, but a working knowledge of typography and typographic terms will never be wasted.

With the dawn of the twentieth century, it was time for the fussiness and clutter of Victorian design to be thrown out in favour of a new cleaner look, called modernism. Clarity and legibility were promoted by graphic designers such as Herbert Bayer (1900–1985) of the German Bauhaus art school and Jan Tschichold (1902–1974) whose influential book *Die Neue Typographie* ('The New Typography') was a manifesto of modernist design, in which he condemned all fonts but sans-serif. He also favoured non-centred design and advocated the use of standardized paper sizes. His work led to the Swiss Style, developed in the 1950s, which emphasized cleanliness, readability and objectivity, using grids and sans-serif fonts such as Univers and Helvetica. Play, irreverence and chance interested the Dadaists, a cultural movement that began in neutral Zürich, Switzerland, during World War I and peaked from 1916 to 1920. German Dadaist John Heartfield (1891–1968) developed photomontage to create powerful political posters satirizing Adolf Hitler and the Nazis. As a result of World War II, many European designers fled to the UK and USA, taking the modernist message with them.

The term graphic design had been coined by the US book and type designer William Addison Dwiggins in 1922. The new profession of art director – the person who oversees the design of magazines or advertisements had been recognized in 1920, when the Art Directors Club of New York was founded, but as yet there was no job title of graphic designer. The art director controlled the overall concept for the look and feel of a page and commissioned others to do the illustrations, photographs and layout. By the 1950s art directors had established the importance of teams of 'commercial artists' in advertising and corporate identity design.

The 1950s and 1960s were the era of mass media, when television and cinema challenged the power of the press. Graphic designers such as Saul Bass (1920–1996) broke new ground by designing title sequences for films by Alfred Hitchcock and Otto Preminger, among others. New print technologies such as photo-lithography replaced hot metal and sought to appropriate some of the visual power of television and cinema by its increasing use of photography – layout was confined only by what could be cut and pasted and put under the process camera. Graphic designers began to cross over into television advertisements and title sequences for film and television. Pop culture emerged from the synergy of the music, graphics, film and fashion industries. In the light of these changes the term 'graphic designer' was more widely adopted in the 1960s and 1970s, replacing the term 'commercial artist'.

▲ A typical design studio before computers were widely adopted. Most design was manually created with pre-digital tools and involved a great many skills.

Meanwhile an entirely new form of media was in its infancy – the Internet – although it would be many years before it would appear on the radar of the graphic designer. Back in 1945, Vannevar Bush (1890–1974) was a chief scientific adviser in

Franklin Roosevelt's wartime US government, and proposed a solution to what he considered the most important challenge of the day: the increasing amount of information that needed to be accessed by scientists, researchers and politicians. In an essay entitled 'As We May Think', he described a machine called Memex that could gather, store and access information. Although Bush's machine remained only a concept, it had a profound influence on the evolution of the personal computer and the Internet. In wartime England, Alan Turing (1912–1954) had worked on code-breaking machines and in 1947 he moved to the University of Manchester to work, largely on software, for the Manchester Mark I which was then emerging as one of the world's earliest stored-program computers. It led to the Ferranti Mark I, the second commercially available general-purpose computer (the first one being the German Z4), with the first machine delivered in February 1951, just beating the US UNIVAC I. Also among the Mark I team were mathematicians Conway Berners-Lee and Mary Lee Woods, who would later marry; their son, Tim Berners-Lee, is acknowledged as the inventor of the World Wide Web.

In the early 1960s, inspired by Bush, Douglas Englebart formed the Augmented Research Centre (ARC) at Stanford University in California. Englebart and his colleagues transformed computers from specialized pieces of equipment that only trained scientists and technicians could use into networked systems that almost anyone could operate. User-friendly devices, such as the mouse, windows, electronic mail and teleconferencing, were among the inventions for the 'augmentation of the human intellect' developed at ARC. In 1963, Ted Nelson coined the terms 'hypertext' and 'hypermedia' to describe a new media format that harnessed the power of the computer to link texts, pictures, animations and sound, and allowed users to choose the order in which they accessed information by interacting with the system.

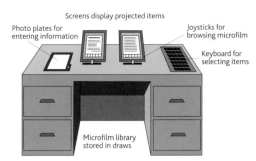

Screens display projected items

Photo plates for entering information

Joysticks for browsing microfilm

Keyboard for selecting items

Microfilm library stored in draws

▲ 'A memex is a device in which an individual stores all his books, records, and communications, and which is mechanized so that it may be consulted with exceeding speed and flexibility. It is an enlarged intimate supplement to his memory.' This is how Vannevar Bush described his invention.

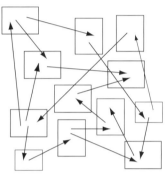

▲ An illustration of how hypertext works, adapted from Ted Nelson's 'Ordinary Hypertext' diagram in his book *Literary Machines* (1982), in which the author describes Xanadu, the original hypertext system.

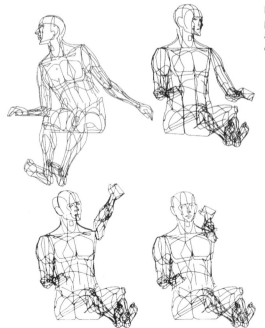

◄ In 1960, the term 'computer graphics' was coined by William A. Fetter. He used it to describe the process of visualizing cockpit designs for Boeing aircraft. In 1963, Fetter created the First Man, a digital human for cockpit testing.

▲ Ivan Sutherland, also at MIT, produced Sketchpad in 1963, the first interactive computer-graphics system.

▲ In 1962, the first video game, SpaceWar, was created by Steve Russell at the Massachusetts Institute of Technology (MIT). SpaceWar used a screen to display duelling spaceships operated by two players using a keyboard.

Internet jargon

- **Internet**: the worldwide, decentralized, publicly accessible system of computer networks that move data by packet switching using TCP/IP (Transmission Control Protocol/Internet Protocol). It is the infrastructure that carries email and the World Wide Web.
- **Internet 2.0**: (or Web 2.0) refers to a supposed second generation of Internet-based services that let people collaborate and share information online through social networking sites, such as MySpace and Flickr, and wikis, websites that allow users to add, remove or edit content.
- **World Wide Web**: a global, read/write information space, in which web pages, containing text, graphics and other resources, are identified by URLs (Uniform Resource Locators).
- **Browser**: software that enables a user to display and interact with text, images, and other data located on a web page at a website on the World Wide Web or a local area network (intranet).
- **Client server**: a network architecture in which the client (such as your browser) sends requests to the server (the computer on which the website you wish to access lives).
- **Search engine**: a program to help find information stored on the World Wide Web by typing in keywords.
- **Rich media content**: term used to describe interactive digital media, such as Flash and QuickTime, which exhibit dynamic motion, using video, audio and animation. They normally require an additional plug-in to the standard browser.
- **Blog**: short for weblog, a personal online journal, containing text, images and links.
- **Podcast**: from iPod and broadcast, a method of distributing audio or video (vidcasting) files, over the Internet using RSS (Really Simple Syndication) format, for playback on mobile devices, such as iPods, and personal computers.
- **CSS (Cascading Style Sheets)**: a method for separating a web page's content (written in HTML or XML markup language) from its presentation and layout (written in CSS).
- **FTP (File Transfer Protocol)**: a protocol for exchanging files over any network that supports the TCP/IP protocol. Commonly used to upload webpages and transfer large files between users.

With these developments in new technology, computer graphics started mainly at research centres in universities, where the possibilities for using computers to display more than just statistics and numerical information on punched cards were being investigated by mathematicians and scientists. Artists soon became involved as the need to visualize the extraordinary potential of this emerging digital world started to be recognized.

Real-world applications for computer graphics quickly became a viable alternative to the traditional methods of production in television, film and print. A wonderland of multimedia experiences was just opening up, combining books, magazines, television, film, radio, music, games, the telephone and computers. Early experiments in computer graphics seem crude by today's standards. Computers didn't even have displays back then and output was to pen plotters (or dot-matrix printers) – animations were made by plotting onto acetate cells and then filmed using a stop-frame 16mm camera. When displays did become available, their screens were green on black, and any input was by keyboard.

In 1970, the Xerox Corporation gathered together a team of world-class researchers

▼ One of the first computer-generated films was produced by Edward Zajac at Bell Labs in 1963. He used it to demonstrate how a satellite would face the Earth during orbit. *Reprinted with permission of Alcatel-Lucent*

to form Xerox PARC (Palo Alto Research Center) in California. Their mission was to create 'the architecture of information'. Many of the technologies we take for granted today were created at Xerox PARC – networked personal computers, email, word-processing and laser-printing. In 1972, Alan Kay formed the Learning Research Group at Xerox PARC and oversaw the most crucial development so far in human–computer interactivity: the Graphical User Interface (GUI). By manipulating graphical icons on their white on black computer screens with a mouse, users were able to interact with ideas in real time using familiar representations of objects that they recognized from their real desktops. There was no longer any need to learn lines of computer code. The GUI made computer graphics part of the working environment; the computer screen displayed images and typefaces exactly as they would be printed, prompting the term 'WYSIWYG' (what you see is what you get) to enter the language of digital communications.

Kay's research led him to the belief that hypermedia, or 'dynamic media' as he called it, would provide the radical interactivity that would form the character of future multimedia communications. Kay also recognized the potential for computers to replace books, so he designed a prototype for the first portable personal computer, the Dynabook. This was capable of combining text, pictures, moving images and sound in a creative, dynamic and responsive way. In 1971, Kay is famously quoted as having said: 'The best way to predict the future is to invent it!'

The culmination of this work was the Alto, a workstation developed for internal use at Xerox. They marketed the GUI on its Star workstation, but it was expensive and ahead of its time and Xerox was more interested in selling photocopiers. Others, however, were quick to see its potential. In 1983, Apple Computer launched the Lisa with a GUI based on the Star; and in 1984 Apple launched the first true

'The best way to predict the future is to invent it!' Alan Kay

▲ The Dynabook, Alan Kay's prototype for a portable computer.

▲ The Alto Star, 1981, showing the graphical user interface; WYSIWYG screen display, keyboard and point-and-click mouse: the desktop metaphor that defines the personal computer today. Xerox produced the first system that allowed users to create and share complex documents by combining computing, text editing and graphics, and access networks around the world using simple point-and-click actions.

▶ The Apple Macintosh with its desktop metaphor and WYSIWYG interface. Although Xerox did not market the GUI, others were quick to see its potential. In 1984, Apple launched 'the computer for the rest of us' with a TV advertisement based on George Orwell's book *1984*. The 'Mac' was quickly adopted by graphic-design professionals because it ran programs like MacPaint and MacDraw which allowed users to paint and draw directly into the computer.

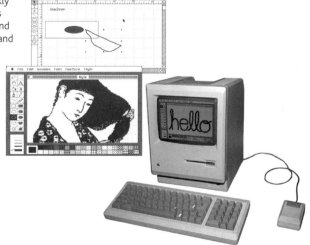

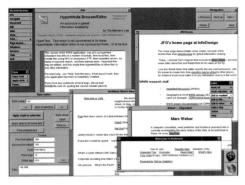

▲ Tim Berners-Lee's first web browser, 1990.

Macintosh computer, and presented it as the first affordable 'desktop' personal computer with the ability to display on its screen what would be printed on the page. Apple shipped the 'Mac' with a mouse and software that supported word-processing (MacWrite) and painting (MacPaint), though only in black and white. Drawing was added later. In 1985, the combination of the Mac, Apple's LaserWriter printer, and Mac-specific software such as Aldus PageMaker (which evolved into Adobe InDesign) enabled users to design, preview and print page layouts complete with text and graphics, an activity that became known as desktop publishing. Although the IBM 5150 PC was launched in 1981, it didn't get its rudimentary Windows GUI until November 1985 as an add-on to MS-DOS. Microsoft Windows version 3.0, released in 1990, was the first version to achieve broad commercial success, and has been playing catch-up with Apple ever since.

In 1980, Tim Berners-Lee, a British independent contractor working at CERN (Conseil Européen pour la Recherche Nucléaire), also known as the European Organization for Nuclear Research in Switzerland, proposed a networked system that would enable the storing, sharing and updating of information by hyperlinking researchers' documents at CERN. He had the idea of bringing hypertext and the Internet together and in 1990 he created the first web-browser software. A year later he began distributing the World Wide Web, a rich, open hypermedia environment, to research scientists. The software was free for anyone

New Media Terms

- **Pixel**: short for picture element, the dot that makes up the representation of a picture in a computer's memory or on the screen.
- **Screen resolution**: the number of pixels horizontally by the number of lines vertically, i.e. 1680 × 1050. A 5.2 Mmegapixel digital camera can produce an image with a resolution of 2560 × 2048 at 72dpi (dots per inch) – 72dpi is also called screen resolution, the image resolution required for websites.
- **Print resolution**: images for print publication need to be 300dpi (dots per inch) or higher, depending on the target printer's halftone screen measurement in lpi (lines per inch). The rule of thumb is that the resolution should be 1.5 to 2 times the lpi of the target output device.
- **Vector graphics**: software such as Adobe Illustrator stores images as mathematical equations (PostScript) and are thus resolution independent, being rasterized (converted to bitmaps) before output.
- **Bitmap graphics**: or raster graphics, in software such as Adobe Photoshop, images are stored bit for bit with the image displayed on a screen. The colour quality of a raster image is determined by the number of bits that are allocated per pixel.
- **Page layout programs**: QuarkXpress and Adobe InDesign are drag-and-drop WYSIWYG page layout programs that input text and images as objects and outputs a complete print-ready document as a PostScript file.
- **Font creation programs**: FontLab and Fontographer (now owned by FontLab) are software applications for designing complete fonts using Bézier curves, similar to a vector graphics program.
- **Colour space**: print uses CMYK (cyan, magenta, yellow and key, or black), a subtractive colour model; computer screens use RGB (red, green, blue), an additive scheme. RGB has a bigger and slightly different gamut (more colours) to CMYK, so converting from RGB to CMYK can result in a disappointing colour match.

to use. Marc Andreessen of the National Center for Supercomputing Applications designed and programmed Mosaic in 1993, a breakthrough graphical Internet browser that could display text and pictures. Widely distributed, Mosaic was once described as the 'killer application' of the 1990s because it provided a multimedia graphical user interface at a time when access to the Internet and personal computers was expanding rapidly.

Early computer systems for graphic design in the 1970s and 1980s were very expensive and mostly in the hands of printers and reprographic (repro) houses. They automated some of the graphic designer's decisions about typography and layout, but designers were generally excluded from the loop. Since new media became a possibility in the 1990s, the era of convergence and connectivity, the graphic designer has been able to exploit the extra dimensions offered by digital technologies. Affordable computers have made it easier to combine text, pictures, moving images and sound. The new-media designer can now draw more on narrative and dramatic expression to unfold messages on screen and, in addition, engage the audience through interaction design.

Graphic design and the impact of new media

The digital revolution really hit the profession in the mid-1980s when the first computers began to appear in graphic-design studios. A magical new tool had arrived that not only enabled text and other elements to be positioned quickly and accurately, but also allowed the designer to visualize and make changes to a layout before it was fixed in place. Graphic designers could input text without involving a typesetter and make large or small alterations without having to rework cut and paste layouts (mechanicals) glued to boards. Output from a laser printer was always pristine.

▲ Airside design studio. Today there is an abundance of computers in the working environment.

In the 1980s the first personal computers were only able to display and print 'bitmapped' letterforms, which were made up from 'pixels' or picture elements; the 72dpi (dots per inch) of the computer-screen display and dot-matrix printer gave very limited resolution, and bitmap typefaces appeared rough and were often displayed with jagged edges. The graphic designer Zuzana Licko exploited these limitations with her Emigre font designs for the Apple Macintosh computer. At the same time, Adobe Systems were developing a 'page description language' called PostScript, which could output typeset-quality text and graphics, and in 1985 the Apple LaserWriter was the first desktop printer to ship with Postscript software. The Macintosh computer and the LaserWriter, along with software called Aldus (later Adobe) PageMaker, sparked off the desktop publishing revolution whereby the traditional activities of the typesetting trade and the designer's studio merged.

▼ Dorling Kindersley's CD-Rom *Nature 2*, 1997, rolled text, illustration, video and sound into one screen. Dorling Kindersley were among the first traditional book publishers to seriously adopt the interactivity offered by the emerging CD-Rom technology. *Dorling Kindersley*

Graphic designers trained in print-based traditions inevitably began by thinking of the screen as a page: in other words, as a flat, two-dimensional rectangle with edges within which all the content should be fixed. Over time, however, designers started to think of the screen as a window into a virtual space beyond, extending in all

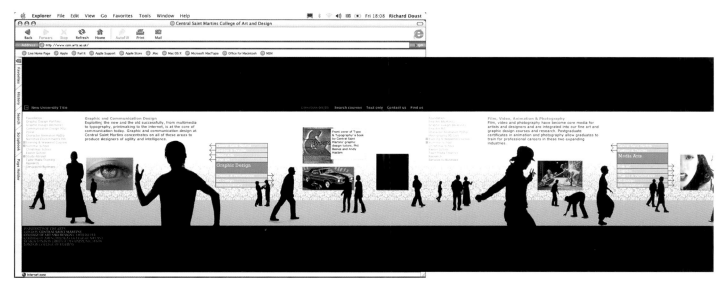

▲ The Central Saint Martins website was designed in 2001 by Jannuzzi Smith as a panoramic landscape that extends beyond the edge of the screen. Visitors scroll along the landscape using their home screen as a frame.

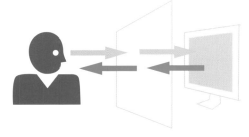

▲ Human-Computer Interface (HCI) is the term to describe the interaction between the user and the computer. It is illustrated in this diagram, which shows an imaginary plane between the user and the computer where the interaction takes place, usually by means of the use of an input device such as a mouse or keyboard.

directions. That same space could contain audio, text, moving-image photography, video and animation. Moreover, there is no fixed sequence of information as in, say, a printed magazine, which has a cover, followed by a contents page and then the various sections of the publication, with the small-ads section traditionally at the back. Graphic designers used to working in print had to begin by unlearning all the conventions about how a publication needed to be structured if they were to move into web design. Hyperlinks opened a door to a new way of organizing information. This was a radical shift, and an exciting challenge to many members of that generation of graphic designers.

Designers working in new media were persuaded to leave the page metaphor behind and envisage the network of information beyond the screen and how they could build structures to store and link information. They began thinking about ways of engaging the 'user' and looking into the ideas about the Human–Computer Interface (HCI) that were emerging from research centres across the world. HCI is the study of interaction between people (users) and computers. This interaction takes place at the user interface (or simply interface) and involves both software (the GUI) and hardware (the mouse or graphics tablet).

The Macintosh, as we saw earlier, implemented many of the HCI ideas from Xerox PARC, and because the Macintosh was a lot cheaper than the turnkey (or package) systems around in 1985, many graphic designers saw the potential of working in a new way and quickly adopted it as the new design tool. This completely changed the practice of designing for print. Since that time, desktop publishing has all but taken the traditional processes of preparation for print production out of the hands of specialists (such as typesetters and reprographics bureaux, or repro houses), who were a highly skilled bridge between the designer and printer, and placed the emphasis on sophisticated software and the responsibility for production onto the designer's desktop. These added demands required graphic designers to equip themselves with levels of technical and practical skills well beyond those of previous generations, but also gave them unprecedented access to and control over the entire design-to-print process.

Since 1995, the widespread use of the Internet has added yet another dimension to publishing. This period in time is often referred to as 'the second information revolution', the first being the invention of printing from movable type by Gutenberg over 500 years earlier. Some greeted the Internet with caution; others were thrilled by the access it afforded to a huge new global audience and its potential as a platform for their work. Graphic design is rooted in the mass production and circulation of messages. Suddenly computers seemed to simplify and accelerate that part of the process beyond all boundaries.

At the same time it became clear that digital work was more fragile and in many ways less reliable than its paper-based equivalent: electronic signals lack material substance; the screen image itself is unstable, changing dimensions on different machines. Typographers realized that the refined letter shapes or typefaces that had evolved over the 500-year history of print lost their crisp definition on screen. However, the challenge with any medium is to turn its characteristics into advantages. As such, typeface designers began to find that they could use the computer to come up with a huge variety of computer-friendly typefaces formed from outlines and shapes that suited both the computer display and high-resolution print. Some typeface designers explored the potential of computing by using code to generate typefaces that moved in sync with sound.

▲ Toshio Iwai used computing to translate the sound of the piano into slithers of light that streamed upwards from the instrument as the pianist played.

Another very exciting realization was that computers enable designers to break free from the screen. Images and words can be projected into physical space accompanied by sound to create extraordinary mixed-reality immersive experiences. In Japan, Toshio Iwai was exploring the integration of sound and image as an interactive experience. He used the computer to create 'visual music systems'. In 1992, as artist-in-residence at the San Francisco Exploratorium, he created 'Well of Lights', using video projection to create and animate creatures that swim and play in space. In 1999, at the ZKM Institute for Visual Media, Karlsruhe, Germany, he produced virtual computer scores by placing 'dots' onto a moving grid that triggered the keys of a real piano and in turn released a flight of projected computer-generated images on a screen. Iwai continues to produce visual musical performances.

It takes time for people to learn to use a new medium; it took more than half a century of experimentation in the fifteenth century to evolve the conventions of typeface, page numbering, paragraphing and chapter divisions in books. New-media graphic design started on screen but is now progressing beyond into the physical world. As the technological revolution continues, it offers a huge range of new challenges and opportunities to the graphic designer working in new media, and we will look at some of the changing and emerging areas of practice in the next section. Nevertheless, there are some constants in this ever-evolving domain:

▲ Toshio Iwai's 'Well of Lights', at the San Francisco Exploratorium in 1992.

Trailblazing in New Media

John Maeda, E. Rudge and Nancy Allen Professor of Media Arts and Sciences at The Media Laboratory, Massachusetts Institute of Technology (MIT), is part artist, part computer scientist and part educator. He is one of the world's leading figures in digital art and graphics. He experiments with the way software can generate print and interactive screen-based work, and the crossover between the book and the computer. He views the computer not as an inferior substitute for brush and paint but as an expressive medium in its own right. Among his best-known abstract works are *The Reactive Square*, a simple black square on a computer screen that changes shape if you shout at it, and *Time Paint*, in which paint flies across the screen. In 2004 he launched a research initiative called 'Simplicity', designed to make computers easier to use and less intrusive.

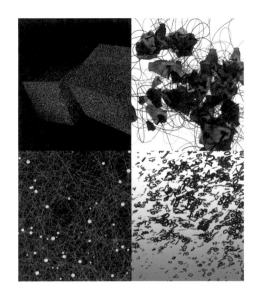

▶ Examples of projects by John Maeda that explore the graphic possibilities for creative expression through computer programming. *www.maedastudio.com*

Yugo Nakamura is based in Tokyo. Trained as an engineer, he developed an interest in people and their surroundings. Inspired by John Maeda, he has been fascinated by the web as an environment for several years now. His use of Flash to create fluid, naturalistic images and sequences has caused a sensation in the design world. His website plunges you straight into an enchanting, playful and finely crafted world of interactive forms. You can distort or repeat forms and generate new images by simple gestures. Nakamura demonstrates how small logical procedures can be used to develop beautiful, elegant and often humorous results. He says: 'There's usability but there's also joy; there's that simple fun of being able to touch and feel, that can draw you deeper into a web experience.'

◀ A selection of projects by Yugo Nakamura. Through his personal website, www.yugop.com, he explores the complexity of interactive experimentation and animation. *www.yugop.com*

Golan Levin studied with John Maeda in the Aesthetics and Computation Group at the MIT Media Laboratory. Between his first and second degree he worked for four years as an interaction designer and research scientist at Interval Research Corporation, and is now Assistant Professor of Electronic Time-Based Art at Carnegie Mellon University in Pittsburgh. Artist, composer and engineer, he has attracted a worldwide reputation in the design community for his simultaneous sound and image performances, produced using cybernetic systems. In 2001, he created *Dialtones*, a work made up of the choreographed ringing of the audience's mobile phones. In 2004, he developed the *Manual Input Sessions*. Performed live on stage, this was a series of audio-visual acts that probed the expressive possibilities of hand gestures in creating sound.

▼ The *Manual Input Sessions* probe the expressive possibilities of hand gestures and finger movements. Performances involve a combination of custom interactive software, analogue overhead projectors and digital computer video projectors. The analogue and digital projectors are aligned so that their projections overlap, resulting in an unusual quality of hybridized, dynamic light. *Golan Levin and Zachary Lieberman with Joan La Barbara and Jaap Blonk*

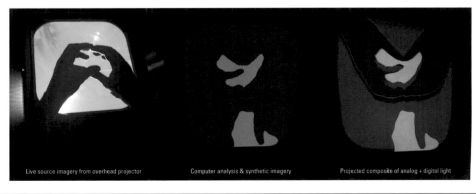

Live source imagery from overhead projector · Computer analysis & synthetic imagery · Projected composite of analog + digital light observation, wit and imagination are the essential ingredients in creating effective messages.

Changing and emerging areas of practice

The basic goal of the graphic designer – to find exciting and relevant ways to communicate information – has not changed, but the areas of practice have morphed and multiplied with the widespread use of computing. For example, illustrators are moving into animation, games and film; information designers are developing dynamic maps; graphics are being used for new kinds of learning and journeys of discovery experiences, interactive information hubs and hybrid music/visual events. As technology develops and markets change, there is a constant need for new creative minds to participate in the evolution of the industry.

Web design

Web design is probably the best-known area of new-media graphics. There is a great deal of demand for websites from governments, businesses, institutions, communities and individuals. Websites have become one of the main ways for people to access information on products, services, company performance and lifestyle choices.

Jakob Nielsen has written extensively on usability and website design. His website, www.useit.com, gives a list of more than one hundred attributes you need to consider, such as basic page layout, page width, 'liquid' versus 'frozen' layout, page length, frames, fundamental page design elements, logo, search, navigation, site map, etc.

Websites need to work fast, be engaging and sustain user confidence. Web designers juggle structure, navigation, visual appearance and appeal, usability and accessibility with business goals and technological constraints. This is a rich mix of factors and usually requires team collaboration.

Commercial websites that use screen-based versions of magazines, commonly known as 'brochure ware', can look rather stilted and only really represent the computer's ability to mimic other media. At one time there was much talk about repurposing print design for the web. There is an alternative, though. Online gaming, blogs, subscriber social networking websites such as Friendster and MySpace, and e-commerce (shopping and selling) websites such as eBay and Amazon store details of your personal profile, and their real-time feeds and cookies (small parcels of information stored on a user's computer by websites, to identify the user across multiple sessions) give the appearance that they know you're there. You don't simply consume the information on these sites; you use them actively to pursue your interests, friendships and even your personal identity.

A check list of operational and graphic elements (also known as assets) is a useful aide-mémoire in building a website, but a successful design is not measured

▲ Websites, such as that for Bureau for Visual Affairs shown here, can be accessed from almost anywhere in the world. Wireless and satellite connections ensure fast and easy access to information on the internet. *Tom Elsner BVA, London*

▲ The Mies typeface, created in 1995 by Jannuzzi Smith, took advantage of the early constraints and unpredictability of the Internet. It was designed using as few pixels as possible while maintaining legibility, visual impact and elegance.

▼ Animated pixels of the 'virtual catwalk' for the Central Saint Martins fashion show. Pass your mouse over the virtual models to reveal high-resolution images and a window of designer details. *Jannuzzi Smith, London*

simply by how many attributes are included or how smoothly the technology functions. It's also about how the website is structured to express the content while including the needs of the user.

Tom Elsner of UK design consultancy Bureau for Visual Affairs says: 'Making a website is like making a real object.' It has a front end – that is, what appears immediately on your screen – but behind that is an architecture created by the designer that structures content into pages, levels and links, and at the back end there is a content-management system usually only accessible to the site operator. Many people don't realize it, but the designer often works out the structure of the whole site.

Max Bruinsma, a design critic, writes: 'Web design is not just making things look good or work well but it is an editorial activity organizing disparate elements into a structured whole on the basis of content-driven choices.'

From this you can move forward to more ambitious designs. Websites offer an opportunity for invention. A good example is the typeface Mies, created by the design consultants Jannuzzi Smith in 1995. At the time, print-based typefaces that had been refined over many centuries were being blurred or corrupted by the new screen technologies. Jannuzzi Smith therefore decided not to try to copy the styles of the past but instead to design a font that would use as few pixels as possible, be quick to download and be compatible with all systems.

The same design team extended this visual grammar to the fashion page of the website for Central Saint Martins College of Art and Design, London. They wanted to capture the vitality of the catwalk but, thinking that video would take too long to download when people clicked on the page, they combined movement with low-resolution images to depict distinctive but blurred walking figures; when users moused over the blurred moving forms, high-resolution still images appeared.

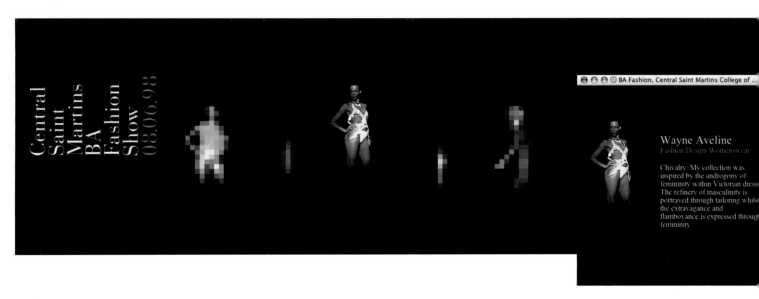

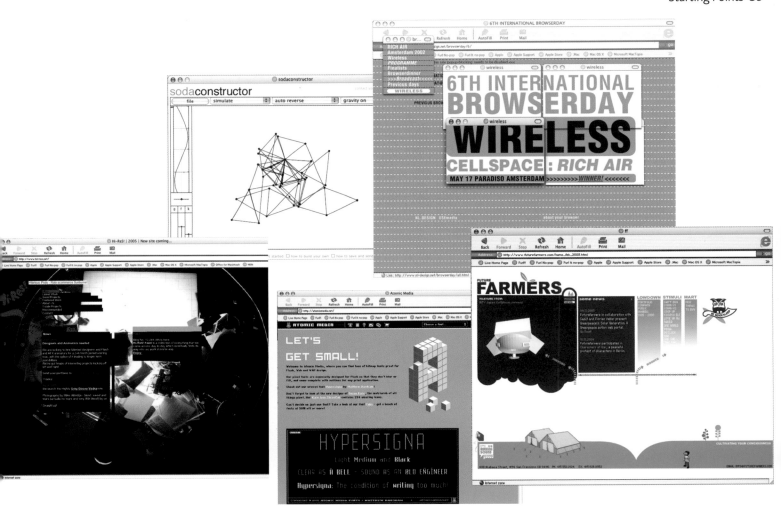

▲ Design companies and individual designers use the web to showcase experiments with software and share their discoveries. Shown here are SodaPlay, Browserday, Hi-Res, Hypersigna and Future Farmers.

Jannuzzi Smith have also used database systems derived from new media to revolutionize print-based systems and products. These are described as 'cross-media' products and demonstrate that new-media thinking can also be applied to revitalize traditional graphics.

There are many experimental websites that explore the expressive and interactive possibilities of the web interfaces. These are of particular interest to graphic designers pursuing innovation, but they are unsuitable for mainstream use because they deliberately flout standard conventions.

Computer games

The worldwide sales of computer and video games have already almost equalled those of the box-office takings of the movie industry and are forecast to continue to grow as new hardware and software systems are developed and launched. It's hardly surprising then, that of all the areas of new media, the opportunities for designers and illustrators in the computer games and interactive entertainment business are perhaps the greatest.

Almost everyone is familiar with computer games, either as home entertainment or from the pleasure arcades in almost every town. From football, golf, tennis, adventure and space to games associated with major movies, it would be difficult not to recognize some of the electronic heroes and heroines in contexts outside their gaming genres. Like their now more traditional counterparts in comic books and graphic novels, these cyberbeings pursue sporting excellence, or good or evil deeds through the passions and dexterity of game players. In the early days, characters from electronic games played on the first dedicated games machines embedded themselves in the public's consciousness as a worldwide phenomenon. Characters such as Pac-Man and Mario from *Donkey Kong* to the semi-realistic Lara Croft character from the *Tomb Raider* series and games associated with major movies such as *Star Wars*, are all played on modern interactive games consoles.

Today, the popularity of computer and video games can be judged by the presence of dedicated stores in our high streets and shopping malls. However, a big market also exists for online games. One such game, *Star Wars Galaxies*, is a Massively Multiplayer Online Role-Playing Game (MMORPG) in which players create their own characters and shape their own destinies. This game allows players to become nearly anything that they can imagine and to some extent write their own Star Wars stories, which has contributed to its success. Like many other games, there is no actual ending to *Star Wars Galaxies*, which allows players to engage with the game for years. Part of the success of *Quake*, another multiplayer game with a huge following, depends on player interaction. Its developers recognized the player base as an asset and provided open access to the game engine so that players can program in their own characters.

While player loyalty to particular genres, titles and platforms often ensures that the latest versions of games such as *Grand Theft Auto*, *Halo* or *The Sims* are a success, versions of popular and new games are appearing on mobile phones and portable entertainment devices that are always connected to networks. Electronic billboards have also been used to display interactive games.

What is a games designer? This is quite a difficult question to answer, because there are in fact several answers. Electronic games are relatively new and although there are established organizations that represent the various factions of the computer games industry, some mystery still surrounds the precise nature and role of the designer. Some games companies do not even have a position called 'games designer'. Most games are the result of the work of teams whose job titles range from artist to programmer, producer, tester, etc. Games companies range in staff numbers from a handful of people to more than 5,000 globally in the case of Electronic Arts, so this may further confuse the job titles of their employees. Smaller companies will often also use publishing partners, cooperating on aspects of game development, from scripting to design, illustration, coding and marketing.

▲ Entropia Universe is an online games community for entertainment, social interaction and trade, with a real cash economy. Multiplayer online games attract large numbers of players across the globe.

Some colleges and universities offer courses and degrees that treat games design as an artistic pursuit, others as a more academic 'computer science' aspect of

Computer games design has come a long way since the simple interactivity of *Pong* (1968). Realism is now demanded by sophisticated game players. *Left:* Lara Croft of *Tomb Raider* fame has swapped her blocky fractals for smooth idealism. *Right, from top: Pong* (1968); *Donkey Kong* (1970); *Mario* (1981); *Tomb Raider 2* (1990); *The Sims* (1995); *FIFA Soccer* (2001); *Grand Theft Auto – San Andreas* (2005).

programming. Both definitions may be right but this will depend on whether the institution is arts based or science based. Individuals often become either technically oriented artists or programmers with design skills. Essential requirements, however, are a good sense of storytelling and strong communication skills.

It is worth noting that a design education gives you a broad set of skills that will be very valuable in getting a job as a games designer. But passion, energy, ability, the drive to make things happen and a willingness to work long hours are what you really need to make a successful career in games design.

Illustration and animation

The opportunities for digital illustrators are as broad as they are exciting. Traditionally, illustrators have mainly worked 'freelance', which means self-employed and working on their own rather than on the payroll of a design company. Success has often depended on styles of work being appropriate to that being commissioned at the time, but the international nature of new media, enabled by the computer and the Internet, has changed the way that illustrators and digital artists work. Illustrators have seen their horizons expand beyond their wildest dreams: from a mainly print-based discipline, through collaboration and the possibilities of a truly worldwide client base, to areas of new work facilitated by expanding opportunities in film, animation, television, the World Wide Web, advertising, concept and games development. Thanks to broadband Internet, an illustrator is no longer a lone figure drawing at home with only a cat for company.

Illustrators are increasingly contributing to new media, having embraced the extra opportunities that the computer offers to create new work, not only in print media – book and magazine publishing, and advertising – but also in less traditional areas such as website icon design, animation, 3D illustration, computer games, film and television title sequences, and music promos. Illustrators now often collaborate with animators or Flash designers, sometimes in different locations, using computers as the means of developing and transferring their contribution to a collective artwork.

Drawing is an invaluable skill for every graphic and new-media designer, particularly for illustrators who have quite rightly considered good drawing the basis of all good illustration. However, many designers and illustrators are now likely to combine computer skills with their more traditional drawing abilities. Digital tools are available to illustrators and designers alike, and have become a medium in their own right like the pencil, ink and watercolour before them. As commissioning design director Peter Grundy says: 'The value of drawing within contemporary illustration is to communicate in an alternative way to writing.'

The challenge for the illustrator now is to find an individual style or voice, which previously might have been acquired through conventional drawing, by taking advantage of mixing imported elements on the computer screen in order to

▲ Andy Martin has successfully used the computer as a drawing tool. He has also branched out into filmmaking using similar techniques. www.andy-martin.com

▲ Dave McKean, *Dream Chair*. Illustration for *D** magazine, 1996.

Jeanne Verdoux: Illustrator, Filmmaker and Graphic Designer

Photograph © Graham MacIndoe

go home

▲ Jeanne Verdoux lives and works in New York, where she designs for both American and French clients.

Jeanne Verdoux first set up her own practice in the heart of Paris in 1998. She shared a studio with a Dutch and a Portuguese designer, creating 'a little European island, very inspirational'. She set out to apply her knowledge of print design to multimedia work. In 1999, she won the Villa Medicis Hors-les-Murs award to go to New York and after a year of drawing and filming the city, established her studio in Brooklyn.

Her recent work demonstrates how she incorporates different media into her creative process. She usually starts a project with just a pen and paper. This could be anywhere, sometimes on a train. Then she goes to her computer with the initial sketch, which offers her a multitude of ways to develop her idea. The decision-making is critical and she is careful to choose a form that is appropriate: typography, photography, drawing or a combination of these. She loves being able to make an animation or mix hand-drawing with type. The screen also gives her a necessary distance from the

initial idea that helps to enrich the primary concept.

When she made the animated film *Das Buch/Le Livre*, the idea came from reading the script. She noticed the etymology of the words *le livre* (French for 'book') and *das Buch* (German for the same word) derives from the word 'tree'. She decided to use wood as the main material. Popsicle sticks seemed ideal: small objects that would allow her to create any kind of shape. As the story was about words, their similarities and differences, type was a good way to visualize it. She created a 'typeface' with full popsicle sticks for stems and broken sticks for crossbars. She storyboarded the sequence and shot the film as separate stills (hundreds of them) on a digital camera. Then she imported the stills into AfterEffects to animate them in time with the narration. The drawings were done by Bérangère Lallemant.

She says: 'In the future new media will not be new any more. Media will not matter. There will be infinite possibilities to create and

▲ *New York Times* letters page. The street signs were drawn, then scanned, manipulated on the computer and traced in pencil, then rescanned for the printer. Hand-computer-hand-computer was the process.

▲ *New York Magazine*'s Intelligencer, a weekly photomontage depicting key events taking place in New York City.

distribute images. These images will float from screen to screen. The graphic designer will remain the creator of images, only his/her palette of tools will widen. As for me, I will keep practising in the same way: using my eyes and mind to observe the world we live in and come up with imaginative concepts, using technology to concretize my ideas.'

◀ *Das Buch/Le Livre*, an animation for French TV channel Arte on the etymology of the words *das Buch* and *le livre* (the book) and their inherent similarities.

▼ *Typographie*, a film based on a typeface inspired by the digital screen font used on New York subway trains by the MTA. The animation was shot on digital video, each sheet of paper is the equivalent to one pixel of the original font. The message is: 'it's hot in NY, no air.' A fan eventually blows the sheets of paper away.

TYPOGRAPHIE

produce a different and personal interpretation of an idea or text. The computer has not just changed the way that illustrators work; it has created a new kind of illustrator, equally ready and able to use a pen or a computer, or a combination of different media.

Although some illustrators may not create their images purely by digital means, they will often use the computer to put the final piece together. Some scan their drawings into the computer and then manipulate, colour, assemble or animate them. Others, notably 3D illustrators and animators, work directly on screen. But the overarching goal and requirement remains strong concepts and ideas and an understanding of composition.

Computer animation is a diverse and exciting field that offers the opportunity for illustrators and new-media designers to tell stories and get ideas across to audiences in ways that cannot be achieved with live-action film. Most animators work in teams, often mixing different styles and 2D and 3D techniques – whatever is appropriate for the task in hand. Expertise with software is important, but whatever computer application is used, the quality of the final image is what counts. Animation is a very broad field, spanning cartoons, model animation, collage, 3D and even live action. Although we are tricked by the animated image into believing the otherwise unbelievable, animators of all kinds have to ground their work in reality; audiences need to see things with which they can identify.

Post-production is the process in the development of movies and television programmes in which film or video is edited, manipulated and composed into its final form. Illustrators and animators work with 2D and 3D software to model and render scenes and objects: for example, dinosaurs, digital humans, landscapes and outer space. Here more than in any other area, the computer has exercised a tremendous influence. From editing and cleaning up film and video footage, to the production of major feature-length movies, story editors and digital-effects artists play a key role in producing the finished film. Movies such as the *Lord of the Rings* trilogy, *The Matrix* and *King Arthur* used extensive post-production techniques to add seemingly impossible sequences to the live action. Completely CGI (computer-generated imagery) movies, such as *Shark Tale*, *Shrek 2*, *The Invincibles* and other full-length 3D animated works, required the development of production and visual-effects techniques capable of rendering fantastic environments in such a way that ever more sophisticated movie audiences will believe in them. The demand for increasingly realistic effects in movies, including lighting and sound design, has widened the opportunities open to illustrators, digital artists and designers.

In a recent trend some movies are now beginning to include in the actual studio set digital effects formerly reserved for the post-production stage. In these cases the new-media artist is called upon to design, and probably program, sequences that will run in actual time on the movie set. An example might be computer screens showing data changing in reaction to the dialogue.

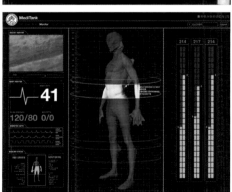

▲ These interactive computer screens, designed and programmed by Toby Glover for the movies *Batman: The Beginning* (top) and *Hellboy*, were filmed on the set as live action with the actors, rather than being created in post-production afterwards. *Warner Bros and Sony Columbia*

Film-industry experts have said that the advent of CGI and special effects, coupled with the visual skills of new-media artists, has made new kinds of movies possible and helped regenerate the industry.

Motion graphics

Motion graphics are film title sequences, trailers and teasers; stings and idents – short identity graphics used, for example, between programmes on television to remind you which station you are watching or added to the end of advertisements to reference the brand identity; promos and advertisements on film, DVDs or television, music videos, and moving sequences on websites.

Designers have been working with moving text, moving image and sound since the advent of film; some of the most famous pre-digital examples include Saul Bass's title sequence for *The Man with the Golden Arm* (1955) and Maurice Binder's 1960s James Bond title sequence where the zeros of the 007 turn into the barrel of a gun. Many graphic designers look to the title sequence for the film *Se7en*, made in 1995 by Kyle Cooper, as the classic of that decade. *Wired* magazine describes how 'In it, the letters hand-scratched by Cooper with a needle onto film stock, frame by painstaking frame – disintegrate to the industrial rhythms of a remix of Nine Inch Nails' *Closer*. The oft-imitated setup perfectly captured the addled mind of the movie's serial killer and set the tone for the entire film.' Images of turning book pages, handwritten leaves of a diary, and close-ups of fingers and razor blades were filmed and overlaid with dark shadows cast by the killer's hand and the scratched title lettering, and edited together on a computer.

Before computing, motion-graphics designers had to use complicated optical printing techniques in a lab to matte, or overlay images. They had to project and re-photograph images to achieve the desired results, or place a static camera in front of a sheet of glass onto which is painted a landscape to obscure a portion of the frame. Computers have made the manipulation of images much easier and enabled more graphic designers to expand their vocabulary to include time-based media. The key components here are movement and sound. A moving image seems to capture our attention more easily than a static one; it unfolds over time and allows the designer to play with rhythm, pace and narrative – all of which make a very direct appeal to our emotions and can create a strong mood. This increases the graphic designer's palette but also the complexity of the task.

Motion-graphics designers are most likely to work as part of a team put together by a director. The team would typically consist of a musician or sound designer, a programmer/developer, possibly an animator, and a production manager.

When advertising agencies commission adverts, they usually start with a script and a storyboard written and visualized respectively by the copywriter and the art director. The design team starts with the visuals and commissions a musician. The visual team produces a storyboard or short visual sequence using Flash and the musician makes a preliminary scratch track. The visuals and sound are then

▲ Poster for *The Man with the Golden Arm* (1955), a film by Otto Preminger. Saul Bass designed the title sequence using similar elements.

modified in relation to each other. Sometimes a composer is commissioned to produce a variety of soundtracks that can be cut and pasted to different scenes. As UK-based production company BDH say: 'Computers enable you to cut unusual samples of sounds, for example, a jet engine and a gentle breeze next to each other, which creates unexpected drama and sound texture.'

Music videos are different. The music usually comes first. The design team generates a visual concept by listening to the music and responding to the brief. Through a process of discussion and associative thinking, they use their imaginations to devise powerful metaphors. They may develop a visual vocabulary based on existing images and motifs that are already part of the identity of the client or product. For example, when Julian House and Julian Gibbs at Intro created the video *Kill All Hippies* for the band Primal Scream, they reinterpreted the graphic language they had already originated for a CD cover for the band. This used images of fighter pilots in which strong flat colours were combined with cut-out rounded forms. To make the video, they sourced additional clips and stills from film archives, cut them into coherent sequences that mirrored the rhythm and development of the soundtrack and added in flat background colour and further images and text.

Computer software such as Flash that synchronizes images and audio has opened up a whole new creative process in which visuals and sound are developed simultaneously. One example is *Anamorph* by Matt Anderson, a video and audio artist working in New York, who is admired by many motion-based graphic designers. 'When first conceptualizing something, I usually think of an image or a visual concept first,' says Anderson. 'For me, it's important to build the visual narrative before I do anything else. Then I have a good sense of the pace and mood of the piece. As I create the music I get a sense for how it will affect the visuals and what the audio demands from them.' The computer will generate sound as you

▶ Stills from *Anamorph* by Matt Anderson, a promotional film for New York interactive and rich media agency WDDG. The film footage, motion graphics and music work in concert to create an overall mood unlike traditional broadcast media. *WDDG, New York*

create images, but you still need to start with an idea. Computers are not going to come up with their own stories. Nor can a computer decide what is successful and what is not – this is down to the designer's judgement.

Information visualization

Information visualization describes the process whereby vast amounts of data or complex flows of information are mapped and represented visually: for instance, the data from the Human Genome Project or the second-by-second fluctuation in the financial markets. Just like traditional maps, information visualizations aim to give you a way into complex information sets that, at first sight, might seem daunting or incomprehensible and reveal more of the world than you could possibly ever experience by yourself. The word 'map' immediately brings to mind the image of a miniature pictorial representation of mountains, seas, roads and towns, but it should be remembered that maps are in fact navigational devices that indicate boundaries, changes, nodes and continuity, and that anything can be mapped: bodies, beliefs, histories, ecologies or data sets. The challenge for the graphic designer is to visualize the information in such a way that it can be easily used and understood.

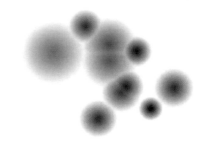

▲ IBM monitored various metrics in their buildings, from keystrokes and mouse movements to movement around the buildings themselves. The aim of this project was to draw out from this dry statistical data an inference as to the volume and type of activity being carried out, and ultimately the emotional state of the buildings' occupants. It was this emotional state that the suite of visual and audio software applications created by Rom and Son attempted to represent in this piece called *Time and Emotion*.

Information visualization uses the traditional language of graphic design: signs, symbols, metaphors, labels, typography, layout, information hierarchies, sequencing, colour scales and grids. Like the print-based graphic designer, the new-media graphic designer still needs to strike a balance between the bigger picture and the detail on the screen, while organizing the information into a navigable system.

The success of the work resides in creating a scenario that simultaneously:

- engages the viewer in a rich visual experience;
- explains itself and offers a navigational system that is easy to use;
- makes the information accessible to the user;
- equals the revelatory experience offered by good maps.

To achieve this you must, first and foremost, understand the information that is being conveyed. You must develop a subtle and imaginative grasp of graphic language and acquire a good working knowledge of digital technologies such as XML (Extensible Markup Language), the purest standard for unformatted content. Equally, you must have the imagination and visual flair to develop the pictorial or visual element of the interface and, last but not least, you must understand how an audience may interact with the interface.

Edward Tufte, in his book *Visual Explanations*, discusses the giant conceptual leap made by map-making in evolving from pictorial representations to abstract diagrams such as bar charts and pie charts. The latter sorts of diagrams do not bear any resemblance to the object or situations they describe, yet there is none the less a logic that enables us to read them. The lesson here is that you do not have to represent the objects of interest literally to make their cumulative effect understood. So, for example, people tapping on a keyboard at a computer in an office can be visualized as glowing points on a screen. In 2001, the new-media group Rom and Son developed a screensaver for IBM UK based on this idea. Employees could see at a glance the number of their colleagues in other parts of the organization who were at their computers: the faster the input, the faster the glowing dots moved around the screen. This data was then translated into sound to produce a musical interpretation of the energy of the combined workforce at any point. This interface was designed to heighten a sense of loyalty and community at work.

Apart from utilizing the traditional tools and conventions of graphic design, information visualization offers three key additional attributes. First, it is 'interactive'. In other words, the user can 'drill down' and 'mine', or uncover, extra layers of information by clicking on the screen. Second, it can be 'live', giving you 'real-time' information on a 'dynamic' interface, for example, showing the rise and fall of stocks in specific business sectors. Visualizations such as *Map of the Markets* by SmartMoney are made possible through the interconnectivity of the global network of computers and the constant input of information from businesses, governments, institutions, individuals and digital sensors in the environment. Third, the user can, in some instances, input information and thereby change the map itself. In this case, data visualization is like a growing organism that responds according to input that can, in principle, come from anywhere in the world.

Data on technical infrastructures such as streets or telephone networks, social groups, corporations, institutions or nations can be visualized to reveal hidden patterns and flows. For example, data on companies and social networks can be mapped in such a way as to reveal who is the opinion leader of a group, who influences whom in reaching decisions and who collaborates effectively. You are able literally to see performance and power relations. You can analyse the performance of, say, players on the soccer field: teams such as SK Rapid Vienna, for example, have been observed to record who passed the ball to whom. Once this information was transformed into a map, you could see which player initiated the most passes, who was receiving those passes, who controlled the team's play, which players were involved in combination passes, who played together with whom and who didn't, in other words which players made the backbone of the team. This enabled new playing strategies to be developed. An equivalent look at a business or institution could provide similar insights.

Network visualizations are a huge area of interest because they bring to light the previously intangible and fleeting dimensions of group and organizational behaviour; as such they are useful instruments to many scientific disciplines and almost any industry. The technique has also been used as a tool for collective communication and has formed the basis for experimental artworks. This emerging practice could not have been developed without appropriate software, of course, but the graphic skills to represent the information intelligibly are of no less importance.

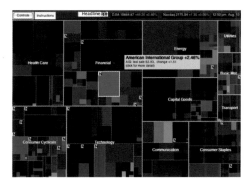

▲ *Map of the Markets* by Martin Wattenberg of SmartMoney. Global stock figures are displayed for investors in real time.

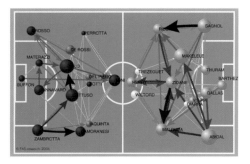

▲ Rapid Vienna's ball passing during the last 15 minutes of a soccer match between Rapid and Sturm Graz on 7 December 2003 (data by Harald Katzmair and Helmut Neundlinger). *Analysis and visualization by FAS.research. www.fas.at*

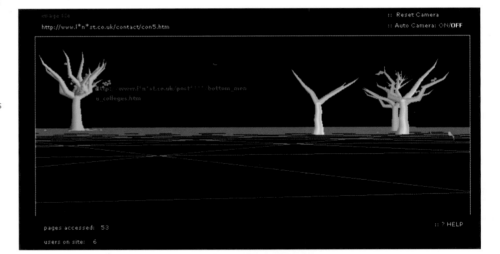

Information visualization takes complex data and represents it in a graphic and often interactive form.

▸ The idea behing the Semantic Map is to present graphically the content of the netzspannung.org database and to visualize metadata about the content. The graphical visualization presents the data in an intuitive way, so the constellations of data form a statement about their contextual surroundings. Semantic Map by Monika Fleischmann, Jasminko Novak, Wolfgang Strauss with Kresimir Simunic and Jochen Denzinger.
www.esono.com/boris/projects/knmaps

▸ Tracking visitors to a website by Rufus Kahler, cyberForest is a dynamic, screen-based forest of trees which 'grows' in real time as users visit pages of a website. It records the time spent and information accessed.

▸ Mapping word associations by ArtText. The complete text of *Alice in Wonderland* set out in an interactive format. Frequency and use of language is demonstrated by the association words used in the text.

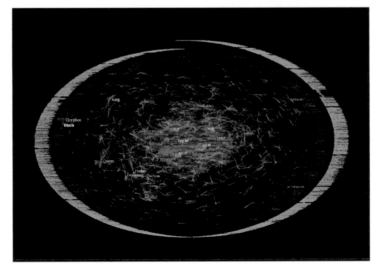

Photography

Digital photography has become one of the main image sources in new media, so much so that most photographers routinely manipulate their photographs on a computer. For many, the digital method has replaced the traditional processes of conventional photography involving film, exposure, developing and printing in a darkroom. Digital images have the advantage of being instantly transferable from the photographer, able to be immediately transmitted, copied, manipulated, published and stored, with little if no degradation in quality.

As new photographic technologies and communications converge, the possibilities for innovative creativity and methods of interaction with images and audiences increase. Cameras have been released from a linear process and static way of recording the world to one in which digital image capture has become ubiquitous. Cameras are in our phones, in PDAs (personal digital assistants) and in surveillance devices; in fact, we take the technology so much for granted in everyday life that we now turn to digital evidence, and particularly images, for safety and proof of our whereabouts. We also take for granted that visual news coverage is transmitted instantaneously from anywhere on the globe to our television screens by digital communications networks, and that sometimes this will be from small devices such as mobile phones.

The popularity of digital cameras shows that in the world of photography, makers of photographic tools, information technology, telecommunications, software and hardware, printing technologies and consumer electronics have converged to push conventional photography aside. The famous names of film camera equipment persist – Leica, Hasselblad, Rolleiflex, Sinar, Nikon, Canon – but they are now partnered by the giants of new technology – Epson, Hewlett-Packard, Panasonic and Sony, who now consider themselves to be at the forefront of the photographic industries. They, in turn, have been joined by computer-software companies such as Adobe and Microsoft to create a seamless process from image capture to output, either electronic or in print. Kodak, possibly the most famous brand name in photography, recently stopped producing film cameras, moved their business to digital, and began marketing complete camera-to-print solutions.

In professional photography the availability of high-end digital cameras has changed the way in which many photographers work. In some commercial studios, the digital workflow has revolutionized the process of shooting and production. In most cases, digital capture shortens the time in the actual studio or on location, decisions are made faster and processing, editing and manipulation of images take place on the studio computer screen. Some photographers no longer need a large studio as they can work remotely and on location. Powerful portable computers, high-resolution digital cameras and wireless broadband communications mean that practically every aspect of a photographic commission can be managed at any distance. Clients, creative directors and photographers routinely work together from around the world. Often without meeting face-to-face, they can work collaboratively online, with the ability to communicate instantly and even discuss the progress of a shoot as it takes place.

◄ ▲ This digitally modified image (above) of the River Thames in London was used in an advertising campaign for Smirnoff vodka. Commissioned by the advertising agency J.W. Thompson, Jason Hawkes photographed London from the air over a period of three days and sent the images to The Dairy, a London post-production house, where 26 different shots were combined and retouched in order to produce an image in which the river has been straightened but the city still looks believable. Compare it with the photograph which shows the River Thames as it really is, snaking its way through London (left), and you will see how digital photography and post-production techniques can alter reality in very convincing ways. The photograph of the 'real' River Thames was taken from an aeroplane as it approached London City Airport by John Stote.

▲ Photographic libraries distribute their collections online and on CD-Rom. Pictures are always available to download. *Getty Images*

The Internet has revolutionized the way photo libraries promote, license and distribute their images. Online picture searches have replaced the need for researchers to search manually through prints and transparencies, and then send out the original. Clients are now able to conduct their own searches online with far more choice, and when an image is selected it can be sent out electronically. Libraries also sell stock images on CD-Rom. For photographers, photo libraries have been and remain a useful means of marketing their work. Digital photography is now the concern of every photographer and new-media designer. Understanding digital imaging techniques is an essential part of professional photography, which in turn greatly widens the scope of image-making through creative manipulation and vision. Opportunities range from the photographic image, barely altered, to highly original, digitally created photo illustration.

Experience design

Experience design is a contested term and is used here following the American Institute of Graphic Arts (AIGA) usage, which defines it as an approach that has wider boundaries than traditional design and strives for creating experiences beyond just products and services that connect on an emotional level with the customer or user. Thus, it is used to describe the ways in which graphics surround visitors or users in a walk-in experience: for example, in an exhibition, a shop, a trade fair, a theme park, an event. The term is appropriate because interactive graphics which are effectively combined with sound and embedded in objects and architecture can not only communicate ideas but provoke very strong bodily and emotional responses as well.

Experience design owes a debt to many well-established design disciplines: the design of environmental signage and way-finding systems, exhibition and interpretive design, spatial design, theatre design, film and interaction design.

Experience design involves thinking in a new way about how you engage the user. You need to consider where they will look and what they will see as they move through an exhibition or shop; you need to visualize ways of enabling people to browse or investigate something, whether this is a rack of clothes or a history of science. Interactive kiosks were first installed in museums in the 1990s. At that time they were conceived essentially as interactive books, screen-based and only able to address one person at a time.

Antenna Design in New York has produced technologically enhanced objects and environments. Their 'Civic Exchange' for the Van Alen Institute in New York is a public interactive information installation (see page 13). Based on the image of people gathering under a tree, the installation features multiple screens for local public information. It also functions as a shelter and as a space for the display of social interaction. The main information screen is a multi-user interactive map table that provides direct access to place-based news. Individuals and community organizations can annotate the map with their own information. Different kinds of information are distinguished by colour and motion.

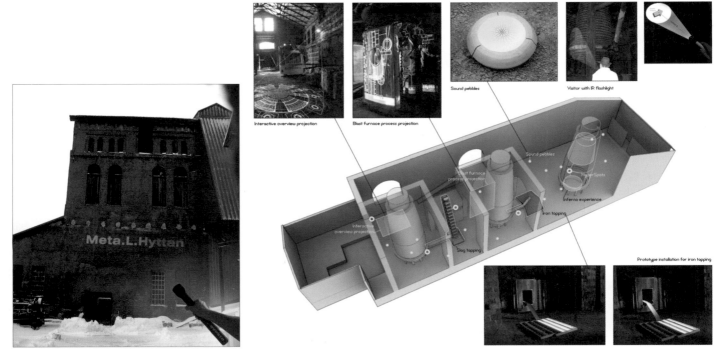

Interactive overview projection

Blast furnace process projection

Sound pebbles

Visitor with IR flashlight

Sound pebbles

Blast furnace process projection

HotSpots

Interactive overview projection

Inferno experience

Iron topping

Slag tapping

Prototype installation for iron topping

▲ The Meta.L.Hyttan visitor centre in the abandoned Avesta steel mill is a joint project between the Smart and the Emotional Studio at the Interactive Institute, Stockholm. Project team: Peter Becker, Thomas Broomé, Peter Ludén, Magnus Lundin, Tobi Schneidler, Ingvar Sjöberg.

By contrast the Meta.L.Hyttan project, developed by the Interactive Institute, Stockholm, in the abandoned Avesta steel mill in Sweden, demonstrates how a site can be transformed into an interactive environment in which visitors can learn, experience and be surprised by history, science and art. This is a dark and mysterious space that visitors explore with special flashlights that are equipped with a coded and invisible beam. When pointed at special hotspots, the beam triggers a variety of audio-visual media, spotlights, projections and even physical effects, such as the moving of mechanical parts. For example, a diagram of the inside of the blast furnace projected onto its outside enables you to 'see through' the exterior and examine its interior workings. The flashlight becomes a navigational instrument that works on two content levels: the educational and the poetic. The educational flashlight releases explanations of the steel production process, while the poetic flashlight makes the environment respond with personal stories and evocative effects.

All Of Us are a young company in London who focus on the development of interactive applications for interior environments and physical spaces. They believe there is opportunity for interactive design that currently remains unexplored. They work on the principle of collaboration. They created the identity, print and event design for Great Ormond Street Hospital for Children in London. They created an interactive projected logo that responded to the children's voices: the more noise the children made, the more the logo moved. The treatment was carried through to print and promotional media, including advertising, tickets and souvenirs, where snapshots of the identity were generated to set alongside the static logo.

Cyberhelvetia Pavilion: 3deluxe, Germany

The Cyberhelvetia Pavilion was commissioned by the Credit Suisse Group, Zurich, for the Swiss National Exhibition Expo. 02. **1** An initial concept sketch. **2** The completed installation. **3** Computer-generated concept diagram illustrating the installation and some of the virtual creatures that inhabit it. **4** Interface for virtual creature development. **5** Virtual creature projected onto a user's hand. **6** 'Players' interacting with virtual creatures in the 'pool'. **7** 'Tourist' wearing a 3D headset lying on a pool mattress. **8** Interactive virtual world viewed through a 3D headset.

Partners: Sun Microsystems; overall concept Belleville Services; programming Iogram, Nuncom, Zurich; platform operation and project management In&Work, In&Out, Zurich; *Concept and exhibition realization 3deluxe, Weisbaden; pavilion architecture Glogger & Prevosti, Zug.*

Joachim Sauter: Artistic Director Art+Com, Berlin

▲ Joachim Sauter, one of the founders of Art+Com, Berlin, Germany.

Joachim Sauter studied graphic design and film in Berlin in the 1980s and became fascinated by the potential of computing. Fuelled by his interest in the capabilities of this new (mass) medium, he co-founded Art+Com in 1988 with other designers, artists, scientists and technicians. Their goal was to research new ways of using the emerging medium in art and design. As an interdisciplinary group, Art+Com developed projects for cultural institutions, industry and the science community as well as pursuing self-initiated schemes.

In 1991, Joachim and Dirk Lüsebrink, Art+Com programmer, made *Zerseher* (*De Viewer*), to promote interactivity in the realm of art practice. The observer faces a framed, rear-projected image of a painting hanging on a wall. On close inspection, the viewer notices that the exact area of the picture he is looking at is distorting under his gaze. As his eye scans the picture so the image dissolves. Joachim and Dirk used an eye-tracking system, which detected the exact spot the viewer is looking at and fed that information back into the machine which then instructed the projected image to distort in real time.

▼ *De Viewer* was developed to demonstrate interaction as a prime ingredient of new media.
All images © Art+Com

In 1995, Joachim and Dirk worked together again on *The Invisible Shape of Things Past*, in which they researched how information architecture could be constructed and used in real time synthetic space. Here they designed a system, by which film can be transformed into spatial info-architecture.

▲ *The Invisible Shape of Things Past*, film sequences transformed into interactive virtual objects based on views from an actual camera.

In 2002, Joachim collaborated on a virtual interactive stage design for the opera *The Jew of Malta* (written by Christopher Marlow, composed by André Werner). The system enables the actors to interact with real-time generated, projected architecture on the stage. Additionally, a system was developed that projected images onto the singers' costumes to symbolize their inner feelings.

In recent years Joachim has focused on interactive, intelligent and dynamic surfaces

▲ Computer generated costume and stage set for the opera *The Jew of Malta*.

of objects and architecture. His numerous projects include *floatingnumbers* (2003), an interactive table measuring 9 x 2m (approximately 30 x 7 feet). A stream of projected numbers bubbles up and floats across the surface of the table. Up to 24 people can simultaneously interact with the piece by touching the numbers which then reveal their historical, religious, mathematical or sociological meaning.

▲ The significance of 'floating.numbers' materialises form various perspectives on science, religion and art.

Joachim has exhibited at the Centre Pompidou in Paris, the Stedelijk Museum in Amsterdam, the Venice Biennale and the ICC in Tokyo. He is professor of Interaction Design at the University of the Arts, Berlin, and adjunct professor at the Media Art and Design department at UCLA, Los Angeles.

The URBIS visitor centre, Manchester, UK: Land Design, London

◀ ▶ These photographs show the life-size projected people pods and the bespoke blue-screen sequence and carefully constructed video matte that engage the visitor with real people and their cities.

▼ Floor plans of the two galleries designed by Land Design Studio for the URBIS visitor centre. The third-floor Change gallery (top) explores how people influence and are influenced by the cities in which they live. The first-floor Explore gallery (bottom) was designed as a matrix to enable visitors to explore six cities and five themes through custom-built interactive media.

Third Floor Plan; Change

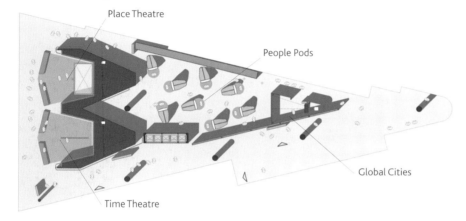

Place Theatre

People Pods

Global Cities

Time Theatre

▼ The photographs below show parts of the city displays for Paris (top) and Los Angeles (bottom).

First Floor Plan; Explore

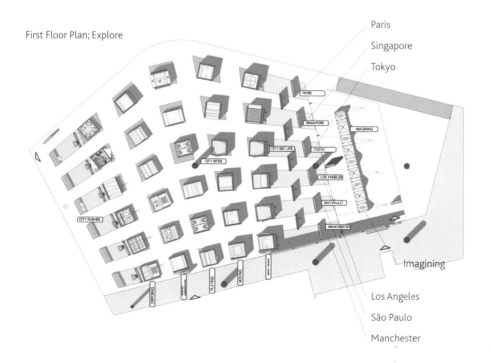

Paris

Singapore

Tokyo

Imagining

Los Angeles

São Paulo

Manchester

Music graphics

From the earliest days of popular computing and multimedia, music and graphics have enjoyed a close relationship. Experimenters in electronic music quickly discovered that they could also capture the digital display capabilities of computer graphics. Using these new-found capabilities in computers, they could sample sound from almost any source, remix it, add graphics and so create a new form of musical expression.

Designers and artists were quick to follow the trend, to the extent that most new-media designers now have a close relationship with musical output. Graphic designers have moved almost effortlessly from producing printed sleeves for vinyl records to facilitating web-enabled mass access to music downloads. Reputations have been built on producing visual interpretations of popular music. It's little wonder, then, that music and sound are such a dominant part of the multimedia experience. With the prevalence of personal computers and digital music players, such as the iPod, DVD recorders and mobile phones, the emphasis has shifted from producing printed materials to providing on-screen support in offering an enhanced experience, through the Internet and video, and broadcasting or sending directly to web-enabled devices. As broadband and wireless develop, 'always on' will mean just that – music and graphics streamed to personal mobile devices at any time and anywhere.

▾ The Optronica festival, organized by Addictive TV, Cinefeel and the British Film Institute, showcases a wide range of international audiovisual artists, VJs and electronic musicians at the BFI IMAX cinema and BFI South Bank, London.

▸ VJ (video jockey) performances. VJs mix graphics and video on their computers and the sequences are projected at live events. The VJs shown here are based in London but perform in Europe, India, Japan and the US. **1, 2, 8** Yeast; **4** The Light Surgeons; **3** Addictive TV; **5** Exceeda; **6** Boris Brüllman; **7** The Mellowtrons

▲ Graphic designer Fred Deakin of Airside also has an international reputation as a member of the music group Lemon Jelly.

Lurking within many a graphic designer is a DJ (disc jockey) keen to demonstrate their talents on the decks. Recently, this outlet has been given even greater scope with the advent of VJing (video jockeying). Taking the lead from musicians and DJs who use computers to cut sections of existing tracks together to make new sounds, VJs, or video jockeys, sample and mix motion graphics on video. This is not sampling in the systematic, scientific sense. Video sampling is an intuitive skill akin to collage and it is performed live. The VJ mixes either from a database of images and video or live video streams to produce a visual mix in response to the music and the mood of the audience. The streams of images are projected onto large screens or directly onto a wall at clubs and concerts. VJing, an experimental practice, derived from the psychedelic light shows of the late 1960s and developed in the 1990s in cities with vibrant club cultures. It has been incorporated into lighting and performance design for major rock concerts, as well as events and performances for theatre, product launches and international exhibitions.

The interactive design practice Rom and Son developed out of Antirom, a collective of new-media designers who exploited the Internet to show off their individual interests – animations, sound tools and creative on-screen playthings that demonstrated the developing power of computer graphics. In one recent project, Rom and Son worked with the Horniman Museum in London, which has one of the most important collections of musical instruments from around the world. The designers' brief was to make an interactive music installation that would allow visitors to access the sounds of the fragile instruments displayed in museum showcases. Rom and Son's solution was to create three interactive 'scanning tables' that enable visitors to listen to the sounds and histories of the instruments, as well as to access projected images of them.

Design group Airside have an international reputation not only as leading interaction designers, but also for their close musical association with the pop group Lemon Jelly (one of Airside's directors, Fred Deakin, plays in the group). Like other design groups worldwide, Airside have exploited their musical interests by

marketing T-shirts and toys connected with their musical output through their own online shop.

Computer graphics are used extensively in music promotion. Many new-media designers started their careers by submitting video sequences to MTV and then moved on to produce 'promos' for major pop groups. Computer applications for sound and video have placed professional sound studio and post-production tools on the designer's desktop, making it possible for anyone to experiment with audio-visual materials and create pioneering visual designs for clubs, commercial events, music tours and exhibitions. Foremost among these design pioneers are the Light Surgeons, a collective of designers, filmmakers and musicians who are at the cutting edge of multimedia sound and light installations, and Addictive TV, a group whose work tries to bridge the gap between cinema, club culture and digital arts.

Collaborations between musicians and new-media designers (sometimes referred to as 'mixotologists') can be seen across the wide range of graphic design. From pop-music videos to interactive installations and experimental audio-visual soundscapes, the opportunities in this area are among the most exciting currently available to new-media designers.

Summary

Computers can be used in the production of 'old media': to produce drawings, paintings, print, film and audio – and it would be extremely difficult to produce anything these days without them. They can also be used in new ways to produce 'new media'. They present an array of possibilities that extend the ways in which designers can manipulate, sample, combine, add and subtract material. In addition, hyperlinks can facilitate users to make associative leaps across global information and entertainment networks, while interactivity can enable users to input, output, modify and sometimes inhabit online worlds. Pioneering designers are showing us how computers can give us fluid, dynamic participatory environments.

If you want to be part of this driving force you need to acquire design skills and apply design principles. You need to learn about layout, colour, sequence, continuity, associative thinking and usability in order to develop your own design voice and direction. You will also need to acquire an understanding of business goals, clients and deadlines, and knowledge of the different industry sectors. The following chapter provides an overview of new-media vocabularies and techniques, and explains the design process for commercial website design.

Designing for New Media **2**

Traditional Production

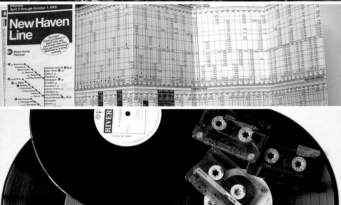

New Opportunities

▲ *Top down:* TV programme graphics produced using an optical rostrum camera. TV programme graphics for *Dr Who* produced using optical effects only by Bernard Lodge at the BBC.
Paper-based railway timetable. Analogue sound discs and tapes.

▶ *Top down:* On-screen page layout replaces mechanical artwork. Digital illustration, detail from a promotional mailer, *Massiv Industries, New York.* TV Motion graphics, 'Static Shock', *Mark Hough.* Visualization of data in a computer file directory. Music and audio visual downloads and 'podcasts'. New-media installation in a New York shop window. *Antenna Design*

The difference between art and design is that while a fine artist generally works on speculative, self-initiated and free-ranging projects, making something in the hope that it will sell, the designer – whether architectural, product, graphic or new media – will be expected to work to a client's brief. A brief is a document prepared by the client that outlines the aims of the project and describes what the client would like to see when the project is completed, in as much detail as possible. An 'open brief' gives a star designer free reign to come up with something.

For all designers, the design process is a series of tasks and events that result in the finished artefact – the building, mobile phone, brochure or website. For new-media designers, the process involves the use of audio-visual and conceptual design methods drawn from a wide mix of disciplines that enable them to give form to the client's message. In this chapter we will look first at the vocabulary and techniques of new-media design and then show how these are used in the design process – particularly in commercial website design.

New-media design vocabularies and techniques

New-media design has evolved from a diverse range of art and design practices. Its most obvious precursors are print and motion (film and television) graphics. Print graphics combines words and static images to produce books, magazines, newspapers, posters, stationery, packaging, maps, charts, environmental signage, business cards, badges, logos, etc. Motion graphics combine words, images, sound, movement and narrative to make film titles, cinematic effects for film, music videos and animated sequences for the web, television, interactive kiosks, PDAs (personal digital assistants) and mobile phones.

New-media graphic design also owes a debt to product design, sound design, fine art and performance art. Product design explores how people touch, hold, move and use objects. The interactive nature of new media means designers need to determine ways for people to open, close or move objects on screen, and indeed how those screen actions can be triggered by using keyboards, smart pens or sensor networks in the environment. Sound is an added dimension that can structure, dramatize, inform, create mood and evoke associations. Fine-art investigations into coding, poetics, meaning and social significance of new media are a source of inspiration for designers. Fine artists question and reflect upon prevailing conventions, so are useful in pointing the way to possible new processes that open up the designer's imagination. Performance art and theatre offer a wealth of experience in dramatizing, narrating and conveying a message.

Layout and Grids

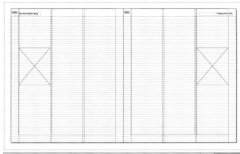

▶ In this book we have used a grid, shown here in miniature, to help order the elements, text and illustrations throughout the book. Designers and printers used grids before the wide adoption of the computer in the printing, design and publishing industries. For print designers, the transition from drawing board to using grids on screen was fairly easy. Software developers used the working pattern created over the years and adapted it in their applications.

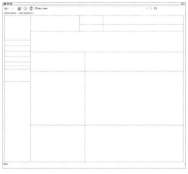

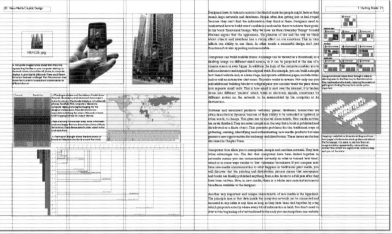

▲ Artist, publisher and designer Jake Tilson uses his website to promote his work and sell his publications. Tilson was an early adopter of the Internet who did some pioneering and experimental design work through his website The Cooker. The illustrations above show how an underlying grid has been used on his online shop and studio website.

▼ Boag Associates are creative graphic information designers. They use grids in printed material as well as for their website to help make complex information clear and easy for people to use.

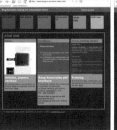

New-media designers have adopted methods from this wide mix of disciplines and have consequently extended the traditional graphic design 'vocabulary'. Below is a short summary of the main terms and techniques used by new-media designers in the production of their work.

Layout

Layout is concerned with how words and images are organized on the page. Invisible 'grids' are normally used as the underlying framework to give a page or a whole book visual coherence. More or less taken for granted by the reader untrained in graphic design, the grid specifications fix proportions, control the height and width of columns, and provide horizontal guidelines and the space available for locating illustrations, photographs, headlines and captions. The grid also defines the position of elements that are repeated on every page, such as margins and page numbers.

Grids both divide and unite the page. They are used to break the page down into blocks of text or image while arranging these blocks in a system. Grids enable designers to create consistency from page to page in a book, magazine or on a website, which in turn aids legibility and navigation for the user. In a paperback novel, for example, the grid will be very simple – a single column of text – but in a newspaper, where space is at a premium and white space is to be avoided, the grid will be quite complex, comprising many columns.

Designers use grids to control the alignment and proximity of text or images and create an overall rhythm that contributes to the look and feel of the publication. There are fixed conventions for newspaper and magazine grids, but skilled graphic designers can create an infinite number of subtle variations in the layout using juxtaposition, scale and contrast to reflect the content and the hierarchy of information – that is, which information is most important and should be read or viewed first, and how subsequent information should be ordered and positioned.

The graphic designer's job is to lead the user's eyes through a layout, from headline, to subheading, to cross-heading, and to tease them with image placement, captions and tasty quotations plucked from the text and set in bigger type to break up any visual monotony as a 'pullout quote' (call-out, liftout or breakout). Many readers are attracted to an image first, then read the caption and are then led into the story. Other devices, such as kickers, a summary line of text above the main headline, and hammers, a larger headline above a smaller main headline, are used to attract attention. Sidebars are smaller articles or lists that appear in boxes alongside the body copy to give background facts to a current story.

Many print-based designers are fascinated by the possible permutations within a grid and sometimes subtly or explicitly break a grid to create unexpected visual impact. David Carson's layouts for the youth market, for example, are almost unreadable to the majority of readers but are appropriate for the target audience.

This is not so easy on the web. Traditionally, web designers have used hidden tables and invisible spacer images to lay out their words and pictures. Prior to this, whole chunks of text were made into images to preserve their typography. However this has disadvantages: the text is not searchable (by search engines) and is also inaccessible to sight-impaired people (speech software cannot 'read' them).

Tables are systems of rows and columns used to constrain certain words, images or videos so they appear in the same place regardless of which browser is installed on the computer. This can produce a grid and table look that lacks the spatial and rhythmic subtlety and flow of print graphics. More flexibility in the layout is available if the graphics are programmed in customized templates created by web developers using software plug-ins such as Java or Flash. This requires that the designer has an understanding of software as well as layout. Often designers collaborate with developers, but this also makes the process more expensive. Software is constantly being developed or revised to enable graphic designers to be more accurate on screen, but the challenge is to work within the attributes of the medium rather than try to make web graphics mirror print graphics.

More recently, there has been a move to separate content from layout using CSS (Cascading Style Sheets). CSS has been used extensively to exert some kind of typographic control over web graphics – defining fonts, size of headings, text colour etc., in a style sheet similar to those used in page-layout programs such as InDesign. If you make changes to the style sheet, everything in the document updates automatically. It is impossible for a designer to know what fonts users may have on their computers, so font is defined as a list such as Verdana, Helvetica, Arial, sans-serif, and if the user doesn't have Verdana installed, then the browser will use Arial. In the worst-case scenario any sans-serif font will do. Now, instead of tables, designers are using CSS 'div' commands to position 'containers' for text and images, providing more versatile layouts.

Print-based graphic designers use scale to balance or emphasize elements and spacing to keep information clear and legible, and they select particular styles of lettering or type to trigger psychological or cultural associations and create mood. This stability of appearance is lacking in web design. Webpages will look different on different computers because users' screens vary in size and typefaces will only appear as designed if the browser on the receiving computer is able to recognize and display them. If the browser does not recognize the typeface, then a default typeface appears and the length of text lines, paragraphs and size of margins will start to change. Legibility is reduced and the look and feel of the page is distorted. People might rearrange the items such as the file icons on screen or import their own desktop image to personalize their screen. They may scroll down the screen and so lose half the layout. Short-sighted users have the capability to increase the size of type on the screen, so thwarting the efforts of an exacting designer. Thus, screen-based new-media graphic designers have to think in completely new ways to convey information in this fluid environment.

Navigation

To find the way around a book or magazine the reader can consult the contents list or, if there is one, look up a topic in the index. This gives a page number to which they can turn. A DVD is often divided into 'chapters' that can be instantly accessed by pressing a menu button. These are simple forms of navigation. Websites also have menu buttons, and a good website will have a site map in case the user gets lost. However, it may be more convenient however to use a search engine such as Google! 'Breadcrumbs' are devices (named after the Hansel and Gretel fairy tale) on a webpage that enable you to find your way back to the home page, for example Home > Products > Clothes > Shoes where each category above the current page (Shoes) is a link to the corresponding page.

Diagrams, charts, graphs and maps belong to an area of graphics known as information design, which aims to make large quantities of complex information sets accessible and navigable. The incredible capacity of computer memories presents an interesting challenge to information designers. Print-based graphic designers compress information into symbols; they use colour codes to guide the eye through a large chart. With a book in hand, perhaps with running headlines describing the chapters, readers can always see where they are and turn back to previous pages. New-media designers cannot unfold the screen to make a large map. They can encourage readers to scroll down the page, but readers can easily lose a sense of the size of the document and their location within it. Interface designers invented the scroll bar to tell users where they are and buttons to take them back up to the top of a document. However, these lack the physical context of a book or even an ancient papyrus scroll, where readers can feel the weight and see how far they have read.

Some designers prefer to fit the text to the screen and divide the information into many smaller pages. Users drill down through the menu options to get to the additional pages or use a search facility. This design strategy requires editing the copy down to the bare minimum. Information architects are helpful in planning the site structure, links and clear navigation devices in relation to the content. The site structure is envisaged in a tree diagram that lays out each page and level in the site and indicates which pages are linked. The navigation devices consist of, for example, the logical and consistent placing of menus, backwards and forwards buttons, and the use of breadcrumb lines. Words positioned on the screen to show users where they have been can help but the thoughtful naming of the content, together with the clarity and consistency of the design, also aids navigation.

Images

Graphic designers use images to communicate their message in an instantaneous and evocative way. Illustration was traditionally drawn by hand using pen and paper. Illustrators still use paper but many incorporate screen-based work too – drawing and collaging with the mouse or using a graphics tablet and stylus, such as a Wacom – in pursuit of their own recognizable style. They also produce images through photography, video, film or 3D modelling and construction on screen.

▼ Icons are graphic images, small pictures or on-screen objects, such as the mouse pointer below, which represent a command, action, software application or piece of hardware. Icons help users interact and navigate their way around a computer or interface quickly and easily. They help users open applications and execute commands simply by recognizing and clicking on an image that they associate with a particular task or action. For example, documents using similar applications or extensions will have a similar icon: a pencil or paintbrush for writing and painting, a page for a document, a folder for storing documents, etc.

Some image-makers interpret words, characters and stories through resemblance and representation for book jackets, magazines, posters, CD covers, web animations, games or post-production. Some make purely abstract images that can be used to set the tone for books, magazines, films and websites. Illustrators have found new freedoms in using the computer. They can make their characters move – and add sound. The computer has brought still images to life. Images can be used in banners at the top of a web page or to illustrate the body text. A small image that links to a page containing a larger version is called a 'thumbnail'. A small image used as a navigation device is called an 'icon'. Images should always have an 'alt' tag to describe the picture to a sight-impaired person, and have their width and height built into the HTML tag so that the layout doesn't move around as they load.

Colour

Colour is another essential tool. Graphic designers use colour to distinguish between choices – for example, subway routes; to 'colour-code' or categorize sets of information such as products in catalogues; and to guide people, for example through the green 'Nothing to Declare' sign at customs. Graphic designers also use colour to provoke a psychological response and evoke associations. For example, banks and financial services often use sober colours on their websites, stationery and signage to create an impression of reliability and security. Colour is a vital component in building structure, mood and identity into a message.

Colour theory seeks to analyse colour through the colour wheel, complementary colours, colour harmonies, saturation, temperature and spatial effects. So, for example, cool colours such as blues appear to recede and warm colours such as red and orange seem to move forwards. However, deeply rooted and differing colour associations are embedded in societies over time: for example, white is the colour associated with weddings in the West but with mourning in India and China. In addition, people have very strong individual reactions to colours. There is no simple correlation between colour and message. Graphic designers need to be aware of prevailing conventions and the context of their work but also to have a strong intuitive colour sense. The use of colour, and finding a set of harmonious colours to use on a website, is both a science and an art.

For graphic and new-media designers, there are two ways in which colour is represented in the appearance of work on screen or in print. Additive, or transmitted, colour for the screen is represented by light in the form of three colours: red, green and blue (RGB). Mixed, they add up to transmitted white light, and where they overlap the combinations provide the rest of the colours of the spectrum. Subtractive, or reflective, colour, used for printed material, is made up of the three secondary colours: cyan (blue), magenta (red) and yellow. When combined by placing dots of colour adjacent to each other, they should theoretically add up to black. However, they don't and so an additional colour, black or 'key', is added to make CMYK. Both additive and subtractive colour do accurately represent what we see in the world around us, but neither can reproduce all the colours of nature. RGB has a larger gamut than CMYK, so a conversion from

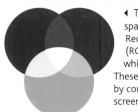

◀ The colour wheel shows the full spectrum of colours, with complementary colours positioned on opposite sides of the wheel.

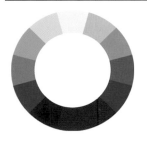

◀ The additive colour space. Transmitted light. Red, green and blue (RGB) combine to form white light at the centre. These are the colours used by computer and TV screens.

▶ The subtractive colour space. Reflected light. Cyan (blue), magenta (red) and yellow combine to form black at the centre. These colours are used to produce full, or four (CMYK) colour printing (K stands for black which is added to enhance the image).

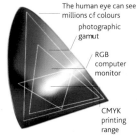

The human eye can see millions of colours

photographic gamut

RGB computer monitor

CMYK printing range

◀ Colour gamut shows where the full spectrum of colours are reduced by the processes of photography, screen design and the printing press.

RGB to CMYK can produce disappointing results. When computer screens could only reproduce 256 colours, designers were recommended to use a 'web-safe' palette of 216 colours that both Macs and PCs could reproduce. Now with computers able to display millions of colours, this is not such a big issue.

Sequence

Sequence is used in print graphics in relation to the succession of the spreads in a book or magazine. As mentioned above, the grid helps to reiterate the permanent features of each page and create continuity. In his book *Understanding Comics: The Invisible Art* (HarperPerennial, 1994), Scott McCloud demonstrates some important principles of sequential structures of still images on the same page: for example, two frames may show 'before' and 'after' scenes and readers will fill in the action in their head. Filmmakers do this when they pan away from a grisly scene to let the audience imagine it for themselves. Comics also show the past and present on the same page. Time is interpreted as a spatial progression as we scan from one frame to the next, usually from left to right.

Graphic designers use storyboards to visualize the unfolding series of images for motion graphics. Storyboards are simple sketches indicating the main action and the composition and thrust of each frame. Sometimes motion-graphics designers make an animatic, a simple digital sketch with movement and 3D action to check the animation before committing to time-consuming 3D modelling. Storyboards allow the designer to get an overview of the structure and development of a sequence and edit it down to the essential and most communicative key shots. Graphic designers work to commercial constraints. One is cost. Filming and editing

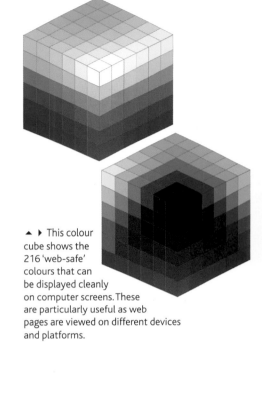

▲ ▶ This colour cube shows the 216 'web-safe' colours that can be displayed cleanly on computer screens. These are particularly useful as web pages are viewed on different devices and platforms.

◀ This sequence from *Jo Jo in the Stars,* an award-winning animated film, illustrates the animator's traditional skills of drawing, storytelling, sequence and image manipulation. This production was financed and produced by Studio aka. Directed by Marc Craste, the story tells the tale of two unlikely lovers: Jo Jo, a silver-plated trapeze artist, and the nameless hero who worships her. *Studio aka, London*

◀ Frames from *Shoxploitation,* an animation for Nike by PSYOP, an independent creative collective based in New York City. Illustration techniques are used in this sequence of drawings which were then manipulated with computer software for the final film. Founded in 2000, PSYOP focuses on blending design, animation and live action with creative and technical flexibility for the broadcast, advertising, music video and games industries. *www.psyop.tv*

◀ This pre-production storyboard for the film *Disponible* (below left) shows a sequence of key shots to guide the director and cameraman. It is common to use still photographs with or as an alternative to the more traditional drawn storyboard. *César Harada, Paris*

▲ These key frames from a film created for a manufacturer of baseball equipment, by director Bill White at the ka-chew! agency, show the products in action. *www.kachew.com, Los Angeles*

are usually time-consuming and expensive, so it's vital to have a clear plan before production starts. Another constraint is time. Television adverts are usually very short (typically 30 seconds) and although there might be a hundred edits, each frame must talk to the others and help to convey the message.

The order of the sequence can affect the message and mood. For example, if you film a conversation between two people, you could start with a wide master shot of both in context, and then follow up with close-ups to establish their individual character, and then make progressively abrupt cuts to suggest tension and anxiety. You might on the other hand start with a close-up of one character and build up an enigma or a sense of mystery.

Continuity

Sound, moving image and interactive screen-based work are always experienced in the present and require some kind of melodic, rhythmic, dramatic or graphic device to sustain continuity. Continuity should not be mere repetition, because that quickly becomes very dull. For example, books and magazines modify the number of columns or image sizes but stay within the overall grid structure. Television and film graphics ensure continuity through careful attention to detail. A scene may be filmed over several days and someone must ensure that the characters' clothes and hairstyles, the direction of the light and position of props or environment are the same at each shoot. Designers can also sustain a particular mood through colour, lighting or typographic style, but vary other elements such as viewpoint, proximity, movement, and sound composition. Elements of action or change can be introduced while building a coherent, progressive order and conclusion to a sequence.

Change in interactive new-media environments such as websites, games or even an ATM (automated teller machine) outside a bank is triggered by the user. This requires the designer to relinquish some of the control over the direction and pace of the sequence. Interestingly, this can make continuity even more essential. Games designers have to ensure they have created visual continuity in the design of virtual environments such as Star Wars Galaxies, but games also rely on rules to create a sense of the whole. Website designers use layout and colour to create continuity, and subtle variations on a template indicate which level or section of the site users are in at any one time. Interactive media seems to lend itself very readily to games. This will be discussed further in Chapter Four.

Nathalie Renard: Senior Producer ka-chew! Hollywood

▲ Nathalie Renard, Senior Producer at ka-chew!, a live action, design and animation company in Hollywood.

Nathalie Renard graduated with a graphic design degree from Pennsylvania State University in 1995 and went immediately into experimental animation with Backyard Animation in Chicago. Print advertising work done as a student provided her with useful contacts in the industry. Even though she had only taken classes in graphic design she knew she wanted to make a career in advertising.

She started as an artworker, helping to create elements for animation. Much of her work involved 'pixelation' or stop motion, so she was more like a prop artist, a miniature set construction crew member or an inker for animation cells.

Typically, in the studio where she worked, crew members progress from artworker to assistant animator, to animator, to assistant director, then director. In the digital area, people start as digital art assistants, then compositors, then motion graphic animators, then move on to be design directors or art directors. On the production side, people begin as production assistants, progress to coordinators, then production managers, then producers. If they are interested in the production support area, they can choose to pursue technical roles in grip, lighting, or camera departments from a production assistant position.

Nathalie worked her way up to assistant director, responsible for supervising the crew and making sure they kept the director's vision in all aspects of their work. She would regularly create the 'dope-sheets' used by animators to check calculations in timing, or synchronizing elements to audio before shooting. She would organize file naming systems and prepare samples or tests for the director to review. Then she decided that she wanted to be a producer so that she could participate in all aspects of a project.

As Senior Producer at ka-chew! she handles budgets, schedules, equipment, locations, crew, travel, client needs and any other arrangements involved in managing a project.

She has teams of production managers and coordinators working for her on each project. She says collaboration, mutual respect and support is important. From preparing a bid, to hiring crew, to editing and sound design, producers and directors or creative directors need to be in sync, so the ultimate vision can be achieved. That is not to say that they have to agree on everything, but they have to communicate about everything.

▲ Velvet Revolver 'Dirty Little Thing', directed at ka-chew! by Chris Prynosk, uses animation.

▲ 'Where they can hear me' for Radio Disney combines the hands-on computer artist's skills of Dave Foss with live action and 2D and 3D animation.

▲ Commercial spot for the Internet service provider EarthLink. The animation, directed by Bil White, shows people talking enthusiastically about the Internet and how they use it.

◄ 'Punk'd' main title for MTV Los Angeles. Bil White started his career in motion capture and moved into animation and directing. He is known for taking the subject of his animations 'a few degrees off skew'.

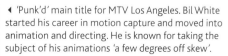

Sound

Although you can't hold a screen in the way you can hold and flick through a book, a sense of physical presence can be enhanced through the use of sound. Interface designers who specialize in the design of the icons, menu bars and configurations such as the layout of email systems use sound to reinforce actions. The swoosh sound of departing email, the thud of arriving chat, the clicks associated with deletion or saving are examples of sound designed to make graphics more legible and interaction more engaging. The designers of the first commercial games, such as Pong and Pac-Man, all used sound to reinforce the experience. Sounds can evoke physical materials, weight, speed and spatial context, and change mood and suggest irony. However, sounds can be extremely intrusive in interface design and need to be used with the utmost subtlety.

▼ Part of a series of sound interfaces that use the language and simplicity of early bitmapped computer games. *Friendchip*

In our daily lives we are now encountering more sound. There is more music available through downloads: iPods and other MP3 players allow us to travel accompanied by an enormous range of music. We hear Muzak in lifts and supermarkets; ringtones of mobile phones on trains. The sounds of traffic fill city streets. Sounds from television fill our homes.

Music software programs, such as GarageBand, enable sound and music composition through graphical interfaces from loops and samples, and have made sound design more accessible to a greater number of people. The emerging generation of sound designers and musicians has a huge range of recordings to reference or quote from. People combine high and popular culture, classical music and their favourite commercials. They experiment with combining debased sounds with high-fidelity sound.

Movement

Movement, like sound, can be used to structure, dramatize, inform, create mood and evoke associations. The computer screen can seem very inert in comparison to the slight movements that surround us in the real world. The ticking of the cursor and the subtle outlining of icons on rollovers are very minimal kinds of movement that work with the static graphic to aid navigation and usability. Interface designers have learnt from film language – for example, how to use subtle transitions: fades, zooms, dissolves – in order to create continuity from scene to scene. On the

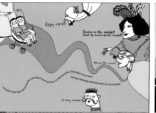

▲ ▶ Narrative illustration for an interactive storybook on CD-Rom by Per José Karlén. Users navigate around the screen pages and discover the interactive characters to reveal more of the story.

▶ *GM Warrior* is an online game which supports and raises awareness for the Greenpeace GM campaign, and which attempts to direct interest to the *Shopper's Guide to GM*, which is a resource to help users discover which foods are GM-free and which are not, and what consumers and supermarkets can do to change things.

In *GM Warrior* the player has to stop GM plants from spreading by shooting them with a sling shot. The player is confronted with a plot of land on which GM and non-GM plants grow, flower and slowly spread over the entire area. The detailed animation and dynamics, as well as the possibility of making a big online score, make the experience something you want to share with your friends. *Artificial Environments, London*

▶ In *Snowstorm* the player has to think and act strategically to clear a parking-lot of snow without piling it up too high in other places and while avoiding obstacles. As the game progresses this becomes ever more difficult, while of course the game becomes ever more addictive...

Snowstorm was developed as a self-promotional tool by *Artificial Environments, London*

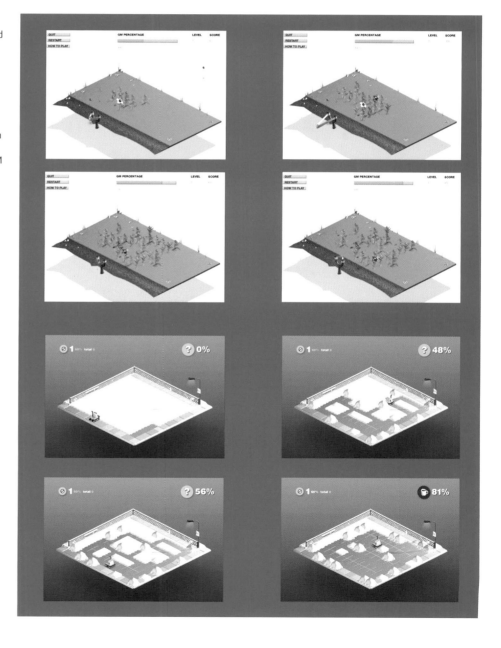

interactive screen we need to feel we know where we are and when we are 'entering' or moving around a space. Transitions and indeed our own ability to pick up frames or icons allow us to get a conceptual picture of the space in our minds. If the change on screen is abrupt and total, it disorientates the user.

Movement on a grander scale is a tool that graphic designers such as Saul Bass and Kyle Cooper have used to great effect in film-title sequences. It is part of the graphic designer's lexicon. Software has enabled designers to animate their images in ways that were never previously possible.

Narrative

Stories have always been an important element of design and the new media continue the tradition. In both old and new media, the story (content) and the telling of the story (expression) are referred to as the 'narrative'. Narrative involves developing a plot that propels the story forwards and structuring events that unfold over time. It provides a way of moving from real to fictional worlds and weaving different characters and themes together to build dramatic tension. Books (except dictionaries and encyclopedias), television and films work on a linear narrative determined by the author. They always start at the beginning, have a middle section and progress to the end, for a set period of time, until the final credits roll. The film director may introduce flashbacks and the author of a book may play around with time within the narrative flow, but the viewer cannot alter the sequence of events as set out by the editor. Although experiments on interactive fiction have taken place, in which the reader chooses what will happen, usually from two alternatives, the results haven't been satisfactory. Magazines are more interactive, the reader picking and choosing what articles to read.

New media offers more opportunities. E-books and CD-Roms have the added ability to be searched. The Internet is one giant encyclopedia, full of text, images and sounds, albeit much of dubious reliability. An action computer game such as *Quake* or *Doom* may have a predefined outcome and conclusion, but there can be many ways of getting there. With multiplayer games the game can go on almost forever. Other games are moving towards non-linear or explorative game play.

In so-called 'sandbox' games such as *Grand Theft Auto*, which allows players to take on the role of criminals in a big city, and *Elite*, a sci-fi trading simulation with space flight, combat, an economy to balance and a huge universe to be explored, the aim is to achieve 'elite' status, but the means to that end are entirely up to the player – it can be achieved by either following a pre-determined storyline or by ignoring it. Role-playing games, such as *The Sims*, and 'God-mode' strategy games, such as *Civilization*, are similarly open-ended. Massively Multiplayer Online Games (MMOGs or MMOs) are online computer games that evolved from MUDs (Multi-User Dungeons) and are capable of supporting hundreds or thousands of players simultaneously. Typically, this type of game is played in a giant persistent world, where the gameplay continues regardless of who is playing. As a result, players cannot 'finish' MMOGs in the typical sense of single-player games.

Outside of games, there are also virtual worlds on the Internet, such as Second Life, in which residents are represented by avatars, computer-generated virtual humans. Here, narrative has all but disappeared, with the virtual world mirroring real life, with property to buy and money to be made. The difference is you can determine how you look, and you can fly. The challenge to the designer is to make the experience desirable and compulsive to the 'player'.

Association and interpretation

All new-media designers use combinations of the techniques listed above to translate ideas into visual or multimedia form. This process of translation could be described as a leap of imagination whereby designers associate ideas expressed in words with scenarios, characters, visual qualities or systems, and thereby create metaphors or analogies that can be substituted for the written concept.

▲ Designers gain inspiration from the things around them such as the contents of their studios or the things they collect. Hyperkit's studio is shown here.

Inspiration and imagination are hard to describe. Sometimes ideas just seem to appear in the mind. However, there are ways in which designers can nurture their inspiration and activate their imagination, for example by building up a personal visual collection from things noticed in everyday life. This is rather like the traditional art practice of keeping a sketchbook and drawing inspiration from natural forms, light effects, shapes and colours. Most graphic designers read lots of magazines on fashion, music and lifestyle. They draw inspiration from television, film and comics. New-media graphic designers are no different; they need to read widely, not just the technology press. Inspiration can be found in anything from music to car-boot sales, science, architecture, illustrations in books read as a child, people's behaviour, the process of working with materials and technology itself. There are no rules about personal inspiration except that you need to know what inspires you and how to sustain your inspiration. It's important to look at other people's work and think through the qualities of the work you like best.

Prototyping

A prototype is a first version of a design solution built to exact technical specifications so that it can be tested. This is an extremely important stage for software development and usability testing of graphic and interface design. The process is iterative: that is, the prototype is manufactured or constructed, tested, and then the design is modified; a new or modified prototype is built and retested. Prototypes will often go through several iterations before they are signed off for production, online launch or publication. A website must be shielded from the public while it is in prototype form. Usually the designer will upload it to a server, whose address is known only to the client and other professionals involved in the project. Because websites can be updated instantly, it is tempting to launch a site before all the bugs have been ironed out. However, only when it is fully working and finished should it 'go live' to the public on the client's web space.

Style guide

A style guide is a detailed document that sets out visual and functional guidelines for the organization of information. Design, typography, photography and

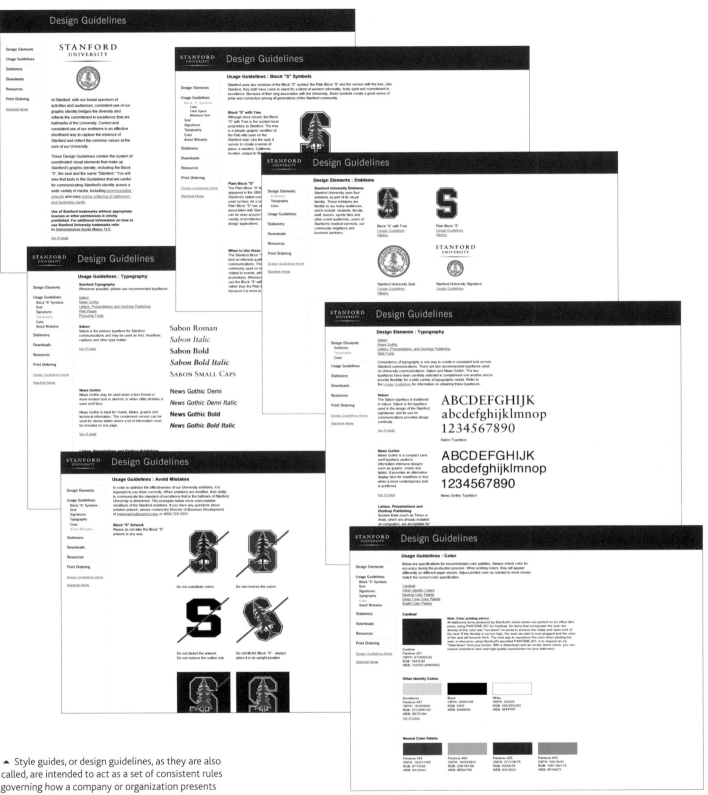

▲ Style guides, or design guidelines, as they are also called, are intended to act as a set of consistent rules governing how a company or organization presents itself visually and publicly. Consistent use of colour, typography, logotypes and symbols are vital. *Stanford University, Palo Alto, California*

illustration must all, in turn, convince an audience that the information presented to them is consistent, accurate, worthwhile and useful.

We look for order, clarity and trustworthiness in information sources, whether in printed documents or web pages. Graphic design creates a visual logic by providing a balance between information and visual sensation. The spatial organization of text and graphics on a page engages readers with graphic impact, directs their attention, prioritizes the information presented and makes the viewer's interaction with the design more efficient and pleasurable. A systematic approach to page design makes it easier for readers to take full advantage of the information, and in the case of a website it can reduce user error and simplify interaction and navigation.

Style guides are usually written throughout the design phase of a project. This is to maintain the design style, and ensure that after the project is launched any subsequent modifications or additions will be consistent with the original design. Style guides record the brand or message being conveyed: the colour palette, for example, in hexadecimal or RGB values for the web, so that it can be precisely reproduced in digital formats; the fonts (typefaces) for headers, body text, captions, etc.; image sizes and instructions for use of any future images, including perhaps angle of view, facial expression, and types of background; and pixel-by-pixel layout for different kinds of pages or subsections.

In some established companies and organizations, style guides may already exist, detailing the way that their people, programmes and procedures are presented through editorial text and visual 'look and feel'. Publishers and newspapers have a style book that sets out spellings (organize or organise), how a date should be written, whether book titles and ship names are italicized, the way to treat acronyms (HTML or html) and rules on all other areas of possible contention. When a company has a corporate identity makeover, the design company will not only redesign the logo, but will also provide a style guide, explaining how it should be implemented in the field, on stationery or signage.

Usability

Usability is a term describing the ease with which the user of a product can understand how it works and how to get it to perform. There has been a great deal published on this subject. Jakob Nielsen (www.useit.com) and Donald Norman (www.jnd.org) are particularly well known for their contributions. Usability can be applied to the design of everyday objects such as telephones and the interface of products such as washing machines and video players. The same principles can be applied to websites, search engines, games, museum interactive kiosks, ATMs or cashpoints, anything that you interact with. There are graphic lessons to be learnt. Crowding a page with information does not mean that the reader will read it and take it in. On the contrary, overcrowded pages can prevent people from reading easily. Providing long menu lists may be accurate, but the detail can be overwhelming. The 'look and feel' of the user interface is created partly by graphic elements such as colour and typeface; the flow and integration may also depend on the choice and ordering of the words used.

A good deal of scientific and behavioural research has been done on the Human–Computer Interface (HCI) design, watching how people use computers and the web in order to test and develop better ways to design for interaction. General standards have been established and commercial websites are thoroughly tested for usability before they are launched. Focus groups are used to test how long it takes to complete a task, or to ask users to 'think out loud' about what the website offers, where they get confused or what difficulties they have in reaching their goal. User-testing demonstrates that while the client and designer attend to every detail, users often glance through a website, pick a small fraction of what's there, take the first reasonable option and muddle through, often missing useful information.

Usability experts advise keeping pages and language simple, and making them obvious so that people don't have to puzzle over what something is or what to do next. Commercial web and information designers need to prevent users from being put off by wondering where they are, how they should begin, where they went or put something, what the most important information on the page is, or why particular language is being used. Experts recommend that every layout should be self-evident.

Accessibility means that people with disabilities or older people can use, and contribute to the web. Web accessibility can also benefit people *without* disabilities,

Designing Effective Websites

The computer screen may seem very small yet it is a window into huge volumes of information. Here are some key pointers for effective website design:

- It helps to design an uncluttered interface that is easy to use. Designers create clear layouts by defining areas using grids, colour, positioning and typography. A generous use of space makes the screen easier to read. Remember: visual confusion undermines user confidence and it's easy for people just to click away.
- Create a coherent look from page to page. Drastic changes of palette, scale or image create a jarring effect and disorientate people.
- The topics or content should be relevant to the goals of the website.
- Good navigation is vital. It is about reminding people where they are and letting them know where they could go next. You can tell how long a book is by looking at how thick it is and flicking through the pages to see the size of the font and the ratio of images to words. You can't tell how big a website is by looking at the homepage. Websites should allow you to find your way around; you should never have to click through more than three layers to find what you are searching for. The links should always work. Make sure there is an accessible menu that is always visible.
- Include links to other relevant websites.
- Include easy-to-find contact information such as phone and email details.
- Show that the site is being continually updated. Websites are ongoing projects.
- Illustrate some experimental or distinctive quality – something that differentiates your website from others.
- Frequently, something funny or entertaining engages the user.
- Conduct usability and accessibility tests, and modify the website accordingly.
- Use search engines, postcards, television and newspapers to spread news of the website. Otherwise no one may ever know it's there.

such as people using a slow Internet connection, people wanting to print off information, or with 'temporary disabilities' such as a broken arm or RSI (repetitive strain injury). When developing or redesigning websites, evaluating accessibility early can identify accessibility issues when it is easier to design for them. This can mean providing alternative modes of navigation, colours that don't confuse colour-blind people, 'text-only' pages to augment a Flash-based site, or simply adding 'alt' tags to images.

User-centred design

User-centred design is a slightly broader notion than usability, whereby designers see themselves at the service of the public at large, and take a philosophical position that design should empower individuals and improve society. For example, the design of teaching aids improves learning, the design of traffic signs saves lives, the design of newspapers and websites informs audiences and enables them to make decisions about all aspects of their lives. Graphic designers construct visual messages that affect people's knowledge, attitudes and behaviour. They have social and ethical responsibilities. Design is not just a question of creating a seductive aesthetic (the 'look and feel'). Designers should understand the needs and value systems of their audience and the potential impact of their design.

Audience research is vital to user-centred design and especially important in new-media design. Sociologists, psychologists, ethnographers, market researchers and consumer advocates are employed by large companies to investigate audience needs and desires.

The design process

The design process starts when a company or organization's marketing department identifies a need for a new product or website, or feels that it is time their current one has a revamp. They will then approach designers and new-media companies and ask them to pitch for the job. This pitch may be paid or unpaid – a paid pitch is obviously better for the designer and shows that the client is serious about going ahead. From an initial brief, the designer will then come up with some presentations. The client will choose one or negotiate a combination of parts of different presentations, the brief will be tightened and there will be talk of timescales and fees. The chosen designer will then get to work in earnest, perhaps with a contract under his or her belt. The client may supply the 'assets' – the words and pictures for the website – or special photography and illustrations may be commissioned. As the project progresses the client may wish to comment on the emerging design, but any serious changes of mind will have to be paid for. Finally, when everyone is happy, the project will go live to the public. In reality, all projects will be different, and the designer may be required to hand over the project to in-house designers at any time.

Designers do not work in a vacuum – unlike fine artists, they invariably work to a brief from a client. The client pays the bills so must be listened to, but the client has presumably engaged the designer because of his or her reputation and ability to come up with the goods, so a degree of give and take will be acceptable. The relationship between designer and client is crucial, however, and can make or break a new-media project.

The design brief

Regardless of the area in which a designer works, the design process normally starts with the client. The client could be a television company or a rock band, a large multinational corporation, a publisher or a friend. Sometimes the client will approach a designer because they know their work. Often the designer has to pitch for a job; in other words, compete against other designers by talking through their approach and presenting an initial design concept. To support these ideas, it is useful to show examples of previous work. As stated earlier, the pitch may be unpaid (architects frequently participate in 'competitions') or, preferably, paid. The client may ask several designers and consultancies to pitch for the same job, each working to the same initial brief. A designer may have put in a lot of time preparing for the pitch and if they are turned down, may feel that their time has been wasted. The pitch may, however, stick in the mind of the client, who may approach the designer again when another project comes along.

Once the designer has been chosen, the client supplies a more detailed brief, or project description. The brief is usually a written document that outlines the target audience and the business goal the client wants to achieve, and gives the project deadlines. Each brief will have its limitations: it could be budget, low band-width connections, restrictive colour palettes, timescale or an anxious, interfering client. The challenge for the designer is to find an inventive way to fulfil the brief within those constraints.

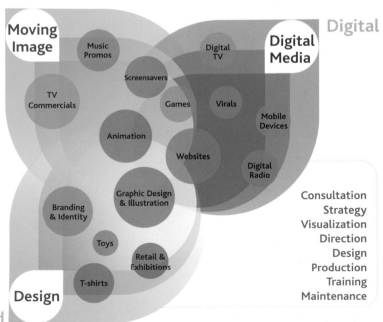

◀ Airside devised this diagram to help its clients understand what the company can do for them.

Sometimes the brief doesn't necessarily capture the client's real desires. By asking questions and listening carefully a designer can begin to discover what the client really believes and wants. It's best to establish good communications and involve the client from the very start of the design process, and remain open to their feedback. Each client is different in how they work with designers. Some expect the designer to work almost entirely independently. Others like to be consulted at every step. At this stage, a designer's role is to gently help the client to identify what they most want while getting a feel for a brand or a message.

In his book *MTIV (Making the Invisible Visible): Process, Inspiration and Practice for the New Media Designer* (New Riders Press, 2002), Hillman Curtis encourages designers to listen to their clients and include them in the design process: 'The key is never to alienate them. Think of yourself as their tarot card reader, gently coaxing them towards their fortune, helping them uncover what they want most.' Every project has a story, what is unique about the company or product, and it's the designer's job to interpret the client's desires. The client and designer have a joint responsibility in the success of the project. What didn't they like about the site that is to be replaced? What didn't they like about the previous designers? A client's feedback should never be dismissed or treated as an annoying interruption to the creative process. A good designer will tap into the client's creativity.

The client's marketing department may have commissioned market research to establish that a revamp of the existing product or website is required. Market research will also identify any deficiencies in the previous design and give pointers as to how it can be made more successful. This research will be made available to the designer or design group. However, if the project is a large, lucrative one, they may commission their own. Some of the larger design groups have associate companies that develop design strategies for companies, using futurologists to spot any new developments in technology or fashion that can be exploited.

Commercial web design

An important part of the design brief for a website is to define the strategy and aims of the site. Commercial websites can fulfil several business objectives: for example, business-to-business, business-to-investor or business-to-consumer communications. Business-to-business sites provide business listings of stakeholders, services, products, news, jobs, etc. Business-to-investor sites publish company reports, provide downloads, frequently asked questions (FAQs), help functions, etc. Business-to-consumer sites showcase product lines, and sometimes express the brand through providing immersive lifestyle experiences by including music, games and video to give a feel for the product. They may also provide interactive services, such as help, registration and downloading functions. These websites form part of companies' marketing and communication strategies. They don't make money directly, but are very important in developing or sustaining a company's profile and its investors' and customers' confidence. These websites have to be reliable, easy to use and engaging, reinforcing positive images of the company that in turn feed into its commercial success.

Some websites support online financial transactions. This is called e-commerce. These websites actively make money. They have to demonstrate return on investment (ROI). In other words, they have to make or save money for a company, and the design process is streamlined to achieve these goals.

Whether websites need to be designed to inform, showcase or actively sell goods and services, they also need to express the company's brand throughout. Brand values are the characteristics or qualities of the company that staff and customers hold in their minds. For example, some companies are considered youthful, energetic and innovative; some secure, reliable, traditional, and so on. The brand or reputation is worth a lot of money in itself.

The process for designing commercial websites runs as follows. First, there is a discussion between the creative director and the client to agree the two or three principal brand values to communicate through the site: for example, 'innovation, quality and passion'. A brand strategist from the client's company or the design company may help to identify those values. Next, through discussion, the goals of the site are clarified. A client may want to showcase an entire range of products or promote sales of a particular line. Equally, it may want to disseminate a financial report to shareholders or develop a list of FAQs for consumers. Alternatively, it may be developing a customer help function so that existing customers can email questions to an online support team. It is important to get core values and goals

▲ In America amazon.com started selling books via the Internet in 1995. It now has websites worldwide and Amazon has grown to become one of the runaway success stories of online shopping.

A communications company can comprise a wide range of different roles

- The design team, who create the look and feel and detailed graphic design of the site. The team is usually led by an art director.
- Information architects, who design the site structure: in other words, the layers, links and navigation, headers, footers and sidebars.
- The user-interface designer, who reminds the team of the wide range of web-related abilities among customers.
- The content strategist, who takes responsibility for the content management, overseeing the sourcing and editing of the words.
- The front-end technologist, who translates the content into web-compatible code: for example, HTML or XML or VRML, Flash or Javascript – in effect, the equivalent of the printing function in traditional graphics.
- The back-end technologist, who is not concerned with design at all but rather with file formats, databases, server site programming and configuration.
- Accountants, who are responsible for ensuring projects work within the allocated budgets and make a profit.
- The creative director or producer, who is responsible for concept development, communication and effective collaboration between the design team and technical teams. The creative director has an overview of the creative process, the business strategy and customer experience.

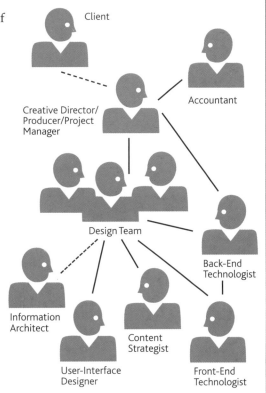

clear from the start. These first discussions also serve to establish deadlines and budgets. Some clients are very well informed about web design and web technology and they see a website as a core part of their business. Others may not be so informed or so convinced. The design company has to be very clear in explaining the process and justifying costs.

The first question a new client will ask is 'how much does a website cost to produce?' The simple answer is the same as the one to the question 'how long is a piece of string?' It is important for the designer to get the client to specify in the brief as much detail as possible, in terms of pages and assets, and set out what is required of them and what the client is expecting at the end of the project. The cost of maintaining the site must also be factored in. Websites quickly go out of date, so who is expected to update it? The client or the designer? It is also important to cost changes of mind and 'kill fees' should the project break down at any point. Budget and deadlines, what should be paid and when, should be in a written document or contract. This is especially important for the freelance designer or small practice. When everything is agreed and everyone understands what is expected of them, the project can begin in earnest.

The creative process

At the concept stage of design, some designers use flow diagrams, mind maps or spider diagrams; some sketch preliminary ideas; some write lists or use collections of images or sounds to work towards a visual solution. Some people use characterization and narrative to suggest new ideas. Imagine a company, a product, a natural phenomenon as a person. How would they behave? What stories would unfold? Imagine the future, build scenarios using a 'what if' approach.

Some designers advocate creative techniques such as brainstorming associations, enjoying the range of ideas that come up; and not worrying about producing the obvious clichés – they should be got out into the open quickly and dismissed. It sometimes helps to reverse situations or think of opposites; considering what is missing rather than what is there. Thinking of what is unlikely or impossible can give a fresh and oblique angle on a situation, object, person or product.

The technology and production process can generate ideas too. Many new-media graphic designers get inspiration from computing in the same way that painters have always been inspired by mixing and applying paint. Basic programming can produce screen-based 'sketches', such as abstract patterns, shapes, sounds and movement, in much the same way that an artist uses a sketchbook. Designers usually present two or three ideas to the client at a presentation. There is usually one favourite the designer personally prefers and it is down to diplomacy to guide the client towards this one. Presentations used to be made using print-outs on boards, or a flip chart, but they are now more likely to be PowerPoint projections from a laptop. Obviously a website presentation should look as much like the finished website as possible, and be produced using the designer's program of

◄ Two websites from Nike, the international sports brand. *Top:* Nikeid, a consumer site that allows visitors to order and 'style' their own products. *Below:* Nikebiz is a website for businesses and investors.

▶ A planning meeting at Airside's studio. This is where ideas and design strategies are discussed between the designers before a client presentation. *Airside*

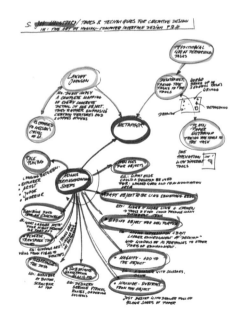

▲ A mind map produced as part of a research project. Designers often use this approach to help clarify their thought processes. *Axel Vogelsang*

choice, Dreamweaver or GoLive, with Fireworks, Flash or Director used for motion graphics. For games, stills of characters and vehicles will have been modelled in 3D software such as Maya or 3D Studio Max; with backgrounds in Bryce or Photoshop. In other forms of design it is important at the presentation stage for the designs to have some rough edges – the clients should not feel that the design is 'set in stone' and cannot be tweaked. At the end of the presentation, the client should have settled on one design (or elements from all of them) and the design process can move on to the next stage.

The next stage involves devising a key concept, which will form the basis of the design brief. Many quite different companies have similar brand values. As such, they need the design company to come up with a new way to communicate these values for them so that they appear fresh and distinctive. In a large design company, the concept is devised by the art director and the creative director/ producer. The brief is then delivered to the internal design team, which interprets this concept and develops two or three examples of the 'look and feel' for the site. This is a major inventive and expressive stage of the design work. While the information architect develops proposals for the structure of the site, the design team produces mood boards, storyboards, sample layouts with different colour palettes and typefaces, sample images, Flash movies and music to evoke and express the design concept. The design team also considers how the company's products may be featured in other media, for example, in print or on a home-shopping television channel. When the client has reviewed and selected one of the proposals for the 'look and feel' and the structure of the website, the team moves on to the detailed design. The concept stage is short. Much more time is spent later working up design details and structures.

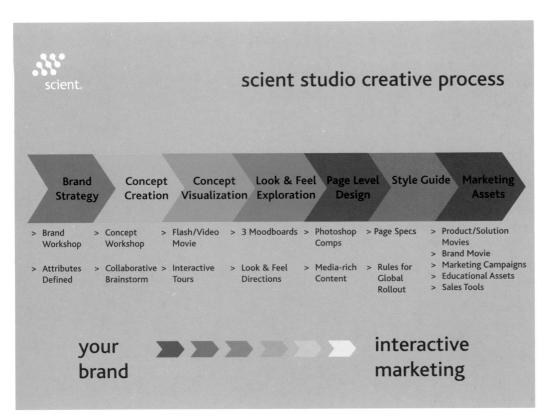

◀ Diagram of the creative process developed by Scient showing the progressive steps in online interactive marketing.

The detailed design of a website starts with the entry point, the homepage, plus the site map that defines a series of pages, such as the index, contents or product pages in order to establish the overall pattern and consistency of the whole site. This is the second inventive stage, where the designers are solving problems within the parameters of the agreed 'look and feel'. It is a process of trial and error, and constant modification is needed until the different pages sit well together. The visual decisions also have to be made with the technical constraints in mind, so the designers need an understanding of the software and bandwidth limitations. A wireframe template, which defines the layout, is developed to hold the content. Once the main design decisions have been made, this template becomes invaluable. The designer may have 70 or more similar pages to lay out, and it is tedious and costly to spend unnecessary time creating each one from scratch. The design team not only work on the 'front end' of the website – the linked pages users can access on screen through the Internet – but also on the content management system, which mirrors the front end and contains instructions and templates that enables companies to change the content. So, for example, when a museum needs to update the information on new exhibitions or opening times, an administrator, rather than a trained designer, can easily enter words, images and sounds that flow directly to the right page and conform to the overall style. A prototype website will be produced and uploaded to a secret (to the public) server, usually the designer's own. Here it can be shown to the client, tested for functionality and usability, and exposed to focus groups. The designer working on the site every day can soon become blind to any deficiencies in the navigation.

Stages in designing a website

▲ Planning interactivity: the brief, designer's layouts (drawings), layout diagrams, who-does-what plan and timeline schedule, with prints of screen pages.

◀ Websites are built using code such as HTML and interactivity is engineered at this point. The site can be updated by returning to the application that first generated it, or by using a CMS (content management system). *The Royal Anniversary Trust website, Axel Vogelsang and the Royal College of Art*

These problems would be immediately spotted by someone new to the site who is searching for specific information, or merely wondering what the website is for. Focus groups are a random selection of users meant to represent the target audience. If the budget doesn't run to neutral focus groups, a small practice or freelance designer can test the site on friends or other designers not involved with the project. The favour may have to be reciprocated, however.

The next stage is development and testing. The front-end designer or programmer codes the website and tests it to ensure functionality: for example, the elements must appear in the correct place, in the desired typeface and colour, and every link

Address of website

Quick navigation

Web browser navigation bar

Website address(URL) http://

text only version

Logo

Banner image/company name

Navigation
buttons
link to
internal
website
'pages'

Heading

Image

Search this site ▶

Hypertext link to more information

Body text

Alternative navigation

▲ Typical elements of a website homepage. The rest of the site is linked to this initial window and usually follows an interface specification or a template design so that all content has a similar 'look and feel'.

wireframe

page design

UI specifications

▲ In the process of developing complex webpages, the design passes through these three main stages: the 'wireframe' sets out the information and is used to check that all the material and links are provided for; based on this, the page is then designed; finally, the UI (User Interface) is accurately specified to ensure consistency throughout the site. *Charles Hayes, Scient*

must work as planned. The programmer also tests compatibility: for example, the website must be consistent across different browsers and machines from an online test site. If necessary, a back-end technologist develops file formats, databases, server-side programming and configuration.

Usability testing is conducted with small focus groups to discover any problems in ease of use. The usability findings nearly always result in design changes. Once all the final changes are made, the website can be launched. Post-launch, further changes will be necessary because companies frequently update their products and information, and consistency is vital. To facilitate these, a detailed style guide outlining the design rules is written.

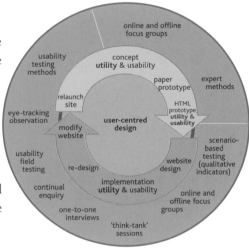

▲ Usability process for testing websites. The process is intended to show any weaknesses in the design and functionality of a website.

Summary

New media evolved from the old media of print, film and television, but new media is much more than old media updated, and it is beginning to throw off the shackles of its forebears and move into new areas and opportunities. Just as cars once resembled horseless carriages, new media began by adopting the working methods and terminology of old media. Print technology terms are still in common use and are unlikely to disappear in the near future, and much can be learnt from a study of layout and classic design methods – why re-invent the wheel! But there is no reason why a website should look like the printed page, and a new generation of new-media designers are seizing the opportunity to throw away the rule book and break new ground.

Strategy for website design and production

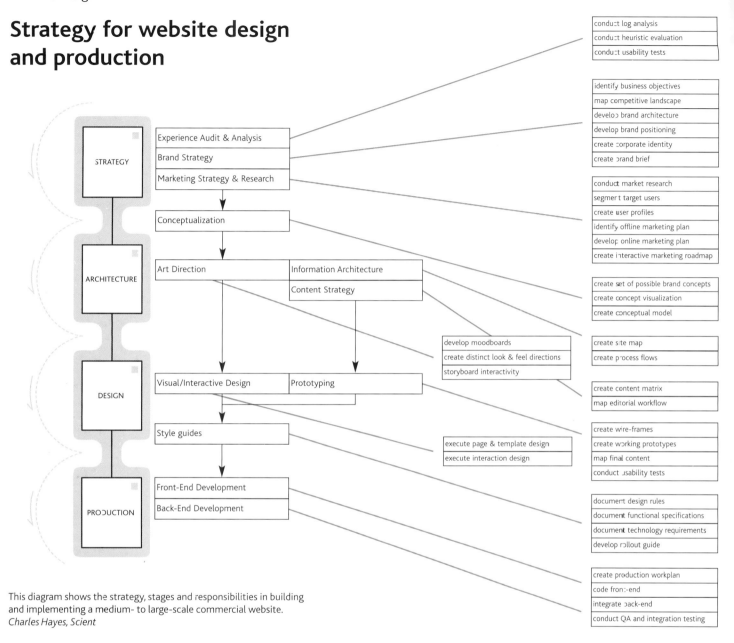

	conduct log analysis
	conduct heuristic evaluation
	conduct usability tests

identify business objectives
map competitive landscape
develop brand architecture
develop brand positioning
create corporate identity
create brand brief

conduct market research
segment target users
create user profiles
identify offline marketing plan
develop online marketing plan
create interactive marketing roadmap

create set of possible brand concepts
create concept visualization
create conceptual model

create site map
create process flows

create content matrix
map editorial workflow

develop moodboards
create distinct look & feel directions
storyboard interactivity

create wire-frames
create working prototypes
map final content
conduct usability tests

execute page & template design
execute interaction design

document design rules
document functional specifications
document technology requirements
develop rollout guide

create production workplan
code front-end
integrate back-end
conduct QA and integration testing

STRATEGY
- Experience Audit & Analysis
- Brand Strategy
- Marketing Strategy & Research

Conceptualization

ARCHITECTURE
- Art Direction
- Information Architecture
- Content Strategy

DESIGN
- Visual/Interactive Design
- Prototyping
- Style guides

PRODUCTION
- Front-End Development
- Back-End Development

This diagram shows the strategy, stages and responsibilities in building and implementing a medium- to large-scale commercial website.
Charles Hayes, Scient

Old media was analogue, static and linear; new media is digital, dynamic and interactive. Designers can introduce sound and movement into their new-media designs, and rather than being pigeonholed into being a designer just for print or films, can widen their horizons to embrace all the media, new and old, and be equipped for the challenge of media as yet not invented.

The Internet Environment ³

Traditional Media

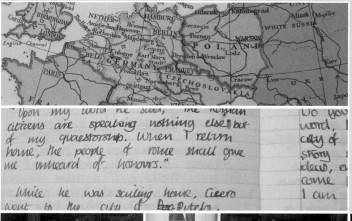

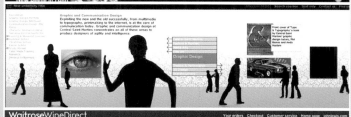

▲ *Top down:* Traditional printed school atlas. Handwritten school exercise book. Museum display case, *Worcester Museum and Art Gallery*. 1960s Press advertisement for Volkswagen cars.

▶ *Top down:* Digital map showing Internet worldwide traffic, *Atlas of Cyber Spaces*. School homework on a computer. Interactive museum display, *Land Design Studio*. Web advertisement for Volkswagen cars. Website for Central Saint Martins College of Art and Design. Internet shopping website, *Waitrose Direct, UK*.

New media evolved alongside the development of the computer. As discussed in previous chapters, it is perfectly possible to produce print, television and film without involving a computer at any stage, and this is how it used to be done for many years. Computers, however, make the whole of the design process quicker, easier and capable of greater things. It also means that a freelance graphic designer can now tackle all kinds of jobs that in the days of old media required expensive equipment and teams of skilled craftspeople. Computers are now indispensable to the old media, but have also been responsible for creating completely new media, such as the Internet, to which this chapter is devoted.

In this chapter, we will look at the brief history of the Internet, and in particular the World Wide Web, to discover how invaluable it is to the new media designer, not just in his or her daily studio life, but in opening up new design opportunities, in the design of websites. Graphic design is all about organizing and communicating information. The Internet is an enormous living archive of information and the largest communications network that ever existed, and is consequently of primary concern to graphic designers. It is also an infinite opportunity for new work – every web page has to be designed by someone.

From cyberspace to the real world

In the beginning, the Internet was almost all non-graphical, and some parts of it, namely Usenet newsgroups, remain text-only today. It's hard to believe that the World Wide Web was originally text-based. Now even emails are a rich mix of text and graphics, and wherever words and images meet is the domain of the graphic designer. Graphic design online evolved into web and interface design during the 1990s. Although these are very important areas of practice, they are by no means the only area of graphic design on the Internet.

The 1990s saw the notion of 'cyberspace', a term coined by writer William Gibson in his 1984 novel *Neuromancer*, dominate popular views of the Internet. Cyberspace conjures up ideas of a new universe, parallel to the real world, whereby instantaneous communication appears to shrink space and manipulate time, offering escape, adventure and even new forms of personal identity. The idea of virtual worlds, generated by computer networks and located somewhere 'inside the computer network', inspired many designers and filmmakers to conceive immersive digital landscapes and imaginary worlds, which have, for example, spawned multi-user online games and growing numbers of interactive games played on mobile phones. (Games design is discussed in Chapter Four.)

▲ An office building in Berlin's Alexanderplatz enhanced by Blinkenlights to become the world's biggest interactive computer display. Animations were submitted by specialist designers and members of the public. *Chaos Computer Club. Dorit Günter, Nadja Hannaske. www.blinkenlights.de*

▲ Google Earth combines satellite images of practically any location on Earth with information on street names, buildings, etc. You type in a city or an individual address and Google takes you there. You can then zoom in for a detailed close-up.

The first years of the twenty-first century have ushered in new waves of technological development that have created novel design challenges and opportunities relating to mobile computing in our immediate location 'outside the network', in the real world. Advances in wireless computing have created the 'mobile Internet'. Wireless networks broadcast from 'hotspots' to the immediate surrounding area. Data from the Internet can be accessed from hotspots by laptops, high-speed, multimedia mobile phones or other hand-held devices. The mobile Internet enables people to access information relevant to their location as they move through it. Designers are considering how users may want to interact with live feeds of complex information on the move. Will this lead, as Howard Rheingold argues in his book *Smart Mobs* (Perseus, 2002), to new forms of collective action and cooperation between groups of friends, or common-interest groups?

There are examples of user-centred, location-based graphic interventions that can give voice to communities. From 2001 to 2002 Blinkenlights, an installation in Berlin, turned an empty office building into the world's biggest interactive computer display. Lamps were placed behind each window at the front of the building, and a computer was used to switch them on and off so that the eight floors of windows acted like pixels to produce an 18 x 8 matrix. The computer was linked to the Internet so passers-by could text love letters, play *Pong* or send simple messages to be displayed on the building using mobile phones with Internet connections. The building was transformed from a derelict eyesore into an important landmark in the local community. Blinkenlights, inspired by hacking in that it was open for all to contribute to, directs our attention away from the idea of disembodied cyberspace to envisage the Internet as a site-specific communication facility for individuals to express their real lives in a concrete way. It demonstrates how the audience can become the author – another new idea for designers to grapple with.

Recent developments in satellite photography have been used to develop new location-based information systems, notably Google Earth, which is a free virtual globe developed by Google for use on personal computers. It overlays satellite imagery, aerial photography, geographic information systems (GIS) – for example, maps generated from statistics – onto a 3D model of the Earth. In principle, you can zoom in to a close-up of any location in the world, although some areas are represented in sharper detail than others. You can fly over and into 3D landscapes or townscapes and overlay the photographic images with street names or other geographical information. Google Earth also offers an additional paid-for service that allows users to annotate the space: for example, you can click on individual buildings and leave reminders for yourself or messages for others.

Compare this to standardized paper maps that you unfold and scan to locate or calculate your position. Traditional printed maps contain levels of fixed information in an abstract format whereas new-media maps are developing spatially dramatic, personalized, interactive functions tailored to your location, destination, interests and memories. These maps are theoretically infinitely extendable and can overlay many levels of information.

The trend to integrate the computing and the physical environment is also exemplified by the development of 'ubiquitous' computing. Microprocessors and memory have become so inexpensive that they are routinely found in all kinds of electrical equipment, down to throw-away greetings cards that play tunes. As computers have become smaller and cheaper to manufacture, it is now possible to embed them in furniture, objects and the built environment. Imagine your mobile phone, your jewellery or your clothing as remote controls that could enable you to download information from your immediate environment or upload messages. It is envisaged that within a matter of decades embedded networks will enfold the entire earth like an additional communication skin. Exciting as these technologies are, they are incomplete without an interface that allows people to use them. This is the work of the designer.

From the Great Library of the ancient world at Alexandria, destroyed by fire in the third century CE, through medieval monasteries, grand and small museums, botanical gardens and zoos, and right up to the sound archives of modern broadcasting companies, human beings have shown a desire to collect. Libraries have evolved systems of classification so that items or ideas can be stored according to subject and retrieved at will. The most widespread system, the Dewey Decimal Classification System, named after its nineteenth-century inventor, Melvil Dewey, uses identifying codes and numbers that you see pasted on the spines of books on library shelves. Each item is tagged so that it can be easily found and returned to its rightful place. All systems require organizing principles or sets of rules, and throughout history a particular person, group of people or institution has always been in charge of that system.

▶ 'Information Management', the original proposal by Tim Berners-Lee, to CERN in 1989. This describes the distributed hypertext system that eventually became the World Wide Web.

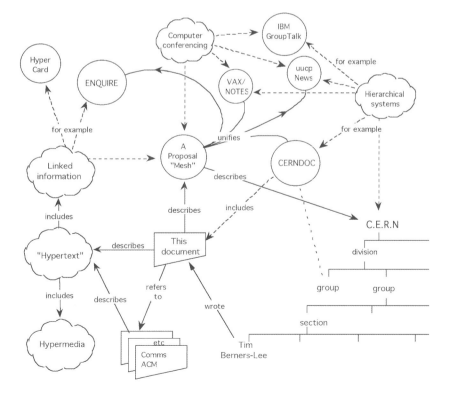

The Internet is different. When Tim Berners-Lee first envisaged the World Wide Web (WWW) in 1990, he saw it as a free-growing mass of links without any overall governing database and with no one organization or any vested interests in charge. The structure of the WWW is created through the contribution of each user and the hyperlinks in documents. The attraction is that, in principle, anyone can contribute to and use the system, not just authors, businesses or institutions. This creates an environment that is at once lawless, complex and unpredictable because it has no overall structure and is constantly changing. It is more like a dynamic ecosystem than a static terrain. This is welcomed by people who see the Internet as a place where they can find adventure, chat, explore, invent, subvert, joke or lie. From this perspective the Internet can be viewed as a free, shared space; and this has great appeal to those who subscribe to the ideal of democracy.

However, the chaotic structure of the Internet presents problems if you are searching for particular information. Imagine getting everyone who lived in the same street to pile all their belongings – clothes, jewellery, food, furniture, magazines, CDs and computers – in one great heap. Even though everything might be there in one big pile, no one would ever be able to find anything in it except by chance. The incalculable amount of information on the Internet presents a similar problem – on a much larger scale.

In an attempt to order and get an overview of the Internet, efforts have been made to map cyberspace. There is a certain irony in trying to create a fixed image of an ever-changing phenomenon, but maps are useful in giving form to the way different people have perceived the Internet.

On individual websites the problem of organizing large quantities of information and making it accessible has been tackled successfully by many design teams. A good example of a large useful archive is the BBC's website (www.bbc.co.uk). The BBC is primarily a national broadcaster, so much of its vast amount of content in

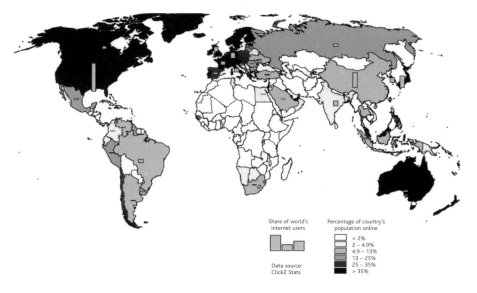

◀ Map showing Internet populations worldwide in 2005 (latest figures available).

Share of world's internet users

Percentage of country's population online

Data source: ClickZ Stats

	< 2%
	2 – 4.9%
	4.9 – 13%
	13 – 25%
	25 – 35%
	> 35%

Internet users worldwide

1975	70
1977	100
1981	250
1983	1000
1995	**30 million**
2001	300 million
2005	**817,447,147 million**
	(12.7% of world population)

Source: Zooknic (http://www.zooknic.com)

all media is linked to television and radio, and it also has a huge archive to call on. It has more than two million pages and its homepage alone receives more than nine million visitors per month, mainly using the links to pages dedicated to news, current affairs, sport, television and radio programmes, and education. This mix of broadcasting, news, education and the Internet is assembled by hundreds of editors, designers, researchers and programmers at a cost of almost £100 million, making it one of the most expensive websites so far created. Over 300 television programmes have dedicated webpages or micro-websites of their own. The BBC's radio stations can be listened to as they are broadcast directly through the website, and many of the shows are archived and can be heard again 'off air'.

As a public service broadcaster, the BBC is not permitted to advertise or to generate revenue by carrying advertising. Instead it receives its income from a compulsory UK national licence fee. Unlike other major websites, it is not dependent on commercial returns, and also makes its web services freely available to Internet users outside the UK.

Although the website represents a flagship British organization, it has international content in 43 languages and has companies worldwide. News and sport sections of the website offer visitors a choice between UK and international versions.

Educational programming is part of the BBC remit and this is one of its major strengths. Learning content, much of it interactive, is brought together on the website and micro-websites from departments and providers such as the Open University, Adult Literacy, Bitesize (examination revision guides) and the Learning Zone. Topics range from art and design, business studies, crafts, environmental studies and information technology to languages, maths, media studies, music

▸ This example of a site map shows some of the primary links from the BBC homepage, *www.bbc.co.uk*. TV and radio pages show channel choices and links that allow the audience to watch or to listen to past programmes on a computer, or to download the programmes to mobile devices. Browsing the hyperlinks reveals a huge range of pages to visit.

and science. In fact, you name it and you are bound to find the subject covered in an interesting and engaging way. The Digital Curriculum for schools is a development that brings the vast resources of the BBC into the virtual classroom.

In terms of traditional portal design, the BBC has made its webpages look great by combining a very high standard of graphic design and excellent technical implementation.

The design approach to websites contrasts with that for printed information. Compare a large website to a complex train timetable, where the reader may run his or her finger along a line on a grid on a large poster to pick out the relevant arrival and departure times. Information online can't be arranged in extensive fixed grids since the screen is a very small space – consider the size of mobile-phone screens – and only a tiny part of a large grid would appear on screen. Information online is organized according to different principles. It is sorted into labelled 'containers' or databases which may grow or shrink and can be sorted by category. These silos of information must be listed by topic in menus and be accessible within a few clicks of the opening page, so that instead of thumbing across a page or flicking through a book you can 'drill down' into the website. So, while the finest grid on the biggest piece of paper contains a limited amount of information, online structures can store much more, in the form of text, image, sound and film, and can be extended and updated at will and, if desired, in real time – for example, adding the latest news items, weather, train delays and sports results as they happen.

Information is understood in relation to what it's next to, what comes before or after it. In a database, all information is equal so the graphic designer and information architect must impose a hierarchy of information through the way they design the interface. It is vital that the sequence of searching through data matches the purpose of the website and the needs and expectations of its target audience. Some knowledge of Human–Computer Interaction (HCI) research may prove helpful to the designer. HCI is a new hybrid discipline that draws on psychology, sociology, anthropology, computer science and engineering. It is concerned with the design, evaluation and implementation of interactive computing systems for human use: for example, the accessibility of new interfaces. HCI research ranges from personal computers through to the layout of spacecraft cockpits and the controls of microwave ovens.

One other key point the designer should bear in mind is that the way in which information is presented sends messages, too. The current graphical user interface (GUI) uses a desktop metaphor, for instance, and is therefore a constant reminder of the workplace: files, folders, wastepaper baskets. Why do we have to access cyberspace via an image as technocratic as the desktop? Is work the most important activity in our lives? Why can't we be reminded of an environment that is more exciting or more humane when we turn on the computer? Sun Microsystems, for example, has explored a new 3D virtual landscape as an interface.

▲ 'Project Looking Glass' by Sun Microsystems is an open platform to explore the innovative use of 3D user interfaces. *www.sun.com/software/looking_glass*

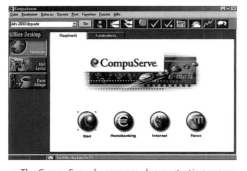

▲ The CompuServe homepage, demonstrating access to services typical of Internet service providers (ISPs). Founded in 1969, it was the first major commercial online service in the US. By the mid-1980s, it was the largest online service in existence and it remained a major player until the rise of GUI-based services during the 1990s such as America Online (AOL).

▲ The Google search engine was founded in 1998 by two Stanford University students, Larry Page and Sergey Brin. It is designed to provide a simple, fast way to search the Internet for information. Google is the largest search engine on the World Wide Web, offering users access to more than 8 billion websites. *www.google.com*

So don't think of the Internet as limited to 'brochure ware' – in other words, hyperlinked scrollable screen pages that look like magazine spreads – and don't think of the Internet mainly as disembodied virtual 'cyberspace' which is somehow separate from the physical world. Consider the Internet for a moment as an extension of the real world in which we live. We use it to imagine ourselves, form friendships, research lifestyle choices and make money. It harbours all the delights, disappointments, virtues and vices of the real world. It raises issues of personal identity, trust and reputation, authority and surveillance, legislation and regulation. These issues cannot be ignored if you are working in new-media graphic design.

Routes into the labyrinth

The Internet is an open structure and as such presents a challenge to businesses that want to control their brands and ensure people notice their adverts or visit their URLs. In the 'real world' you can pay for a billboard advert in the centre of town, but how do you ensure that the equivalent virtual advert gets seen when there is no centre to the Internet?

Companies are well aware that teenagers spend more time online than they do watching television and they want to attract their attention. To achieve maximum visibility they need to appear where users most often go. Where is the main street of the Internet? Not people's homepages, which vary according to their interests, nor people's corporate or intranet homepages at work, which don't feature adverts. One way to get noticed is to offer goods and services through one of the big sites that get a lot of traffic, for example, eBay and Amazon. These are becoming huge trading platforms for other companies whose logos may appear discreetly on the home-page or whose goods or services may feature as part of the content. The other, most well-used sites on the Internet are search engines such as Google, Yahoo! or MSN. These sites make a significant part of their profits through advertising and sponsored links.

Access to the Internet was first envisaged by service providers such as CompuServe, Prodigy and America Online (AOL) as 'portals' or gateways. The first service providers tended to include links their editors deemed useful, thus deterring users from straying into the wider Internet. By keeping users contained within portals, they could advertise to them and perhaps persuade them to sign up for additional services.

Automated search engines that would search across the web were developed in the early 1990s. They used software programs, now known as 'web crawlers' or 'web spiders', which trawl a computer or a network and gather and report information that contains specific words or phrases in a user's query. The first search software looked for words in the meta-tags. The meta-tags are in the HTML headers used to identify the webpage and comprise a brief description of the content plus relevant keywords.

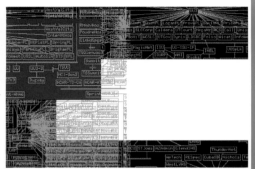

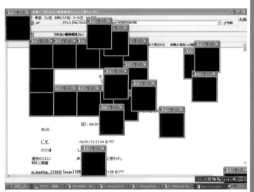

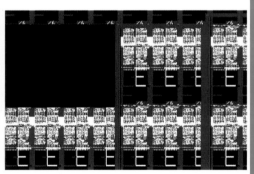

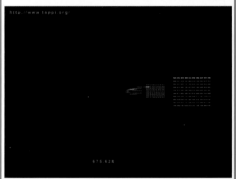

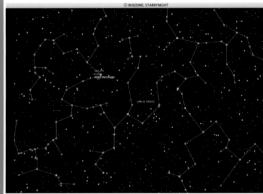

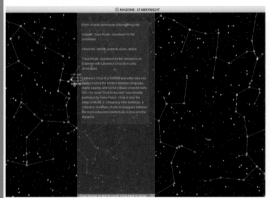

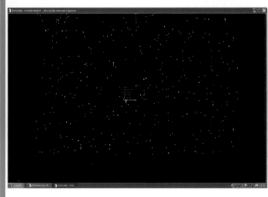

▲ Dutch artists and designers Jodi give you a very different view of the Internet. When you visit their website, your first reaction may be one of alarm. Frames flicker, scrollbars jerk, text leaps about unpredictably. You think your computer has crashed or been invaded by a virus. Jodi don't make web pages; they make environments that expose the underlying mechanisms of the Internet. They find a way to bring the 'anatomy of the code' to the surface and turn the software inside out. Their site offers no explanation of itself or its aims. Jodi aim to subvert the way we take the Internet for granted and make us think about what's going on behind it. They invert our expectations, for example, by making everything go slowly as a critique of the mainstream design quest for speed. They noticed the irony that although we think of the Internet as instantaneous and time-saving, we will spend hours on it, neglecting the real world and real people. *www.jodi.org*

▲ UK artist Simon Biggs explains of Babel: 'In Babel viewers logged onto the site are confronted with a 3D visualization of an abstract data space mapped as arrays and grids of Dewey Decimal numbers. As they move the mouse around the screen they are able to navigate this 3D environment. All the viewers are able to see what all the other viewers, who are simultaneously logged onto the site, are seeing. The multiple 3D views of the data-space are montaged together into a single shared image, where the actions of any one viewer affects what all the other viewers see. If a large number of viewers are logged on together the information displayed becomes so complex and dense that it breaks down into a meaningless abstract space.' *www.littlepig.org.uk*

▲ Rhizome is an online space that features digital art. It contains a poetic visualization of the Internet, inspired by Vincent van Gogh's painting *Starry Night*. It presents art websites as a constellation of stars. The user drags the mouse over stars to trigger key words and clicks on a star to access full information. Each time a star is clicked, it gets brighter so that the interface represents the combined searches of everyone who has used the interface from all over the world. *www.rhizome.org*

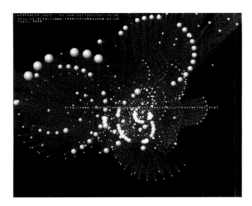

▲ WebTracer is a project that attempts to visualize the structure of the web. There are many applications that analyse websites for structural integrity and diagnostic purposes, but few that reveal the visual structure that web hypertext creates. WebTracer represents this structure as a three-dimensional molecular diagram, with pages as nodes and links as strings that connect those nodes together. *Nullpointer*

In 1998, Sergey Brin and Larry Page had a different idea when they invented Google. They built a search engine that would not only look for the meta-tags but also the page contents. They also developed a system for linking popularity to page rank on the premise that useful pages are likely to have a greater number of other websites linking to them. The more links, the further up the search list the site would appear. In addition, the stripped-down, minimal interface is designed for legibility.

Search engines 'mine' information available in newsgroups, large databases or open human-edited directories like DMOZ (Directory Mozilla). Search engine data collection is automated, which distinguishes them from web directories, such as DMOZ and Yahoo!, which use people to classify information into hierarchies.

Search sites provide search engines free to the user, but companies that build and operate search engines make profits by selling sponsored links. Google lists its sponsored links on the right of its page; Yahoo! puts them in a box at the top. Whoever bids the most for a particular word or phrase gets their link at the top of the page. Organizations pay search-engine optimization companies to help them to maximize their page ratings and visibility.

There are other ways than search engines to enter the Internet. Artists have attempted to find alternative ways in and to provide overviews that are not driven by commercial interests but more by general curiosity, drawing attention to and revealing alternative images or ways of visualizing the Internet. This is the kind of thinking that inspires graphic designers, who innovate by experimenting, challenging conventional thinking and developing new ways of working.

Social space

Millions of people compile their own homepages, incorporating favourite bits of music, photographs of themselves and pets, snippets of poems, unedited writings. They offer an invitation to look into someone else's personal life. Do people build their own websites to construct or reconstruct an identity, to confess, to self-publish, position themselves as experts in a field or just to have fun? Are they using the computer to reflect upon and shape their own identities? Psychologist Sherry Turkle argues that all of these factors play a role: multiple gaming identities, in other words the multiple personalities players can take on in games, are as important to people in constituting their sense of themselves as are their face-to-face relationships. Turkle has studied how children relate to computers as 'sort of alive' and she claims that as a result the Internet can operate as an intimate and self-reflexive medium. She predicts that we will develop further sorts of relationships, including nurturing ones, with computers, as they take the form of toys, robot animals and companions in the future.

▲ A personal weblog (known as a 'blog'), created as part of a student project at Central Saint Martins College of Art and Design, London. Blogs are a means of personal publishing on the Internet; 'bloggers' regularly update their content and invite others to contribute to their site. *Laétitia Cordier*

Blogs (weblogs) first appeared as aide-mémoire lists of discovered links, but evolved into personal online diaries updated regularly, perhaps as often as every day, and presented in reverse chronological order. Bloggers, short for 'webloggers',

▲ Design Observer is a blog for the design community. Hosted by some important names, it features lively discussions. A comment feedback box is shown on the right.

◀ A half-serious, half-fun blog about travelling on the London Underground, updated daily by Anni Mole. Readers can contribute and post their comments.

▲ Wikipedia is a free online encyclopedia to which anyone can contribute and edit. In this English version, started in 2001, there are currently 1,734,248 articles (April 2007) on everything from the arts to technology. *www.wikipedia.org*

▲ The World Starts with Me (WSWM) is a digital learning environment concerned with sexual health education, AIDS prevention and developing creative ICT skills for young Ugandans. *Prix Ars Electronica 2004 Golden Nica.* *www.theworldstarts.org*

have developed as a new form of personal publishing, drawing attention to interesting things they have found elsewhere on the Internet, and providing a link list to other blogs. Customizable software can be downloaded, which automatically archives and indexes your input. Blogs have quickly evolved into a number of different forms. Communities sharing interests engage in discussion about their views, experiences, likes and dislikes outside the editorial filters of the broadcast media. Broadcast media has adopted blogging as a form of reporting whereby the content reflects the values of the newspaper or television channel. There are now commercial blogs, and individual freelance writers are commissioned to write blogs on particular subjects. Vidblogs, or video blogs, are also emerging.

Wikis are another social phenomenon of the Internet. Shared domains containing a set of hyperlinked webpages, they allow all registered users to contribute to them and organize them as they wish. Wikipedia, for example, is a community-created, open-content encyclopedia. Offering information in an encyclopedia format, it's free to use and easy to manipulate. Moreover, anyone who joins the community can add or edit material.

Open-source software is another cooperative web-based phenomenon. The open-source movement emerged from hacker culture as programmers and other computer users advocated unrestricted access to source code, as opposed to proprietary or closed software owned by businesses. 'Open source' refers to the source code of software that has been built and made available on the Internet for other programmers or developers to use and modify, and as such relates to but differs from the free or low-cost software movement that makes ready-made 'shareware' software packages available. Open-source software offers greater flexibility to end-users because any end-user can take the program and modify it for their own needs. The term 'open source' is applied to the entire concept that the creation and organization of knowledge are best carried out through open and cooperative efforts. This movement is sometimes called 'open content' or 'free culture'.

The Internet is also an ideal space for groups and communities that use desk-based computers or laptops. The World Starts with Me (www.theworldstarts.org) delivers HIV/AIDS education to young Ugandans. The German website Krebs-Kompass (www.krebs-kompass.de) provides cancer patients with peer-to-peer message-board forums, a portal to qualified information resources and prompt online consultation from certified experts.

▲ Friendster is a popular online community that focuses on helping people stay in touch with friends and discover new people via member-generated content in a number of forms, including personal profiles, audio, video, images and blogs. It is popular among people of all ages, particularly young adults. *www.friendster.com*

Friendster (www.friendster.com) is a popular online community that connects people interested in dating or making new friends. 'Friendster helps users find dates and new friends by referring people to friends, or friends of friends, or friends of friends of friends, and so on. When signing up, users post a picture of themselves and a list of their interests. Crucially, they are also asked to provide a list of their friends and their email addresses. If their friends also sign up, they are asked to confirm their relationship to the inviter. Once these social links are established, users can traverse the entire web of contacts, finding people they'd like to meet and sending them a message. The service is fun and easy to use, and the invitation feature not only creates a rich web of contacts, it's also the key to Friendster's viral growth. In addition, the system of validating social relationships provides a kind of virtual "vouch" that protects participants from random contacts.' (*Wired*, July 2003)

MySpace (www.myspace.com) is another online phenomenon. Started as a website for unsigned bands to post MP3s of their music, it has developed into a popular one-stop portal for artists and illustrators to portfolio their work. It is also a site for people just looking for dates. Users list their interests and amass a community of 'friends' who can receive messages and bulletins and contribute to the in-built blog. Unfortunately, its appearance can be customized, leading to some horrendous design disasters. Flickr (www.flickr.com) is a community site for sharing photographs and illustrations. Similar sites exist for communities of Photoshop manipulators, Flash animators and 3D modellers.

Trust and reputation have emerged as significant factors in online social interactions and commercial transactions: for example, Amazon's online recommendation system, which lists other books purchased by people with similar interests and eBay's feedback forum and reputation system for buyers and sellers worldwide.

Artists and designers are experimenting with interesting ways to express some of the qualities of new location-based mobile communities. Jonah Brucker-Cohen

▲ Umbrella.net 2004: Jonah Brucker-Cohen and Katherine Moriwaki.

▲ www.theyesmen.org

▲ Adbusters' campaign to promote a 'buy nothing day', its annual worldwide drive intended to embarrass commercial organizations in their push for ever-increasing sales and consumption. *www.adbusters.org*

and Katherine Moriwaki created an installation event in New York in 2004 called Umbrella.net (not a website). As the artists explain on the website (www.spectropolis.info/umbrella.php), in places where rainfall is frequent and unpredictable people carry umbrellas in case they are caught in a downpour. It is not unusual to witness a sea of umbrellas suddenly open up as the rain starts and this connects people in one place through a shared action. In their installations, the open umbrellas are equipped with digital receptors and a wireless network connects strangers caught for a moment in a shared situation. They form a brief community of interest. The network opens and closes according to coincidence.

On a more directly political note, people also use the Internet as a social space in which to organize collective action. A recent example is the phenomenon of so-called 'Flashmobs', people gathering together at a predetermined location to demonstrate before dispersing. Flashmobbing can be organized by sending short text messages to a community of like-minded people via Internet-linked mobile devices, or by online messages in chatrooms, on blogs and forums. Clay Shirky, consultant, teacher and writer on the social and economic effects of Internet technologies, argues: 'We have historically overestimated the value of network access to computers and underestimated the value of network access to other people.' In other words, people, not technology, are the key nodes in a network.

The Internet has enabled artists with a political slant to make new kinds of hoax interventions in unusual ways: for example, the Yesmen (www.theyesmen.org) have infiltrated a number of world economic summits. The group had a fake website that mirrored the website of the World Trade Organization (WTO). Institutes across the world have mistaken the Yesmen's site for that of the WTO and have invited the artists to conferences, believing they are economists. This small group of prankster–activists has gained worldwide notoriety by getting on stage and making ironic speeches and giving performances to puzzled audiences.

This sort of activity is sometimes called 'culture jamming', the phrase used to describe the practice of organizations such as Adbusters (www.adbusters.org), which cleverly plays on the conventions of advertising to critique consumer society.

The audience for Internet pornography is likewise viewed as a community. Internet porn is a thriving industry and, despite the objections of many pressure groups, it looks likely to continue to grow. Most industry participants are individual webmasters who work out of their homes rather than big offices. Although the online porn industry is offensive to many people, it has led the way in several significant Internet developments. It can claim to be the first successful form of online commerce; it was the first to use database storage and broadband for video downloads; and it pioneered the use of windows and cookies.

Social space on the Internet stems from the real world. It can be personalized, comforting, volatile or provocative. It is open for all to contribute to, and if you work in new media you will almost certainly come to acknowledge social space as one of the most dynamic and creative environments facilitated by new technologies. Contributing to social sites is not only a pastime; it can increase your website's Google ratings and get you work.

Discovery and learning

Museums are using the Internet in order to offer a comprehensive guide to their collections. You can now go online to, say, the website of the Louvre Museum in Paris (www.louvre.fr), choose which room you want to visit and even click on individual exhibits to learn more about them.

The Theban Mapping Project (www.thebanmappingproject.com) offers an interactive atlas, where you can visit a number of locations of historical interest: for example, the Valley of the Kings in Egypt. The site holds a database of information about each tomb – you can view a compilation of more than two thousand images, interact with models of each tomb; and measure, pan and zoom over 250 detailed maps, elevations and sections. There are also narrated tours and a 3D recreation of the tombs.

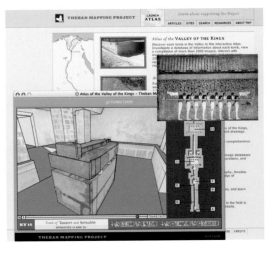

▲ The tombs of Egyptian kings are investigated in interactive 3D on the Theban Mapping Project website. *www.thebanmappingproject.com*

Some sites offer 'fly-through' experiences. This means the user is positioned in the sky and by hitting keys on the keyboard he or she can fly over, move through and land in a virtual landscape or townscape. One of the first 'fly-through' experiences available on the Internet was an extraordinary journey through the human body. Since this early experiment, however, software developers and designers have made such progress that they can now offer users a more immersive experience, as in the case of *Invisible Shape of Things Past* by the new-media designers Art+Com based in Germany (www.artcom.de): 'The project enables users to transform film sequences into interactive, virtual objects. This transformation is based on the camera parameters relevant to a particular film sequence on screen (movement, perspective, focal length). The individual frames of the film are lined up along the path of the camera. The angle of the frames relative to the virtual camera path depends on the view from the actual camera, while the size of the frames depends on the focal length used. The rows of pixels at the frames' edges define the outer membrane of the film object. A spatial/temporal concept was developed for the organization and navigation of the film objects: in the case of Berlin, for example, all the urban development phases from 1900 onwards in the vicinity of the Museum Island and Potsdamer Platz were modelled and the film objects were positioned according to their virtual location, as determined by when and where they were shot. Users are able to move about within time and space, interacting with the film objects. The final stage involved building an interactive installation and a material architectural model based on individual film objects.'

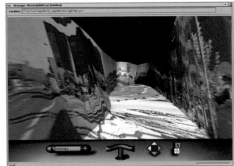

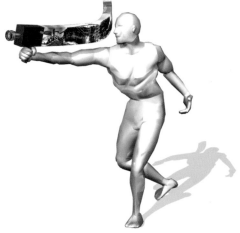

▲ *Invisible Shape of Things Past*. A fly-though map that allows you to land in different decades and move through 3D reconstructions of Berlin. The project enables users to transform film sequences into interactive, virtual objects. © *Art+Com, Berlin, 1995. www.artcom.de*

e-learning

The Internet has opened up so many new opportunities for graphic and multimedia designers. One of these opportunities, online education or e-learning, has only been made possible because of the dynamic nature of the Internet.

Schools and universities can now deliver courses to anyone with access to the Internet, wherever they are in the world. The design of virtual learning environments is another area in which the designer plays a major role. Course content must be presented in a way that is accessible to a truly worldwide audience. For many participants, the delivery language may not be their mother tongue. Local schools and colleges also use the Internet and intranets (see below) to allow students to check their classes and deliver their homework. Help with learning is widely available on the Internet. There is a broad spectrum of sites that specialize in curriculum support, from primary through to research level. All require the information design skills of new-media and graphic-design specialists.

Online courses can provide educational opportunities to people living in remote parts of the developing world, and to people whose mobility is restricted through poor health or owing to social and religious customs. No matter where or who you are, it is useful to be able to access an expert visiting lecturer online. It is also an economical way for educational institutions to deliver high-quality information to more people.

What is e-learning? Online learning means that the student learner and the instructor or teacher delivering e-learning need not be in the same geographical location. They may never meet face to face as they would in a traditional school, college or university, but they can communicate with each other in what can be a truly global 'virtual' learning environment. Students only require access to a computer and an Internet connection. Courses and learning support materials are delivered in any number of electronic and multimedia formats, all of which need the graphic designer's skills in visualization, format design and knowledge of software and web design tools. Of course, as in any other area, graphic designers work with a number of subject and learning and teaching specialists on planning and making relevant, accessible and enjoyable materials that engage and enhance the learning experience. Creating e-learning support materials can involve designing for websites, CD-Roms, DVDs and print.

There are three main ways in which online or e-learning is delivered: distance learning, where students learn anywhere, any time and usually at their own pace; blended learning, where there is some face-to-face contact between the student and teachers, but some of the course must be completed online; and independent learning, where students engage in personal development, perhaps for reskilling or professional advancement.

Many colleges and universities offer distance learning in a wide range of subjects, from practical 'know-how' to higher degree courses that are taken entirely online.

e-Learning Websites

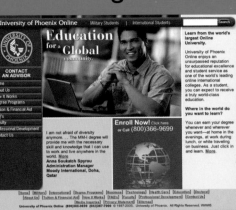

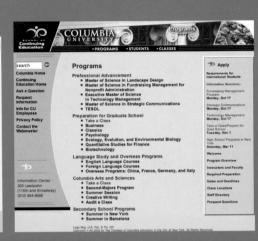

Increasingly universities and commercial training companies offer courses and training online. Their students are very often located in different parts of the world, and for some the convenience of studying for a qualification from an internationally famous university without moving from their home country is the only option. Illustrated here are some webpages announcing online study and training opportunities at universities and companies based in the US, the UK and Australia. Some art and design schools run online courses in practical as well as research subjects.

Top row from left: University of Phoenix; Colombia University, New York; MIT (Massachusetts Institute of Technology). *Above:* University of London. *Right:* VTC software training online. *Left:* University of the Arts London (LCC). *Below:* College of Fine Art, University of New South Wales, Sydney (Omnium), and New School University (Parsons New School of Design), New York.

▲ The Blackboard Virtual Learning Environment is used by many universities and colleges for delivering teaching support online to their students. By using the Internet for delivery, users can work from any location in the world. *www.blackboard.com*

The duration of such courses can range from a few days or weeks to several years. Blended learning is also popular with educational institutions because it provides for contact with students on campus. Some blended learning courses may also have residential sessions. A common factor in distance and blended online learning is the use of so-called VLEs (virtual learning environments). Although commercial VLEs are popular with some e-learning providers, others develop and design bespoke solutions based on 'open source' or free software that is available to adapt and use.

Independent learning can take many forms and can include both distance and blended learning. Much is made of the term 'lifelong learning' by providers such as government agencies, universities, colleges, television broadcasters, commercial and industrial companies. Their output and products range from pre-school education, school homework help, examination and campus tutorials, 'on the job' or workplace learning, to adult education and so-called 'third age' learning. Large companies, and the military and public services often encourage their workforces to use online training materials, relating to things ranging from engineering and workplace skills, to complex social issues, allowing staff to build their own independent programmes of learning. Software manufacturers and specialist training companies provide online tutorial support for computer applications, including those commonly used by graphic and new-media designers.

For designers, this is a very interesting area of work as it offers the chance to practise wide-ranging graphic design and new-media skills. Information design, typography, animation, illustration, photography, games design, video and narrative experience all play major parts in the development and the production of e-learning materials for all types of online learning.

Intranets and extranets

Businesses, educational institutions and organizations of all kinds develop their own internal websites to communicate information that they want only their employees, students or members to access. These internal websites are called 'intranets', which could be local area networks (LANs), that do not necessarily need to be connected to the Internet; however, where they are, they often use a password to restrict access, and are usually 'hidden' from the public behind a secure 'firewall', to protect sensitive and confidential information (firewalls help prevent networked computers from unauthorized access and hostile attack).

Intranets are built using the same concepts and technologies as the Internet and may also look just like normal webpages. For the new-media graphic designer there are a series of special considerations, such as the internal branding, that clients wish their workforce to comply with. This will involve not only design consistency in the 'look and feel' and personality of an enterprise, but also how to deal with large amounts of information from different parts of the organization as well as from external sources. The advantage of intranets is that they enable information that is used regularly by co-workers to be gathered in one place. Typically an intranet will contain downloadable documents and forms, technical information, confidential price lists, internal telephone numbers and staff email addresses. Another important advantage is that the latest and most up-to-date information can be made accessible to users throughout an organization. The disadvantages are that sometimes workers feel that they are open to their employers 'spying' on them or monitoring their work; also by keeping so much data in one place, it can become a target for hackers trying to break into the network to cause damage. If not managed securely, intranets can be easily compromised.

From the designer's point of view, an intranet will be aimed at more specific users than most websites. Intranet users will be more likely to work collaboratively with people they know and share in the authorship of internal documents, both in their origination and in subsequent updating. This will be particularly important if an intranet is serving a large organization that has different office locations and a large workforce, part of which may be mobile, with people who need to keep in touch with each other and the central administration.

For intranets of all sizes, the task of the graphic designer is to help develop the information architecture as well as the 'look and feel', usually as part of a project development team and with the help of existing users from within the client enterprise. Consultation is an essential aspect of this process in order to find out how users work and how they want their intranet to function. The aim should be to improve usability and encourage everyone in the organization to use the intranet in their daily work.

Several component groups of large organizations may have individual intranets that need to share information between one another. Linking intranet sites together within an umbrella organization is sometimes referred to as an 'extranet'. The term is used to describe central repositories of shared data, documents and information that are accessible only through the web to authorized users. Project or research and development teams can share documents, drawings, technical updates, and request potentially sensitive information from other parts of the enterprise through a dedicated project extranet, using a log-in to gain access without leaving the protection of their local network.

Intranets and extranets make a valuable contribution to the success of any enterprise that needs to share resources with its users.

Email

Electronic mail (email) is right at the heart of modern communications and one of the essentials of the Internet, largely replacing paper-based correspondence for many organizations. It has become one of the most popular uses of the Internet. The convenience of being able to dispatch a message to a distant recipient and receive, in many cases, an almost instant reply alters the timescale for many

▲ The Royal College of Art intranet frontpage shows daily events as well as carrying links to important information for faculty and students. Log-in is required to access the intranet from outside the college network, when it becomes an extranet.

▲ Intranet front page for the town of Clermont in France. Note the log-in requirement that restricts access to private local businesses in the site levels beyond this introductory page.

projects. Emails can deliver text and also 'attachments', which could include images or video clips, to computers and mobile devices that are connected to the Internet using existing telephone lines, mobile or cell-phone networks and communications satellites. 'Mailing lists', facilitated by Yahoo! for example, are an important means of networking. All emails sent to a group address will be sent to all members of that group; members can also opt to receive a daily digest or access the emails on the web.

Bandwidth is a measure of the capacity of communications channels. The higher the bandwidth, the greater is the transfer of information at higher speed. New-media designers often attach image and movie files to emails for client approval or in order to collaborate on projects, but many ISPs (Internet Service Providers) impose limits on the amount an inbox can store, so FTP (File Transfer Protocol) may be more appropriate. Bandwidth also means that television reporters and photographers can deliver live news reports accompanied by images from the remotest parts of the world.

Digital broadcasting

With digital broadcasting, radio and television programmes can be accessed at any time. Instead of adhering to a linear schedule, where programmes are shown one after another at specific times, digital broadcasts are interactive: they can be paused, stored on digital media and manipulated for a new use. Radio and television companies can now make broadcast material available online. Bands and charity concerts initially made 'webcasts', using 'streaming media', audio or video clips that are consumed (heard or viewed) as they are being delivered, and cannot easily be stored. It is easy to envisage a future when many television channels will be available to watch over the Internet. YouTube (www.youtube.com) is an example of a video-sharing website.

BBC radio in the UK (www.bbc.co.uk/radio) provides a 'listen again' link on its website. This allows listeners to access radio programmes, usually for a week after broadcast. This consists of a 'streamed' audio channel which can be downloaded on demand to an Internet-connected computer. Many of these popular shows are also made available as 'podcasts', which are downloaded over the Internet – sometimes for a subscription fee – and transferred to a portable media player for convenient listening on the move. RSS (Really Simple Syndication) feeds can automatically update players with the latest version of shows.

The Australian Broadcasting Corporation's '4Corners' current-affairs programme (www.abc.net.au/4corners), which is broadcast to a traditional linear television schedule, offers viewers an interactive in-depth review of programme subjects online through the '4Corners' website. By adding extra material, contributed comment and opinion to the original broadcast, the ABC uses the Internet to provide a far richer, more interactive and enhanced viewer experience than possible with a traditional broadcast.

▲ Email client software organizes your electronic mail so that you can easily keep track of messages. Most email services are also available through an Internet web browser as webmail, making email available anywhere. *Eudora*

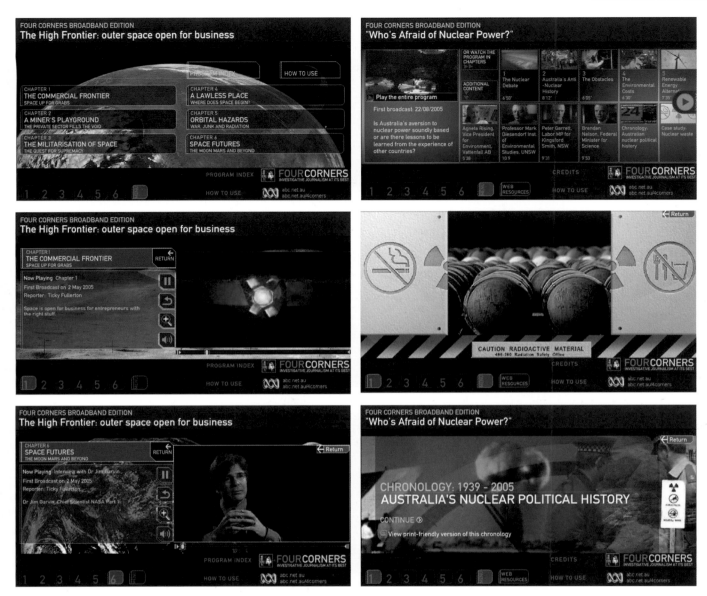

In the same way that sound can be 'podcast', television can be 'vidcast', allowing viewing on the move. These developments are significant for new-media designers who have to design for the increasing number of new and interactive formats.

▲ Screens from one of the Australian Broadcasting Corporation's '4Corners' web specials, showing a mix of broadcast and augmented interactive material that allows the viewer to delve deeper, something that traditional linear television broadcasting is unable to provide. *www.abc.net.au/4corners*

Marketing and commerce online

Over the past ten years, people have been trying to figure out ways to make money out of the Internet. Businesses that understand their customers and the Internet have made millions. Commercial websites have to be fast, convenient, reliable and embody the company's brand values. Consumers are always interested in finding the lowest price, but if they do not like a website they will move on. 'The web is the most selfish environment in the world,' says Daniel Rosensweig, Chief Operating Officer of Yahoo. 'People want to use the Internet whenever they want, how they want and for whatever they want.'

After its widespread take-up, starting in 1995 in the US, Western Europe and Japan, there was a general belief that large portions of the commercial world would migrate to the Internet. Every business wanted a website. This was the era of the dotcom boom. Print designers, artists, programmers, and even musicians found new job opportunities. However, the medium was so new that there was initially little real understanding of dynamic environments, interaction design or information systems, and as a result many of the websites were impossible to navigate and frequently malfunctioned.

Feverish excitement on the stock exchanges of the world was triggered by a vision of vast new commercial markets emerging on the Internet, not only for existing companies, but also for entirely new online organizations that were as yet without a physical identity, known products or target consumers. One of the most interesting challenges for designers was visualizing a company with no physical outlets and no brand image in the bricks-and-mortar world.

The technology bubble burst in 2000 and economic gloom set in. Suddenly working on Internet design became much less lucrative and there was a lot of talk of the constraints and limitations of web design. However, half a decade or so later, it seems that the initial forecast of large sections of global markets moving onto the Internet is indeed coming true.

There are now some extraordinary successes in customer-led online sites. The largest Internet auction house, eBay, was created in 1995. Its commercial activity is driven by user demand. In 2003, eBay traded US$8 billion worth of motor vehicles and parts, making this its highest-earning category; not long before, this category had been Beanie Babies. The most remarkable thing about eBay is the degree to which it is customer-led – the site sets up new pages and online services as customers require. With more than one hundred million registered users worldwide, half of eBay's income comes from outside the USA. Local sites in over 28 countries, franchised from eBay, are tailored to local needs. This is a business dream come true: eBay only benefits from getting larger and, unlike traditional suppliers of goods, which need to invest in more production, it simply matches buyers with sellers, who do all the packaging and posting themselves. eBay makes money by charging fees for listing items for sale. Its purchase of PayPal, the online Internet bank widely used by eBayers, further increased its revenue.

However, eBay is more than just a functional conduit; it also provides a 'trading experience'. Meg Whitman, the company's chief executive, describes eBay as one-part company, one-part town-hall meeting and one-part entertainment. It has grown out of a belief in an honest, open market – these are in many ways eBay's brand values. It understands that customers want information about products and prices; that they want to be able to navigate the site easily, compare offers, secure transactions and have fun. Communicating these qualities and services is the job of the web-design team, which has to get under the skin of the customer but also work within business and technological constraints.

▲ Founded in 1995, eBay manages an online auction and shopping website, where people buy and sell goods and services. The eBay community includes more than one hundred million registered members from around the world. On an average day there are millions of items listed for sale. People spend more time on eBay than any other online site, making it the most popular shopping experience on the Internet. *www.ebay.com*

Artificialtourism: Gonzalo Garcia-Perate and Alicia Comella

▲ Gonzalo and Alicia in their east London studio.

Artificialtourism (www.artificialtourism.com) is an independent design studio based in London. Its founders are Gonzalo Garcia-Perate and Alicia Comella, born in Madrid and Barcelona respectively. They met in London where they both graduated from the Communication Design MA at Central Saint Martins College of Art and Design.

Gonzalo has been involved in digital media for over 12 years, working internationally both in South America and Europe. He spent several years working on digital brand consultancy, directing projects for clients including Royal Mail, BT, Barclays Bank and Volkswagen.

Alicia comes from a fine arts background. After moving to London, she became interested in digital media and spent the next five years designing for several London agencies, leading projects ranging from websites to in-flight entertainment systems for clients including Bentley Motors, the Royal Albert Hall and Virgin Atlantic Airways.

After leaving Saint Martins, Gonzalo and Alicia set up Artificialtourism as a platform for the development of new ideas within an interactive design context. In 2004, it became a partnership that aims to take the same approach to the commercial environment. Together they create websites, experiences, spaces and products, collaborating mainly with arts, cultural and educational organizations. Their approach combines their clients' insights with their expertise, helping organizations take full advantage of the possibilities digital media has to offer.

One of their projects, DataCloud, is a data-visualization system that displays the live weather conditions of major cities across the globe simultaneously. Weather conditions are mapped onto a typographic representation of each city: font size relates to visibility, colour to temperature, and transparency to humidity. The city names move with the speed and direction of their wind readings, while their atmospheric pressure is applied as friction to the movement. The project has been exhibited in New York, Boston, Berlin, Vienna and it is part of the online museum Rhizome's permanent collection (www.rhizome.org).

▼ Data Cloud. *www.artificialtourism.com/dataCloud*

▼ Design for the Ruskin School of Drawing and Fine Art, Oxford University. *www.ruskin-sch.ox.ac.uk*

▼ Modern Art Oxford website design
www.modernartoxford.org.uk

The actual value of transactions online is dwarfed by comparison with the influence the Internet is having on purchases made in the real world. Many customers walking into a Sears department store in the US to buy an electrical appliance, for instance, will have researched their purchase online first, and as a result will know exactly how much they intend to spend. Even more surprisingly, the majority of Americans start shopping for new cars online, though they will then buy them through traditional dealerships. They go to the showroom armed with printouts from the web.

There is a recognizable development in user habits. People begin to shop online for simple, predictable items such as DVDs and then graduate to more complex items, for example, used cars. It is possible that in time physical stores may become showrooms to allow potential purchasers to experience the products before buying them, but that the actual transactions will then take place online. Online and offline worlds are merging. More than ever, a useless website suggests a useless company.

Summary

The Internet can be intimate and personalized, a channel for expression and experimentation, a social space for discussion and action, a medium for commerce – almost anything you want it to be. Fabulous products, fun games and interesting or shocking information are made accessible, visible and meaningful through good graphics. Graphic designers put things in order to make them comprehensible and appealing. They need to understand that no matter how important the message is, people won't give it a second thought unless it is presented in a way that captivates and engages them. Designers must deal with the logic as well as the look of systems. They need to collaborate with interface designers, information architects, programmers and different kinds of clients. They must understand the psychology of Human–Computer Interaction.

The Internet is constantly growing and changing, and both hardware and software are rapidly evolving. New-media designers can't afford to think in terms of static design solutions; instead they need to design for scalability, fluid shifting layouts, differing resolutions, changing hierarchies, continual updates on content, as well as user navigation and user contributions. In addition, they have to factor in technological incompatibility, as people all over the world access the Internet via different machines on different bandwidths. In short, new-media designers are working on shifting sands.

As the spread of broadband connections continues, the demand for content will likewise increase, as will the need for graphics. New-media graphic designers will need to understand the relationship between context, interface, content and visual expression. Most importantly, new-media designers must have a sound grasp of real-world issues if they are to communicate clearly.

Imaginary Worlds **4**

Old World

New World

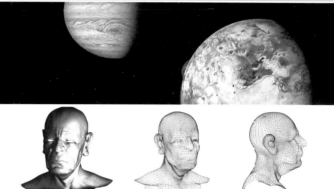

▲ *Top down:* Early star chart. Life drawing class. Traditional studio desk. Actors performing on a stage, *Drama Centre London.*

▶ *Top down:* Digital rendering of planets, *NASA.* Heads modeled in 3D, *Leon Williams.* New studio desk. Modern design studio equipment. Virtual performance, *The Light Surgeons.* 'Ananova', an avatar news announcer, *reproduced with permission.*

This chapter explores the work of the new-media designer in shaping imagined worlds in virtual space. These are the worlds of computer games, virtual experiences that can transport you to a fantasy landscape, or back in time, through outer space or into hostile environments. Also included here are online games and websites equipped with artificial intelligence software, where you can find powerful avatars, computer-generated virtual humans – cyberbeings – who can be your representatives online, your friends or adversaries. This chapter also explores the world of artificial life, imagined creatures or systems that do not exist anywhere but in cyberspace.

How do the graphic artist and designer fit into this emerging pattern of possibilities? To understand this, we need to know a little bit about how computer graphics evolved out of simple coloured lines and shapes on a screen into the complex and super-realistic images of today.

Computer graphics: imaging real and unreal worlds

Computer graphics grew out of the need to envisage the world around us, to test theories about how things might look before they were actually built. Computer graphics were developed in order to make it possible to interpret information and simulate actions.

The Cold War, which lasted from the 1950s to the 1980s, engaged the two superpowers, the USA and USSR, in a nuclear-arms and space race. Both sides needed ways of predicting and modelling what the other was doing. In October 1962, following the deployment of American nuclear missiles in Europe and Turkey, the USSR secretly sent missiles to Cuba and set up a nuclear launch base close to US shores. For two weeks, people around the world held their breath as the Russian leader Nikita Khrushchev and the American president John F. Kennedy threatened all-out war if the other side refused to back down and remove its installations. Disaster was avoided when the US authorities proved conclusively that Russian ships, despite official denials, were indeed carrying their deadly cargo, by producing at the United Nations Security Council highly detailed photographic images taken by spy planes of the missiles on the vessels' decks and the launch sites in Cuba. Faced with the publication of such graphic evidence, Khrushchev ordered the ships to return to Russia and the removal of missiles already in Cuba. The US also agreed to remove some of its missiles from Turkey. The US Secretary of State at the time, Dean Rusk, commented: 'We went eyeball to eyeball, and the other fellow just blinked.' A major crisis was averted.

▲ US reconnaissance photograph of the Soviet ship *Poltava*, turning back to Russia carrying missiles and launch trucks (circled). *Dino A. Brugioni Collection, National Security Archive*

Following the Cuban Missile Crisis, official attention was increasingly directed towards universities and research centres involved in the emerging science of computer graphics. If complex information and data could be visualized as images so that people in general, and not just scientists, could interpret and understand what was going on, the world might become a safer place.

The space race developed into a political duel that saw the Soviets launch the first man-made object, Sputnik, into orbit around the Earth on 4 October 1957. Then, on 12 April 1961, the Russian cosmonaut Yuri Gagarin became the first human to orbit the Earth. A deeply shocked United States responded by promising to put a man on the Moon by the end of the 1960s. The US's Apollo 11 mission successfully landed Neil Armstrong and 'Buzz' Aldrin on the lunar surface on 20 July 1969. Meanwhile, the National Aeronautical Space Agency (NASA) was launching probes into deep space and as a result gathering huge amounts of data on the planets and the solar system. The question was how this entirely new kind of information could be visualized so that scientists and the public would be able to understand and interpret the results.

At NASA's Jet Propulsion Laboratory (JPL), science-fiction artists and illustrators were employed to work alongside their computer experts to interpret the data received from the spacecraft and visualize what the planets looked like close up. Remarkably, when the Pioneer, Voyager and Galileo space probes eventually got close enough to transmit real images of the planets, they confirmed the accuracy of these early conceptual and computer-generated pictures. One such animated sequence was greeted with great excitement when it was shown on television networks around the world as a prelude to Voyager arriving at Saturn in November 1980. The resulting enthusiasm helped secure NASA funding for later missions. This computer-generated animation showed the Voyager probe approaching Saturn and turning to look closely at the rings surrounding the planet. On the NASA website (www.nasa.gov) today, there is a similar computer animation of the current probe, Cassini, as it passes Saturn, as well as images sent by this spacecraft that confirm the visualizations of the earlier missions.

▲ Computer-generated image from Voyager's simulated 'fly-by' animation produced at JPL. *NASA*

Bob Holzman established the JPL Computer Graphics Lab in 1977 at the California Institute of Technology (Cal Tech). Holzman was already working at Cal Tech with a group of technology experts, including Ivan Sutherland, on visualizing the data being returned by NASA missions. JPL now hired James Blinn, a graduate student at the University of Utah. At Utah, Blinn had worked on computer-imaging techniques, which he now developed into a system for the visualization task at JPL. Ivan Sutherland once said of Blinn: 'There are about a dozen great computer graphics people, and Jim Blinn is six of them.'

Holzman described his personal excitement at working with Blinn as he developed the software to simulate the planetary fly-bys. They worked as a team, making short animations of Voyager 1 and 2 at Jupiter and Saturn. 'It was great to see the finished product. Since we released these before the fly-bys, one of the challenges

▲ *Top:* A frame from an animated simulation of the planetary impact believed to have formed Earth's Moon. *Above:* A frame from a TV animation for the Learning Channel, showing Galileo passing Io, with Jupiter in the background. A technical hitch meant that Galileo's cameras were unable to record this view. CGI images by Don Davis.

▲ This painting by Don Davis was commissioned by JPL to commemorate the successful Voyager 1 and 2 mission to the outer planets. Computer drawings were used to create correct size and perspective details.

▶ Computer-rendered image by David Seal of Cassini leaving Earth in its primary trajectory.

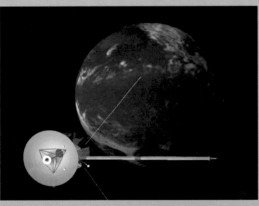

▲ Don Davis produced this digitally rendered image of a Voyager spacecraft passing Jupiter to be viewed as part of a moving sequence on a planetarium computer graphic system.

Artists, modelmakers and illustrators have played a major role in envisaging the work of space scientists at NASA's Jet Propulsion Laboratory since it was established at Cal Tech in the 1970s. Artists such as Don Davis, Rick Sernbach, Charley Kohlhase and David Seal at first painted the planets and their moons using data received from the early space missions. Later, they were able to 'map' their speculative images onto computer-generated globes and render animations of deep space. As photographic images were returned to Earth by the spacecraft and graphics systems became more sophisticated, these artists were able to use computers to create planetary detail. Techniques pioneered at JPL have found uses in film, TV, computer games, planetariums and museum experiences.

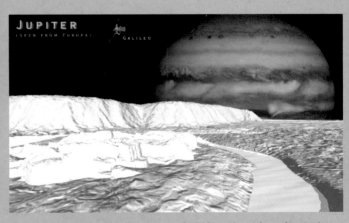

▲ This computer-generated image is rendered from the surface of Jupiter's moon Europa. The Galileo spacecraft can be seen in the sky above.
◀ Computer-rendered image of Cassini firing its engine to reduce speed and enter Saturn's orbit. Both images are by David Seal at JPL.

we had in making the movies was that before we got to these planets we didn't know what the moons actually looked like up close, so we had [well-known space artists] Don Davis and later Rick Sternbach work with us. Don helped us render surfaces of things for best guesses when we didn't know what they actually looked like. We would imagine what the surfaces would look like and Don would paint them. But once Voyager 1 arrived and took the real pictures, we would quickly patch the photographs of the real moons on the animation before we made the Voyager 2 animations. So the second in the series was always better.'

The software created by Blinn was called SPACE. It consisted of a suite of computer-graphics programs that simulated spacecraft trajectories and were specifically designed to produce realistic animated films of the space missions. SPACE produced a series of black-and-white images called 'wireframes' on the host computer. These could be played back smoothly in real time at 15 frames per second. Another computer was then used to map images onto key wirefames that showed the positions and outlines of objects at intervals in the sequence. By adding more frames progressively, using an automated version of a traditional animation process called 'in-betweening' (known also as 'tweening' in computer animation today), a realistic solid object animation was produced and finally rendered onto film.

These films served a number of audiences. The wireframe sequences could be used to analyse and identify any problems in the trajectory design and the rendered fly-by movies showed a realistic computer-graphic vision of what NASA missions to the planets would look like from the spacecraft. This notable combination of science and art defined an important new relationship between computer scientists, graphic artists and designers that continues to this day.

From the early 1960s, a number of artists and musicians were also becoming fascinated by the potential of computers as artistic tools. In 1963 Charles Csuri, a painter and a professor in the department of art at Ohio State University, initiated some of the earliest pioneering work by an artist using computers and in 1967, working with a fellow academic from the department of mathematics, he used a line drawing of a man's head and face and modified its shape using mathematical software on a mainframe computer. Csuri printed intermediate frames created by the computer using a plotter; he then used the resulting prints to produce a primitive animated film. Continuing to experiment with other drawings, he produced a film called *Hummingbird*, consisting of 14,000 computer-generated frames that were then output to 16mm film. In 1968, the Museum of Modern Art in New York bought *Hummingbird* for its permanent collection, one of the first computer-animated artworks. Csuri was one of the artists featured in an exhibition called 'Cybernetic Serendipity: The Computer and the Arts' at the Institute of Contemporary Arts (ICA) in London in 1968. The exhibition catalogue was one of the first publications to deal with 'the relationships between technology and creativity'.

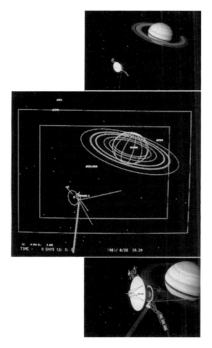

▲ Keyframes from the Voyager 'fly-by'. The middle picture shows the wireframe onto which surface textures were rendered for the final animation.

▲ *Hummingbird* (1968). Charles Csuri, considered the father of digital art and computer animation, constructed his film of a hummingbird in flight from more than 14,000 images. The film was purchased by the Museum of Modern Art for its permanent collection to represent one of the first computer-animated artworks.

Having received a prestigious grant from the National Science Foundation in 1969 to study the role of the computer and software for research and education in the visual arts, Csuri continued to work with graduates and fellow academics on instructing computers to animate drawings and objects. He formed the Computer Graphics Research Group (CGRG) at Ohio State University in 1971. Members included graduate students from the departments of art (including graphic design and illustration), industrial design, photography and cinema, computer and information science, and mathematics. In 1987, the CGRG had became the Advanced Computing Center for the Arts and Design, where significant research work continues to be carried out in the area of computer animation by faculty and students, many of whom have become leaders in the film and computer games industry, working for companies such as Disney, Pixar and Electronic Arts.

▲ Students and staff at the Advanced Computing Center for the Arts and Design at Ohio State University are collaborating with Brave New Pictures and the Burpee Museum in Rockford, Illinois, to produce a documentary-style, one-hour special on the dinosaur that was found in Hell's Creek, Montana, in 2002. It is one of the first large-scale projects to incorporate both live-action footage and 3D animation at an educational institution.

Simulation

The manufacture of increasingly sophisticated jet aircraft led to the need to train pilots on visual flight simulators. Commercial pilots and their crews could become familiar with the controls of new aircraft and the approaches to runway layouts of airports all over the world without actually having to fly there first. Military pilots could fly over realistic, simulated enemy territories and engage in combat without the need for war to break out first.

Visual flight simulators date from the late 1950s. At first, these relied on film or closed-circuit television to provide the pilot's 'point-of-view' film footage. Systems using 35mm or 70mm film were shot from real aeroplanes, providing a projected view of a flightpath to the trainee pilot, who had some responsive interaction with the film. The closed-circuit television system usually consisted of a specially adapted television camera that responded to pilot action, mounted over an accurate model of a landscape. Although high degrees of realism were achieved through both systems, they were of limited value because of the restricted possibilities they created for presenting variations in flight path or unexpected situations that might confront a pilot during a real flight.

Computer-image-generation (CIG) systems were developed in the 1970s for the US space programme, including the animated fly-bys mentioned above. Initially, flight-simulation systems produced two-dimensional images, but later three-dimensional objects were also generated, adding some realism to these mainly real-time interactive landscapes. By the late 1970s, military and commercial visual training systems included simulations for air, land and sea activity.

In 1968, two pioneers of computer graphics, Ivan Sutherland (who developed the first interactive computer-graphics system, Sketchpad, at MIT in 1963) and David Evans (who started the computer science department at the University of Utah, a centre for innovation in computer visualization) came together to form Evans & Sutherland, to produce visual simulation systems. CAE is another world leader in the provision of simulation and modelling technologies and integrated training

▲ Training simulator for helicopter pilots. The realistic landscape and flight-control interaction are in 'real time', giving trainee pilots the feeling of real flight. *Evans & Sutherland*

▲ A full-flight simulator replicates every detail of the aircraft cockpit. It also reproduces, with great accuracy and realism, the visual environment the a appears to be flying in, including clouds, thunderst and the landing approaches to airports around the © 2004, CAE Inc.

▲ Simulators are also used to train ground transport staff for safe operations around aircraft at airports. © CAE Inc.

◄ Simulations are used by both military and civilian aircraft manufacturers to help test and sell concept aircraft as well as those already in production. © CAE Inc.

services for civil aviation and defence customers around the world. Simulators are widely recognized as the closest thing to the actual experience of flight.

Computer-imaging systems for simulation and visualization soon began to find new applications, including the creation of theme-park rides and digital projection. As computers became smaller, faster and cheaper, artists and games designers began to use some of the computer-graphics techniques employed in the development of flight simulators to create images and imaginary experiences on-screen. As game genres developed, flight simulators were among the earliest available, proving enduringly popular on personal computers and games consoles. They are now so powerful that users are able to experience historical combat missions. Players of the latest Microsoft Flight Simulator can download additional accurate flight formation, cockpit and landscape data, allowing them to simulate flying with, for example, the UK Royal Air Force Red Arrows aerobatics team. In the US would-be air force pilots can cite their flight-simulator scores and results from simulation games when they apply for pilot training.

Both government and commercial organizations also use road, railway and maritime simulators. As such, trainees can experience all kinds of possible situations and conditions before venturing out into the real world. The first experience of learner car drivers behind the wheel may well be in a driving-school simulator. Trainee truck drivers are also encouraged to experience simulated road conditions to improve their driving and vehicle-handling skills. New trains are tested and their drivers are trained using CIG simulations of real track routes in all weather conditions.

▲ Highly realistic, very detailed and exhilarating, Geoff Crammond's *Grand Prix 4* can be played on a personal computer and games console. *MicroProse*

All types of simulation use realistic graphic computer modelling delivered in real time. The level of 'realism' achieved is extraordinary. One particular Formula 1 motor-racing game is now so convincing that it is difficult to distinguish it from the experience of watching a real race on television through the lens of a camera mounted behind the driver's head. The parallels between driving and flying games, and training simulators are very close. All draw on similar graphic-design skills.

By the 1980s, developments in computer graphics were beginning to interest graphic designers, but with the cost and difficulty of access to computers, few were able to take advantage of the new possibilities. This situation changed radically in a very short time. It is virtually impossible for a graphic designer to practise now without working on computers.

The virtual graphic-design studio: the digital island

For several years now, graphic designers have had nearly all their tools in one place on their desktop. However, this has not always been the case. In the past, having been briefed by a client who would usually know what form the job would take – a brochure, an annual report, a press advertisement, a poster, a book cover, etc. – the designer would then have had to make a series of rough layouts on paper. After discussing the roughs with the client, he or she would 'work up' an agreed design, specifying details of elements such as type, illustration and photography. On receiving approval from the client, the next stage would be to gather or commission these other elements from other professionals. For instance, a marked-up manuscript and accurately drawn layout would be produced and sent to a commercial typesetter. The graphic designer would finally prepare or specify camera-ready artwork, or the mechanical, by cutting and pasting physical pieces of typesetting on bromide paper onto boards to be sent to a repro house and converted first to film and then to printing plates. All this took quite a long time and involved specialities and trade skills that have all but disappeared, although some traditional print reproduction methods, such as letterpress printing from lead type, are still used by enthusiasts.

Conventional graphic design workflow

rough visuals	detailed visuals	type mark-up	typesetting	paste-up	camera-ready artwork	proofing	platemaking	printing
studio			typesetter	studio		repro house		printer

Digital graphic design workflow

rough visuals	design and typesetting	laser proofing	file transfer	printing
studio			printer	

▲ This diagram compares conventional graphic-design and digital workflows. It shows the differences in both the studio time and how associated external specialists, such as typesetters, were employed in the traditional production process. In the digital workflow, tasks including typesetting are carried out by the designer in the studio and the finished design is transferred directly to the printer for printing and distribution.

▲ The Apple Macintosh 128k, launched in 1984, heralded the 'desktop publishing revolution'.

For graphic designers, the first major contact with computer graphics accompanied the computerization of parts of the print industry in the 1970s. Once the techniques of reproducing photographs and graphics in magazines had been changed by the introduction of scanners and high-quality colour output, controlled by sophisticated computer workstations, the print-production workflow was revolutionized beyond recognition. Today, we take for granted the power of our computers to manipulate images and create computer graphics. Graphic designers in particular are now in control of computer hardware and software tools that are fully capable production tools. These desktop facilities have replaced highly specialized and costly high-end equipment requiring purpose-built industrial spaces.

The first systems in use were expensive turnkeys, such as Quantel's Paintbox, more commonly found in broadcast post-production graphics. However, in 1985, Apple Computer introduced the LaserWriter that, combined with the PostScript language from Adobe and the page-layout application Aldus PageMaker (later taken over by Adobe Systems), produced crisp 300dpi type and image printing. The term 'desktop publishing' is attributed to Paul Brainerd from Aldus, as a marketing catchphrase used to describe the small size and relative affordability of this suite of products,

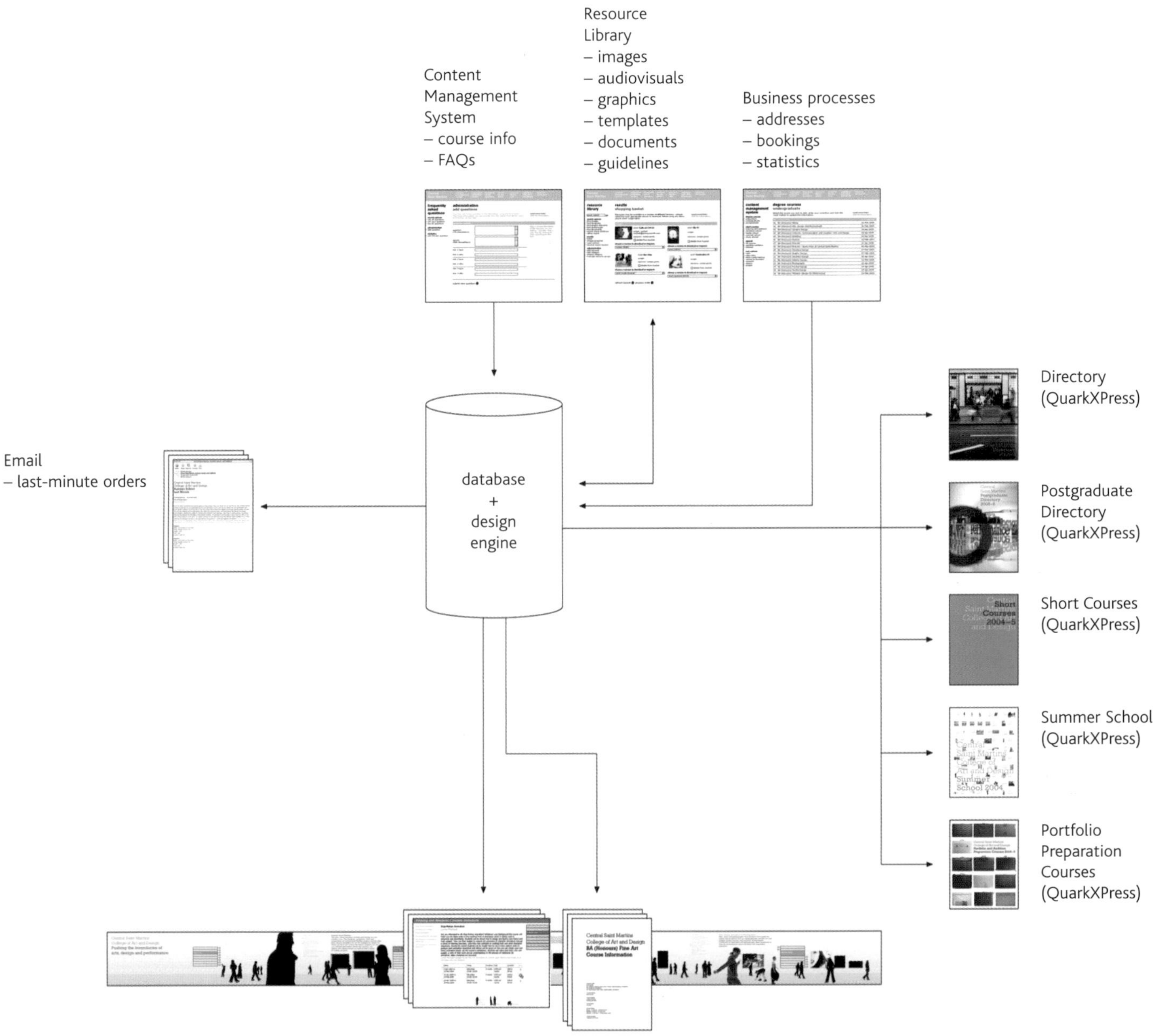

Content
Management
System
– course info
– FAQs

Resource
Library
– images
– audiovisuals
– graphics
– templates
– documents
– guidelines

Business processes
– addresses
– bookings
– statistics

Directory
(QuarkXPress)

Postgraduate
Directory
(QuarkXPress)

Email
– last-minute orders

database
+
design
engine

Short Courses
(QuarkXPress)

Summer School
(QuarkXPress)

Portfolio
Preparation
Courses
(QuarkXPress)

Website
– course info
– FAQs
– news
– bookings

PDF downloads
– course outlines
– application forms

Cross-Media Publishing System
Large volumes of changing information make
it difficult to repeatedly produce effective
communications. A publishing tool, shown in the
diagram (above), produces highly detailed page
layouts, web documents and Portable Document
Files (PDFs), each optimized for their respective
medium. Shared databases with common content
(such as a collection of images) feed the design
engine, ensuring consistency across the range of
media. The graphic designer can set the level of
completion for each document: from text only with

typographic styles for galleys to a completed
document (including images) ready for the printer.
There are key advantages for designers using such a
publishing tool: the design input is already contained
in the pre-determined templates, which empowers
the designer to create marketing materials, embracing
a visual identity on demand. The burden of repetitive,

data-intensive and error-prone tasks is removed; with
improved efficiency, each piece can be produced more
quickly, with less effort, significantly reducing costs
and content can be input and managed independently
from the design and production process, creating a
harmonious, collaborative working environment for
the client and designer. *Diagram © JannuzziSmith,
CSM*

compared with the commercial phototypesetting equipment of the day. Designers could now design and set type on screen; WYSIWYG ('what you see is what you get') applications meant that what the designer visualized was what the printer produced. They might still have had to use a repro house for high-quality output, but the design process could mostly be kept in the designer's studio. QuarkXPress was introduced in 1987 and became the dominant package, until Adobe launched InDesign in 1999 to replace PageMaker. By 2002, it was outselling QuarkXPress, mainly because it integrated with other Adobe products such as Photoshop and could export documents in Adobe's PDF (Portable Document Format).

Multimedia

Graphic designers were liberated and back in control of the process, no longer at the mercy of the sometimes arcane practices of typesetters, repro houses, printers and suppliers. Design for print gained sophisticated professional page layout, image origination and manipulation applications, as well as quality typefaces, all available on the desktop Mac. The workflow model was reduced to a few steps. Suddenly, most of the production cycle took place on the designer's desktop. Print, although old media, has not stood still – nowadays almost everything is printed full colour and small batches can be produced almost on-demand, using digital technology.

However, perhaps the most dramatic change for graphic designers has been the way their work has expanded in its application; they no longer design only for print. Some designers, such as Saul Bass, Charles and Ray Eames in the US, and Bernard Lodge and Colin Cheesman for the BBC in the UK, were already producing outstanding moving-image work in film and on television that would be considered multimedia today – without the aid of computers. Computer graphics are now commonplace and touch every part of our lives, from television, film sequences and programme titles, animated display hoardings, advertising, shop displays, museum experiences, computer games, outdoor events and the Internet, to the screens in front of which most of us spend at least some of our time.

The presentation of information to convey ideas in various formats is not new. For several hundred years, artists and designers have found ways to represent information in innovative ways using more than one of the visual techniques from their armoury without the help of computer technology. However, in the development and use of computers in graphic design, multimedia has played a major role.

Multimedia is best described as the convergence of digital media that has allowed the creative development of computer graphics to spread into many new areas. There are two main reasons for this. The first has been the combination of different types of media into one – text, pictures, video, sound and animation. The other has been interaction – multimedia involves users, turning them from passive observers of information displayed in a predefined order into explorers deciding for

London-based Why Not Associates were commissioned by Kobe Fashion Museum in Japan to be the first designers to use the museum's audiovisual facilities. *Synapse* is a ten-minute installation that takes place hourly in the museum's central square. Twenty-four hidden projectors cast 1,500 individual image compositions onto the four walls and floor of the room. The display explores the theme of 'fashion', with layered imagery depicting nature, shelter, culture, communications, technology and materials, illustrating what produces and affects our notion of fashion.

▼ The installation area before *Synapse* commences.

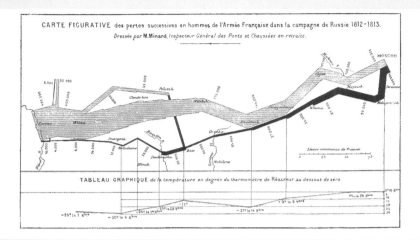

◀ Graphic interpretation dates back many centuries. Illustrated here is a diagram showing the Napoleonic army as it advanced on Moscow and then retreated towards Poland in the Russian Campaign of 1812–1813. The thickness of the line shows the number of French soldiers still alive at any moment in the march. The lower part of the diagram indicates the shifts in temperature. Taken from *La Méthode Graphique* by E.J. Marey (Paris, 1885), p. 73.

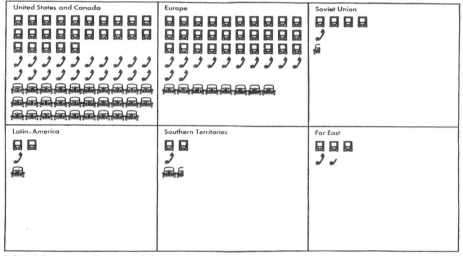

◀ Otto Neurath pioneered the technique of interpreting statistical information by means of graphic diagrams. It caused some political unease when it became apparent that the graphic information showed an uncomfortable balance between rich and poor nations. Taken from *Modern Man in the Making* by Otto Neurath (London and New York: Isotype, 1939).

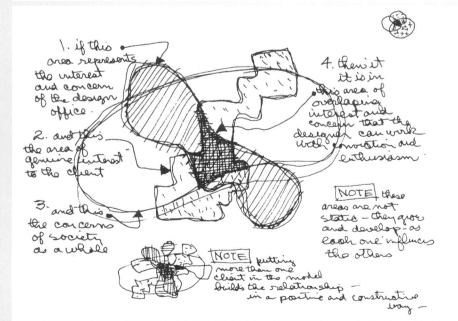

◀ Charles and Ray Eames opened their design office in the 1940s. They believed good design and business could coexist and developed a practice based on a combination of art and technology. Charles Eames carefully sketched out this diagram to represent the balance between personal, business and social needs and it has since been adopted as a general model for design businesses, of whatever size. The Eames office produced some extraordinary examples of 'multimedia', using the older technologies available at the time.

themselves how they wish to access, digest and use information. There are huge design implications in the way that this information is presented, cross-referenced and linked together. The merging of telecommunications, telephone, movie, cable and television companies into one vast network connected by fibre-optic cables, wireless and satellites is already a reality that has provided platforms for the development of multimedia experiences on an ever-widening and ambitious scale.

In 1978, the 30-cm (12-inch) laserdisc, the first optical-storage medium, was marketed as an alternative to videotape and made it possible to realize the potential of digital multimedia. Laserdiscs provided a number of advantages over VHS videotape, which was linear and analogue only. Image quality was much sharper at nearly twice the resolution. Discs could also handle multiple analogue and digital soundtracks, and access was random, allowing any point on the disc to be selected almost instantly. Initially used for movies, laserdiscs could be marketed as 'special editions' with extra information, such as the director's audio commentary, included along with 'behind-the-scenes' documentaries. In 1984, the movies *Citizen Kane* and *King Kong* were released in the US by Criterion, who pioneered 'special-edition' laserdiscs. In the UK, the BBC used laserdisc technology to produce a modern-day Domesday Book to celebrate the 900th anniversary of the original Great Land Survey of England, commissioned in 1086 by King William I (also known as William the Conqueror). In 1986, about one million people, including schoolchildren and community groups, contributed text, photographs, illustrations, film clips and other information about their local area. Maps were used for statistical data taken from the 1981 census, and the result was a multimedia snapshot of modern England, created mainly by the people who lived there. The project was ahead of its time but ultimately sold very few copies because laserdiscs required a special player that was too expensive. Also, newer, more compact technologies were about to enter the field.

The invention of the CD-Rom (Compact Disc Read-Only Memory) in 1983, with its smaller disc size and large, relatively cheap storage capacity, established digital multimedia as a major vehicle for information and entertainment. At the time, the development of the CD-Rom was compared in significance to the advent of the printing press and photography. During the early 1990s, new multimedia titles on CD-Rom were published in hundreds and thousands, and a multimillion dollar industry evolved. Creative and visualization skills ensured that graphic designers quickly became central to the teams of specialists that were required to assemble the complex information and produce the interactivity required by this new medium.

Multimedia applications exploited computers in ways that had not been anticipated, and not only helped to establish the popularity of personal computers, but also extended their use in educational institutions and the workplace. Libraries of multimedia software offered more opportunities to explain a subject than their traditional book-based encyclopedic counterparts. Other sources of reference also

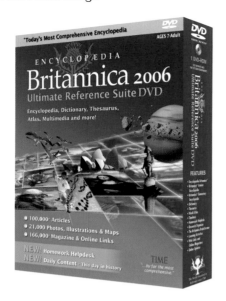

▲ The *Encyclopædia Britannica*, traditionally a 32-volume book publication, is also available on DVD and CD-Rom as an all-in-one reference resource in a multimedia format. *Reprinted with the permission of Encyclopædia Britannica, Inc.*

▲ Mosaic, the first popular web browser for the World Wide Web, was written at the National Center for Supercomputing Applications (NCSA) in 1992 by Marc Andreessen. Mosaic was described as 'the killer application of the 1990s' because it was the first program to provide a slick multimedia graphical user interface to the Internet's burgeoning wealth of information. *Courtesy of the National Center for Supercomputing Applications (NCSA) and the Board of Trustees of the University of Illinois*

adapted well to this new media. The CD-Rom utilized the computer's ability to bring multiple media – images, text, animation, video and sound – together to enhance the user experience and, in educational terms, make it easier and faster to learn.

The multimedia revolution has become broadly categorized into reference, education, entertainment and services. Encyclopedias have already been mentioned; atlases, manuals and museum collections can be threaded with additional material and reference links. In education, the multimedia classroom offers a structured programme, from early to life-long learning through creative tools (writing, drawing and painting), science and maths, languages and storytelling. Multimedia entertainment ranges from computer games and interactive movies to music and animated cartoons. Services include business and workplace training, medical and scientific simulation, point-of-sale and in-flight information.

From the mid-1990s onwards, following the rapid expansion and popularity of the World Wide Web, multimedia increasingly found a new home on the Internet. As networks grew and access to high-speed broadband became commonplace, so did the demand for more challenging and complex media content. The entertainment industry was quick to grasp the potential of multimedia in this new context, developing interactive experiences that users actively participate in, rather than passively receiving information in a predefined order.

With the arrival of DVD (Digital Versatile/Video Disc) in the late 1990s, entire films could be stored on a single small disc, featuring interactivity and extra information. Music on audio CDs could be enhanced with video sequences and even gather information from the Internet.

Multimedia-rich digital television offers channels with multiple choices, such as the option to access extra resources including the possibility to shop online, use the World Wide Web, email, and, in sport, select the game or camera angle of your choice. Most television shows have websites and discussion forums where you can explore additional information about the issues raised by the programme or find out more about the personalities involved.

The digital effects industry

What is real? Much of what we see on television and in films has been subjected to processes of digital enhancement or digital fabrication. Often the television presenter stands in a 'blue or green screen' studio (a technique also known as 'chroma key' that allows an electronic image such as a synthetic set to be shown or 'dubbed', or superimposed, into a blue or green coloured area behind a studio subject), yet what is broadcast is a merging of several sources creating a complete environment surrounding the presenter. Television designers use multiple media – live action overlaid with graphics to illustrate programmes and enhance our viewing experience in this way. Some of the earliest television graphics were developed for weather presenters, standing before animated maps and charts.

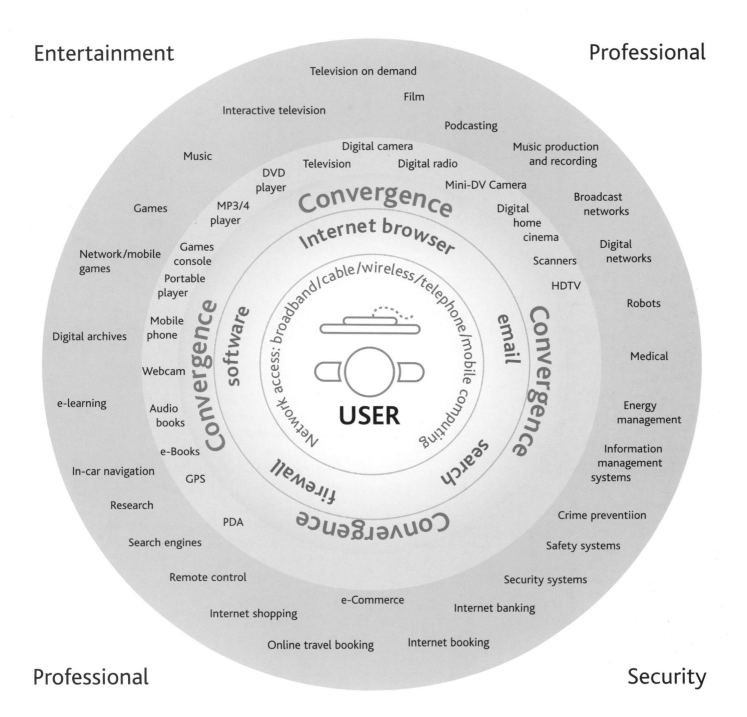

Entertainment

Professional

Professional

Security

Television on demand

Film

Interactive television

Podcasting

Music production and recording

Music

Digital camera

Television   Digital radio

DVD player

Convergence

Mini-DV Camera

Digital home cinema

Broadcast networks

Games

MP3/4 player

Internet browser

Digital networks

Games console

Scanners

Network/mobile games

Portable player

Convergence software

Network access: broadband/cable/wireless/telephone/mobile computing

HDTV

Digital home cinema

Robots

Digital archives

Mobile phone

USER

Convergence email

Medical

Webcam

Energy management

e-learning

Audio books

Information management systems

e-Books

firewall

search

Convergence

Crime preventiion

In-car navigation

GPS

Safety systems

Research

PDA

Security systems

Search engines

Remote control

e-Commerce

Internet banking

Internet shopping

Online travel booking   Internet booking

▲ This diagram puts the computer user at the centre of a 'digital hub' surrounded by the tools of communication. Personal computers and other peripherals of all kinds are connected to networks through telephone lines or by wireless. Software enables the user to access communications globally and also work in many professional and work contexts. Convergence between different media means that new-media designers are forever preparing work for different applications and output formats.

▲ A 'chroma key' background allows a presenter to be filmed in a studio, against a green or blue background colour, and then to be combined with an image from a different source such as a 'live feed' from another, often remote, location, or an image from a picture library. The resulting blend is broadcast as one picture. This technique is widely used in news and weather programmes on TV.

▲ Green-screen, or chroma key, components are combined in software such as the Ultra2 interface before being output to video, DVD or broadcast media. *Serious Magic Inc.*

▲ Sky's Golf application – here for the Ryder Cup – shows just how comprehensive an enhanced sports application can be. Multiple camera feeds are complemented by scrolling scores, a guide to the course, top shots, etc. *Sky Interactive*

Television news and reality programmes may feature real-time 'live feeds' direct from cameras at remote locations ('feed' is a term used in the broadcast industry to describe a link from an external source). Additional studio 'feeds' allow extra material, archive footage and explanatory graphics to be overlaid and interwoven into what the audience sees, contributing to a richer experience for viewers. Broadcast teams include designers who generate graphics, such as maps, on the fly as the programme is being broadcast. Designers work with programmers to develop techniques and mini applications to make this process possible.

Digital television has widened the possibilities for extra material to be provided to the viewer. At the touch of a button, a vast amount of programme-related information can be accessed. For example, a sports event, such as a soccer match, may be broadcast live using multi-camera feeds to follow the action on the pitch. At any point in the game digital viewers are able to replay sequences, look up statistical information about the teams or individual players and even connect to club websites before returning to the game at the point at which they left it. In some cases, viewers can even choose from which camera they prefer to view the game. During the Olympic Games, for example, a viewer may choose which simultaneous event to watch in the stadium: the long jump or the 10,000 metres, for example.

The cinema regularly immerses audiences in imaginary futuristic or recreated historical events and landscapes. Some of these effects are produced using dedicated sophisticated equipment; others require no more than a digital camera and a desktop computer.

Techniques for extending what is possible in a single camera shot are widely used in the film industry. Take what looks like a fairly straightforward sequence in a film, as the camera passes from an exterior to an interior view through a pane of glass in an apparently seamless movement. The pane of glass is not really there. Instead, a layer of reference points has been digitally applied to indicate the plane on which any reflections in the glass should appear. These reflections have then been superimposed to trick the eye into seeing a glass pane, and so allowing the camera to appear to pass through it to the interior.

▲ An Avid post-production suite. Avid pioneered the concept of using computers to digitally manipulate film, video, audio and 3D animation by providing media creation tools to broadcast professionals. *Peak White Studios, London*

Techniques for combining or superimposing film images have existed since the early days of cinema. Motion capture is a more modern technique, commonly used in movies such as the *Star Wars* films. Models of spaceships have been digitally tracked as they were filmed against a blue or green 'chroma key' screen. The precise position of the model and the camera's movement at every frame have been recorded, so that when the footage is replayed, the spaceship's action and position on screen is known precisely and it can be 'matted' into the film's action. The term 'matte' describes the process of superimposing or merging one or more images onto another realistically. Before computers, an exotic scene above the action could be painted on a piece of glass in front of a static camera, or two pieces of film could be superimposed using a matte as a form of stencil mask. Sometimes, a single spaceship is part of a larger complex action involving many others, all shot and matted in a similar way.

In the 1999 film *The Matrix*, directed by Andy and Larry Wachowski, some of the sequences were produced using still frames shot in close succession by an array of carefully positioned 35mm single-lens reflex cameras in sequence. The effect is known as 'bullet time': a moment progresses in slow-motion while the camera appears to orbit around the scene at normal speed. When these were digitally added to the backgrounds it resulted in some of the most spectacular action sequences of the time. In 2001, *Star Wars: Attack of the Clones* was the first major feature film to be shot entirely using digital cameras, which allowed the director George Lucas to apply some groundbreaking effects.

▲ ▲ The film *Titanic* combined live action with digital effects to produce dramatic scenes. In the dock sequence (above), waving digital people were placed on the deck of the ship, using a library of about 20 different waving animations. *Titanic © 1997 Twentieth Century Fox and Paramount Pictures Corporation. All rights reserved*

Digital effects contributed to the huge box-office success of James Cameron's *Titanic*. The film cost US$200 million to make – one of the most expensive ever – and in 1998 it won 11 Oscars. The similarly successful *Lord of the Rings* trilogy also boasts scenes and characters that could only have been achieved with the use of digital effects; for instance, the battle scenes and Gollum himself were created digitally using motion capture from actor Andy Serkis.

The increasing reliance of movies on digital post-production techniques has led to a need to transfer large amounts of film and video data between companies for editing and work on special effects. For example, 'Sohonet' is a network service that allows the transfer of files between linked production houses in London's Soho area, Hollywood and Australia.

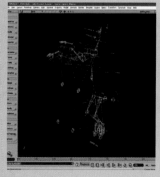

This page illustrates some of the ways in which digital effects make imaginary characters and worlds real.

▲ *Top Left:* A 3D laser scan created a model of a stone knight for one of the *Harry Potter* films. Texture was digitally added for the final sequences.

▲ *Top Right:* Characters created by the director of *Pinocchio 3000*, Daniel Robichaud. The 3D puppets are created using CGI animation techniques and manipulated in digital film sets.

◀ *Left:* Stills from television and film commercials. All have been manipulated using digital effects to recreate historical or imaginary events. Highly sophisticated software and powerful computers are used to create these images. *Images courtesy of BBC/BBC Worldwide/ Framestore CFC*

▼ *Bottom:* Lassie was created entirely by digital means. Hair movement and lighting require special computer animation techniques to produce the realistic actions of a super dog.
Mike Donovan NYC and SoftImage

Advertising on television and in the cinema has also embraced digital effects. To capture the imaginations of audiences and persuade them to buy products and services, advertisers need to call on the experience of the film industry to make their point in 30-second slots.

Public service broadcasters, such as the BBC in the UK and some commercial television channels, have been quick to follow the example of the film industry in the use of digital effects. *Walking with Dinosaurs* further developed the techniques used in the film *Jurassic Park*. Reconstructions of historical events have been created using digitally manipulated images and life-like characters programmed with artificial intelligence (AI).

Although digital effects may not be covered in detail on a college graphic design course, there are opportunities for graphic designers in the film and television industry as computer graphics specialists, creating characters or environments, or as art directors, visualizing productions. This often means that they become key members in movie production design teams. For example, Ridley Scott, who made *Blade Runner* and the first of the *Alien* films, trained as a graphic designer at the Royal College of Art in London.

The computer games industry

The worldwide market for electronic games software grossed US$28 billion (£14.5 billion) in 2005, almost equalling the box-office takings of the film industry in the same year. This profitability continues today.

Early commercial computer and platform games included the on-screen table-tennis program *Pong* (1972), *Space Invaders* (1979), *Pacman* (1980), *Mario* (1981, originally called *Donkey Kong*), *Manhole* (1981) and *Tetris* (1985). The continuing demand for newer and ever more complex games has made this one of the fastest growing areas in computing. With the power of home computers and consoles, games have become a major source of innovation in programming and graphics. Expertly crafted fantasy games such as *Myst* and *Riven* require users to discover their own clues to the game-play through a realistic environment. The success of Lara Croft of the *Tomb Raider* games has made a cyber-personality into a media star. Designers play a major role in the games industry and as a result often take a share in the considerable financial rewards.

Both novice and experienced gamers can immerse themselves in multi-level 3D environments. In simulation games you can fly combat missions in the latest jet fighter over super-real landscapes or drive a racing car on the world's Grand Prix circuits. In martial arts games you can pitch yourself against the computer or another player, role-playing by adopting and manipulating a character. Online gaming over the Internet ranges from one-to-one connections to multi-player action in MUDs (multi-user domains), where players compete in a truly global gaming arena. In classic games, such as *Quake* and *Star Wars Galaxies*, players can

▲ Three of the most popular and endearing games characters. *From the top*: Mario for Nintendo; Sonic the Hedgehog for Sega; Lara Croft from the *Tomb Raider* games.

Electronic Games

- In 1961, *Spacewars*, the first real electronic game to be played on a digital computer with a CRT screen – was produced. It was programmed by Steve Russell at the Massachusetts Institute of Technology (MIT) in the US.
- The first video-game arcade machine was called Computer Space (an arcade version of Spacewars) and it was built by Nolan Bushnell in 1971.
- The first truly portable games console was the Nintendo Game Boy, introduced in Japan in 1989, which has now sold more than 70 million copies worldwide.
- The **first-generation** electronic games machines were 8-bit, the dominant console was the Japanese Nintendo Entertainment System (1985), and the most popular character was Nintendo's Italian plumber Mario.
- The **second-generation** electronic games machines were 16-bit, the dominant console was the Japanese Sega Megadrive (1988), and the most popular character was Sega's Sonic the Hedgehog (1991).
- The **third-generation** electronic games machines were 32-bit, the dominant console was the Japanese Sony PlayStation, first introduced in 1994, and the most popular character was Lara Croft (1995) from Eidos's *Tomb Raider* games, which were not exclusive to the PlayStation.
- The **fourth-generation** electronic games machines were 64-bit and the dominant console was the Japanese Nintendo N64 (1996).
- The **fifth-generation** electronic games machine is 128-bit and the rival consoles are Sony's PlayStation 2 (2000), Nintendo's GameCube (2001) and Microsoft's Xbox (2001).
- The **sixth (and seventh) generation** electronic games machines (still 128-bit) are designed to allow gamers to access media from anywhere on the Internet. Sony introduced its PlayStation Portable (PSP) in 2005 and PlayStation 3 in 2007. The rival consoles are Microsoft's Xbox 360 (2005) and Nintendo's Wii (2006), formerly known as Revolution.

▲ A scene from *Quake,* a multiplayer online game. *Activision*

program themselves into the game by means of a personal avatar. In 'God' games, such as *Black & White*, which let you create and control the lives of virtual people or worlds, you are the controller and you interact with artificial intelligence (AI) that 'learns' how to influence the outcome of your actions. In games such as *The Sims*, players exercise social control and manage populations.

Some games have moved into multi-platform dimensions. The same title is often available in amusement arcades, on games consoles, personal computers and mobile phones. The game graphics and action appear the same, but are enlarged or shrunk to suit the host device. In one example, a car-racing game was played by people dialling from their mobile phones, each taking it in turn to control a racing car displayed on a giant screen in Times Square, New York.

Russell Lowe (New Zealand and New York) uses computer games engines to construct environments where creative people meet and work online. His environments often radically transform real-world constraints such as scale, gravity and materiality.

▶ On a Victoria University (Wellington, New Zealand) course, designed by Russell Lowe, Joneen Wall constructed a floating city made from versions of the Farnsworth House by Mies van der Rohe, and the Johnson Glass House by Philip Johnson. Each unit responded to player proximity, which constantly transformed the city. Players were able to find and use 'jump pads' to make an assisted leap from one building to the other. In this environment the time spent leaping between and on the roofs of each unit equalled that spent inside them.

▼ The 'FarmGate' project extends research by MediaLab South Pacific. In collaboration with Fonterra (one of the world's largest dairy suppliers), the following question was asked: 'How might thousands of farmers use broadband Internet services if it were delivered to their farm gate?' One answer proposed re-purposing computer game technology to facilitate remote education; which in this case involved learning safe practices to operate farm vehicles.

▶ ▶ The vehicles in many computer games reflect themes of aggression and violence. In the project 'MobileHome3000', Russell Lowe produced a series of vehicles for *Unreal Tournament 2004* that were inspired by things found around the home (and even houses themselves). The treadmill and sofa flying vehicles are a tongue-in-cheek response to the relationship between our physical and virtual bodies while gaming.

▶ ▶ Game modifications, or 'Mods', such as, GarrysMod9, utilize the latest generation of computer gaming engines' capabilities for real-time physics simulation. For the first time 'players' are able to create original content without leaving the gaming environment. This opens up huge possibilities for designers to collaborate from opposite sides of the globe.
A group of design students pose for a virtual class photo in front of a fiery landscape installation (right).

Peter Molyneux: Lionhead Studios

Peter Molyneux, founder of Lionhead Studios, is recognized worldwide as one of the most innovative computer-games developers.

Peter Molyneux is one of the best-known names in the international world of computer games. In the UK Molyneux is the acknowledged godfather of the games industry. He also has a high profile in both the United States and Japan, something no other British games designer can boast. His career in game development began in 1987 with the formation of Bullfrog Productions. The company's future was assured with the release of the ground-breaking *Populous*, which created a new genre of computer games, the 'God' game.

Molyneux and his team at Bullfrog developed a string of bestselling games, including *Powermonger*, *Theme Park*, *Magic Carpet* and *Dungeon Keeper*. The company quickly became recognized as the UK's most creative and successful development studio.

In 1997, Molyneux left Bullfrog Productions to form Lionhead Studios. In 2001, *Black & White* was released to widespread acclaim and sales currently top the two-million mark. It has won numerous industry awards including two BAFTAs and three Emmys. In late 2004, Lionhead released its second game, *Fable*, on Xbox and its sales have also topped two million copies. Autumn 2005 saw further releases: *Fable: The Lost Chapters*, *Black & White 2* and *The Movies*. In April 2006, Lionhead Studios was bought by Microsoft and now forms part of the Microsoft Game Studios.

▷ *Top:* A hero in full armour battles with a balverine in *Fable: The Lost Chapters*. *Below:* Two heroes battle it out using magic in *Fable: The Lost Chapters*.

Molyneux is one of the computer games industry's most articulate and eloquent speakers. He has spoken at the American Museum of the Moving Image, the British Film Institute, the ICA and the Tate Gallery in London, and the Dortmund Museum of History and Culture in Germany. He is regarded as the games industry's premier spokesperson and in this capacity he has been featured in national newspapers and on television. He was inducted into the US Academy of Interactive Arts and Sciences Hall of Fame in 2004, the first European developer to be recognized in this way. He was also awarded an OBE in the 2005 New Year's Honours List in the UK for services to the computer video games industry.

▲ ▷ All the creatures in *Black & White 2*, such as this lion, have powerful AI (artificial intelligence) systems. This is recognized in the *Guinness Book of World Records*, 2006 edition.

▼ This screenshot illustrates the variations in alignment between a 'good' and 'evil' city in *Black & White 2*.

▲ The ape gets rather cross in a game scene from *Black & White 2*.
▷ A glamorous star from *The Movies*.

What makes a good games designer? The authors of *Rules of Play*, Katie Salen and Eric Zimmerman write: 'A game designer is a particular kind of designer, much like a graphic designer, industrial designer or architect. A game designer is not necessarily a programmer, visual designer, or project manager, although sometimes he or she can also play these roles in the creation of a game. A game designer may work alone or as part of a larger team. A game designer may create card games, social games or video games. The focus of a game designer is designing game play, conceiving and designing rules and structures that result in an experience for players.' (MIT Press, 2003) The emphasis here is on designing the gameplay, the overall structure, but there are also roles for team members or collaborators specializing in designing characters, both as 2D concepts and 3D models, designing buildings and vehicles, designing backgrounds and environments, designing the user interface – even designing logos and the box graphics.

▲ Using their mobile cell phones, passers-by in Times Square, New York, could take turns to race each other live on the Reuters sign in the world's first interactive video game on a digital billboard. The game and its technology was developed by R/GA, the New York-based interactive advertising agency, to promote the re-launch of the Yahoo! Autos website.

One reason why computer games attract graphic designers is because of the vast range of possibilities they offer for showcasing ideas. The design and manufacture of games bring together an extraordinary variety of skills and kinds of expertise. There are numerous examples of groups of enthusiastic designers and experts collaborating to try out their ideas. In many cases, this has produced games that have been used to explore new graphic-design and illustration techniques. Although some of these creations may at first seem deceptively simple, many have actually helped define the future direction of games design. Innovative programming and graphical experiments on the websites of groups, such as AntiRom (www.antirom.com) and Future Farmers (www.futurefarmers.com), and individuals such as Yugo Nakamura (www.yugop.com) and Daniel Brown (www.danielbrowns.com), provide an important reference point for designers interested in games and new-media design in general, because they show what can be achieved with the creative use of software tools.

Including games in graphic design projects is one way of exploiting the medium. Software tools such as Flash and Shockwave provide powerful and stable platforms to experiment and build interactive games for a number of project solutions. In Airside's website for the 'Jam: Tokyo/London' exhibition of contemporary urban design and culture at the Barbican Centre in London in 2001 (www.airside.co.uk/

▲ Sports games have always been among the most popular interactive computer games. In *FIFA 06* the soccer action achieves an almost photographic realism on screen. *Electronic Arts*

sites/jam), visitors interacted with screen characters that formed an online catalogue and promotion for the exhibition. At New York's P.S.1 MoMA (the Contemporary Art Center affiliated to the Museum of Modern Art), artists and visitors were able to create animations to play on mobile phone screens.

Universities and art colleges are now offering courses in games design either from within art and design departments or from computer science faculties, with the aim of training graphic designers, illustrators and programmers to play a key role in developing games for the major companies. The design and realization of the settings for some of these blockbuster productions make a variety of demands on designers and programmers, and the development of an individual project is usually shrouded in secrecy. Collaboration between specialists is one of the keys to the realization of a game concept where the pressure to produce unique storylines, spectacular visuals and compelling gameplay is paramount. This can be inspiring and at the same time frightening; games that have been hyped in advance can falter when they are finally released because player expectations have not been met, often owing to disappointing design or programming.

What is it about computer games that so fascinates and engages us? Studies have been carried out into the effects of games that suggest some answers to this question. Games are fun to play, so players get enjoyment and pleasure. They are a

Gaming Genres

- Adventure games require the player to solve puzzles and find artefacts.
- Educational games use the game as a vehicle for teaching, mainly the young.
- Fighting games emphasize one-to-one combat and martial arts.
- Multiplayer online games involve players interacting together online.
- Platform games include traditional two-dimensional elements, such as running, jumping from level to level, fighting enemies and collecting rewards.
- Puzzle games require players to solve logic puzzles and navigate locations/mazes.
- Racing games typically put the player in the driving seat of high-performance cars.
- Role-playing games give the player the opportunity to act as an adventurer in fantasy settings.
- Serious games teach real-world scenarios and can be used in corporate environments.
- Simulation games aim to recreate activities such as flying as realistically as possible.
- Sports games emulate the playing of physical sports such as soccer, golf, tennis, etc.
- Strategy games focus on planning and management skills.
- Traditional games are based on popular board and card games.

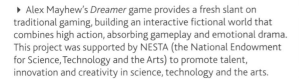

▲ *In The Warrior* by Rockstar Games, players engage in activities outside their normal experience. *Rockstar Games*

▶ Alex Mayhew's *Dreamer* game provides a fresh slant on traditional gaming, building an interactive fictional world that combines high action, absorbing gameplay and emotional drama. This project was supported by NESTA (the National Endowment for Science, Technology and the Arts) to promote talent, innovation and creativity in science, technology and the arts.

form of play that demands intense and passionate involvement. Challenge, competition, opposition and conflict require problem-solving that sparks creativity. Storytelling and representation provide emotion. Games are structured by rules and have goals that motivate. Interactive play provides action and results in feedback that helps to determine the outcome. Winning gives players satisfaction too. Interactive games that involve multiple players can help to develop social groups.

Compelling gameplay unleashes the potential of new media as the digital theatre of the imagination. It allows players access to a time and place beyond their everyday experience, engaging them and suspending their disbelief both at conscious and subconscious levels.

Virtual game worlds may not need to imitate reality, but they do need to be believable to allow the player to identify and interact with the characters and the gameplay. Interaction should also have a sense of emotional depth and aim to move the story forward as well as reveal the nature of the characters.

In recent years the games industry has grown exponentially. Millions have been made by titles such as *The Sims* and *Temple of Doom*. As a result, specialist service areas within the industry have developed, offering services and expertise in character and background design, user experience, sound design, scriptwriting and dialogue, and user-testing. Increasingly, too, games engines are being developed as programming toolkits, which are then made available to games designers and developers as technical solutions that can be plugged together to make ever more complex gameplay scenarios possible while helping to reduce overall development costs.

▲ *Star Wars Galaxies* engages players in a multi-character fantasy environment in which they are able to interact in a story of their own making. *Lucas Film*

▲ Released in 2000, *The Sims* has become the bestselling non-violent PC game in history. The only objective of this 'God' game is to organize the Sims' time to help them reach personal goals. It developed from *SimCity*, launched in 1989, a simulation and city-building game that became the first commercially successful simulation video game. *Maxis, Electronic Arts*

Games developers are also increasingly negotiating deals for their content to be used across different media. This can be a two-way process, in which games experiences are licensed to broadcasters and filmmakers in return for the right to use film storylines and characters, and can lead to rich cross-media content development.

This broadening of the games culture requires designers to be aware of the need to create worlds that will reach across current and future media experiences. Characters with whom players can readily identify and strong narrative threads are just two of the ingredients necessary for a compelling gameplay experience. Lara Croft is an example of a powerful action character that has crossed media boundaries, appearing as the pixellated heroine in the popular *Tomb Raider* games as well as taking on human flesh for the film version. She also appeared in an advertising campaign for an energy drink and as a franchised model toy.

Broadcasters too are integrating interactive scenarios into television production as a way of involving their audiences in branded experiences. Press the red button on your television control and digital channels reveal a menu offering more information about the programme you are watching.

We all enjoy playing games and solving puzzles. In some respects this is a traditional pastime – whether with a pack of cards, a board game or the electronic equivalent, most people have games experience. There is a fairly common belief that within everyone there is an idea for a game. But what does it take actually to become a games designer? Graphic designers should and do have an advantage here, as they are good at visualizing messages and narrative. But how do you go about designing the next blockbuster game? The answer is that you probably cannot do it on your own. You may have the greatest idea for fantastic graphics and compelling gameplay, but the reality is that the industry is already mature and quite well-defined in its structure. Specialist teams have long since taken the place of the few enthusiasts slumped over computers for long hours, even years, coding their way to the ultimate game experience. Now, it is more likely that the concept and narrative, the graphics, the code and the marketing will be developed by a group of specialists, who may well not be all part of the same company or even in the same part of the world.

We have already looked at why games are engaging, but in developing a product it is equally important to understand who your potential players are. Research has identified four types: conquerors, who are concerned with competition and beating games; managers, who are interested in strategic and management gameplay; wanderers, who enjoy open games and play for the sake of playing; and participants, who focus on the emotional context of play – this group can be subdivided into hardcore and casual players.

Understanding the game genre is crucial. The games industry has arrived at a kind of consensus regarding genre definition, and there has been a considerable amount of research into the demographics of which players select which games.

Electronic and virtual worlds

Representations of real life exist both in electronic artefacts and virtual presentations. Robots can now learn from their surroundings, recognize people and respond to commands. Designers play a crucial role in applying cutting-edge technical innovation in the development of special products. Imagineers and theme-park designers incorporate terrifying and thrilling virtual experiences in their newest rides. In virtual worlds, artificial life can take on sophisticated human characteristics: a digital avatar such as Ananova is able to present television news, complete with perfect facial expressions and voice inflections. Ramona, the alter ego of American techno-entrepreneur Ray Kurzweil (www.kurzweilai.net), invites us to question her directly using voice-activated software.

This quest for realistic perfection has had a mixed reception from end users. It seems we like our cyber friends to be slightly imperfect. The game version of Lara Croft appears to be more acceptable to people than hyper-realistic digital models such as Aki Ross from the movie *Final Fantasy: The Spirits Within* or Kaya (www.vetorzero.com.br/kaya). We appear to be unnerved by seemingly real but alien and bloodless characters, which are intended to simulate our own humanity. Disney and Pixar, for example, were thus careful to people the world of *Toy Story* with humans and toys that were highly stylized; they were recognizably human in their characteristics but not conceived to trick the audience into thinking they were all human.

▲ The idea behind Kaya was to make a believable digital girl. She looks almost too natural in an animated movie. *Alceau Baptistão*

Developers of virtual electronic environments have at their disposal some powerful 'emotioneering' tools. The quality of the visual design, whether it is a virtual-reality ride through an imaginary world or the digital resurrection of past events, can make all the difference between providing a rich experience and something short of satisfying.

NoDNA, a German design studio (www.nodna.com), is using human-motion capture techniques to produce 3D virtual characters to host virtual events and populate European interactive television channels with virtual presenters. The studio has created a virtual character agency that licenses characters for events.

Animated avatars or 'chat bots', which use text-to-speech software and artificial intelligence (AI), can provide business and educational support or perform instant messaging tasks on mobile phones. Virtual hosts for e-marketing websites interact with virtual products and provide round-the-clock customer support. They can be proactive or reactive and even knowledge-based, using AI to ask and answer questions based on how you interact and respond. These virtual characters can also act as personal webguides, explaining and helping with filling out forms where appropriate.

▲ 'Chat bots' are animated avatars, on-screen characters used to augment webpages and guide visitors through a website. The avatars are created using motion-tracking and realistic movements by actors. *noDNA, Oddcast*

Designers are working with some of the graphics and programming technologies developed by the games industry to produce groundbreaking digital installations in galleries, museums and theme parks, where the public can walk into multimedia, multi-sensory environments, which respond to their presence. URBIS, in Manchester in the UK, uses responsive technologies to guide visitors through its exhibition space, developing an experience for users individually (see page 56).

Summary

For the new-media graphic designer, the various areas encountered in this chapter offer exciting challenges in shaping the future use of computer graphics. Visual interpretation of the world around us and of imagined or as yet undiscovered worlds creates both fantastic and serious scenarios for audiences to ponder.

Film, television, games and the Internet are constantly changing, and it is a challenge for the designer to keep pace with technology and new skill sets. But it is these new ideas that make this an exciting area to be involved in, and these skills can be applied in almost any of the multifarious areas of new media. Opportunities for collaboration with other designers and specialists are wider than ever, and extend to anywhere in the Internet-connected world.

Next Steps 5

Old Media

▲ *Top down:* Portfolio case. Typeface specimen book. Letterpress type tray. Phototypesetting.

▶ *Top down:* CD-Roms and DVD discs. Type samples on screen. Video camera. Computer studio. Digital printing. Multimedia studio.

Why choose new-media design?

Since the 1980s, the availability of affordable, powerful computers and the wide-spread introduction of broadband Internet have revolutionized the design professions, and graphic design in particular. New media has generated fresh business and career opportunities in all fields of graphic design: web design, television, film, video, games design, animation, exhibition and event design.

The excitement of new-media graphic design is that it never stands still. It is a demanding profession, ideal for people with great ideas who enjoy working at a fast pace and whose personal interests include art and design, magazines, film, television, music and fashion. Almost certainly they will be passionate about drawing, typography and computers and will love the challenge of learning new skills. Graphic designers working in new media will also enjoy a career that involves varied work: no two jobs are ever the same.

All new-media designers get a thrill from seeing their work on screen and knowing that thousands or even millions of other people could be looking at it. New-media designers are very conscious of the computer's power to bring like-minded people together and enable them to communicate with each other. They understand that people with similar interests – for instance, in music, fashion or politics – will con-gregate around particular websites and online communities, such as forums and mailing lists. So not only do they design with these people in mind, they also feel that they are actively contributing to emerging communities. In other words, new-media designers are not simply driven by a fascination for the new tools but also by the way that new technologies change how people feel, think and behave.

New technologies have also helped level the employment playing field – it is possible for a self-taught individual freelancer working from home, or a small design group or collective of art school graduates, to compete with the traditionally large corporations or multi-disciplinary design consultancies.

The qualities you need to succeed

What kinds of people go into new-media graphic design? What qualifications do you need to enter the industry? What are the skills and approaches that typically make for success? What is it like working in the industry? Even a really experienced new-media designer will probably only have been in the business for a few years. New-media graphic design is therefore a young industry open to newcomers. Nevertheless, if you want to work in it you will need a wide range of abilities.

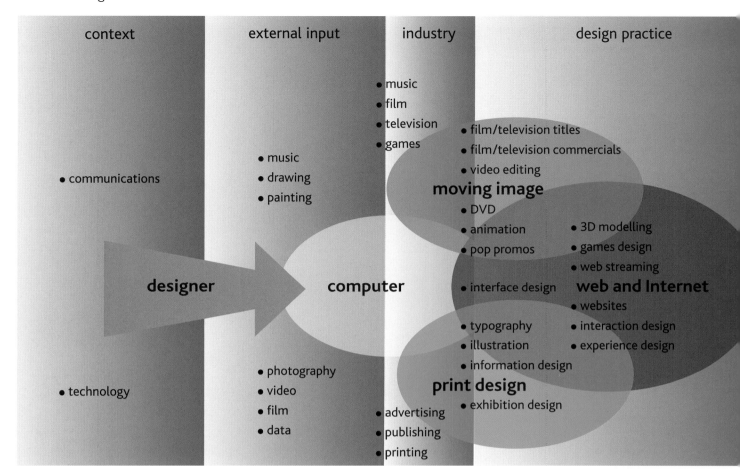

context	external input	industry	design practice
		• music	
		• film	
		• television	• film/television titles
		• games	• film/television commercials
	• music		• video editing
• communications	• drawing		**moving image**
	• painting		• DVD
			• animation • 3D modelling
			• pop promos • games design
			• web streaming
designer	**computer**		• interface design **web and Internet**
			• websites
			• typography • interaction design
			• illustration • experience design
	• photography		• information design
• technology	• video		**print design**
	• film	• advertising	• exhibition design
	• data	• publishing	
		• printing	

▲ This diagram maps new-media design practice against the information and entertainment industries. The designer is commissioned by a client to communicate a particular idea or story to a specific audience. The designer uses the computer as a medium to produce material for television, film, video, games, advertising, publishing, print, fashion, exhibitions or education.

The sectors that use new-media graphic design can be grouped into three main categories: moving image, web and Internet and print design. Those wishing to work in moving image need to learn about sequence and narrative; the web and Internet require an understanding of interactivity; print requires an inventive approach to the combination of word and image. All design practice is underpinned by technical knowledge, but more importantly designers succeed by developing their own creative voice and distinctive style.

Skills and attitudes needed to enter the profession:

- Visual flair – an ability to construct an engaging feel or mood using the elements of the visual world, in other words an ability to make people stop, look, read or listen.
- An eye for detail, sequence and story.
- The ability to think both laterally and analytically.
- Observational skills – an ability to notice what others usually miss.
- Research skills – an ability to investigate a topic using books, magazines, the Internet, interviews, drawing, photography, video and sound.
- Knowledge of the creative process – understanding how to generate and give form to ideas.
- Communication skills – an ability to do presentations, listen, negotiate, and write reports and pitches.
- People skills – an ability to get on with lots of different kinds of people.
- Computer skills – knowledge of the programmes in your area of graphics, plus the relevant hardware and production processes.
- Business skills – including numeracy, especially if you want to run a small business at a profit.
- Entrepreneurial skills – self-belief, determination and an ability to recognize opportunities.

- The ability to stay calm under pressure.
- A willingness to work unusual hours.
- An ability to work in teams and enjoy collaboration.
- An ability to meet tight deadlines.

Personal qualities:
- Ambition
- Curiosity
- Charisma
- Confidence
- Determination
- Discretion and diplomacy
- Energy
- Enthusiasm
- Imagination
- Initiative
- Talent
- Wit and humour

You may have all the above skills and attributes, or just some of them. There is room for everyone in new media – from the go-getting freelance individual to the back-room techie, working quietly on essential back-end and server-side programming, from the fiercely independent maverick to the team player.

Working environments

In a young industry like new media, working environments will vary widely, from the conventional old-media model of design studio with a strict hierarchy of management and employees, to workgroups of individuals that could be located anywhere in the world, communicating and collaborating via the Internet. New media has evolved new working patterns and practices, and they are continually being invented. This section examines some of the more common work experiences, starting with the traditional multi-disciplinary consultancies that might embrace advertising and public relations (PR), as well as pure graphic design. A typical career path for a new-media designer may well be to join such an organization to gain experience in real-world projects and working with clients, and make valuable contacts, before branching off alone or with a group of other designers.

In the world of graphic design, a large company usually means one that employs more than 20 people, but some are much bigger. For example, some companies have offices throughout the world: Pentagram, originally established in the 1970s, has offices in London and New York, San Francisco, Austin and Berlin. Wieden + Kennedy is an independent advertising agency with offices in Portland, Ohio, New York, Amsterdam, London, Tokyo and Shanghai. They work in all media, broadcast, print and online, making commercials for Nike, Heineken, Vodaphone and Honda. The WPP Group has 2000 member companies that employ 91,000 people in 106

countries. WPP companies include famous names such as Fitch Design, J. Walter Thompson, Ogilvy & Mather, and Young & Rubicam. Landor is a multinational company providing brand consultancy and design services; it has 23 offices in North and South America, Asia, Europe and the Middle East. Wolff Olins, a brand consultancy, employs people in Europe, America and Asia, representing 24 different nationalities and 17 different languages, and in turn is part of the Omnicom group, which manages companies throughout the world that operate in advertising, marketing services, specialist communications, interactive/digital media and media buying. These include brand and advertising agencies such as Interbrand, BBDO, DDB and TBWA. Framestore CFC (Computer Film Company), a post-production company based in Soho, London, creates visual effects on computers that are then applied to advertisements, television programmes and films. It has 500 employees and is now the largest visual effects and computer-animation company in Europe. These examples demonstrate that the creative graphics, new-media and communications industries make significant contributions to national economies.

In some sectors, your only choice is to work for a large or medium-sized company, as is the case for post-production for film or video, because the investment needed to buy very powerful computers and software would normally be out of reach of a small or start-up company.

Medium-sized design groups and smaller companies that specialize in new media work directly with their own clients but are often used by bigger companies who commission them for their skills, specialist knowledge and reputation for being in tune with a particular market.

New media is still a young profession in which people can make a name for themselves in a short period of time. There are plenty of small design companies and freelancers in the new-media graphics industry. A thriving network of independent designers exists in cities such as London, Amsterdam, Tokyo, Sydney, Melbourne, New York and Los Angeles. Some of these designers can be found by searching for special-interest groups and design communities on the Internet, looking at magazines or in bookshops that specialize in design. Most countries have professional associations for graphic designers: the American Institute of Graphic Arts (AIGA) in the United States; the Chartered Society of Designers (CSD) in the UK; the Australian Graphic Design Association (AGDA); and the International Council of Graphic Design Associations (ICOGRADA), are just four examples. The Internet provides a truly global platform for the exchange of ideas and knowledge. There are online magazines and websites dedicated to showing the best and most progressive new-media design work.

Young, independent new-media design companies

Some design graduates who are friends and share a common interest in experimentation and innovation set up their own businesses. In recent years, young entrepreneurs with initiative, curiosity and ambition have formed the

◀ Advertisement for the Audi A6 saloon car. Computer graphics were used to explode the car into shapes that then 'fly' through the streets of a city, pausing to form the Audi slogan 'Vorsprung durch Technik', to reassemble itself at the end of the advertisement. Created by the international agency BBH (Bartle Bogle Hegarty), the advertisement attracted wide attention for its computer graphics treatment. *BBH London*

▲ The American Institute of Graphic Arts (AIGA) website promotes the work of professional designers and also reports news and events in the United States. The AIGA also supports education and training initiatives for young designers.

▲ Website for ICOGRADA (International Council of Graphic Design Associations) provides news of events, meetings and competitions worldwide.

3deluxe

Brothers Andreas and Stephan Lauhoff, graduates in graphic design, joined interior designer Nikolaus Schweiger to establish the interdisciplinary creative group 3deluxe in Wiesbaden, Germany, in 1992 (www.3deluxe.de). In the mid-1990s, the designer Dieter Brell, a former member of the group Adieu New York, became the fourth member. The Lauhoffs lead the graphic division while Schweiger and Brell lead the interior division. The teams engage in a constant creative exchange. They do not work in commercial web design but use computer technologies to design interactive graphics into spatial environments for clubs, expos and retail outlets. They have worked for major banks, car companies and government organizations. The company has grown steadily and currently employs about 20 people. Not only is it commercially successful, it has also established a reputation for groundbreaking new-media work.

Their first projects in fashion, music and sports allowed them to develop experimental graphic work, crossing from 2D to 3D forms. They have devised ways for words and images to be displayed on objects or architectural structures and to transcend the desktop screen. These physical structures are interactive: in other words, the visitor can trigger an image by touching a surface, making a sound or movement.

Andreas Lauhoff explains: 'We are always on the lookout for innovative technology that we can use for our virtual spaces and interactive installations. In order to synchronize various media, such as light, sound, film and projections in real time, we use software that was developed by one of our partner companies. This type of interaction between visitors and our productions has only become possible using computer-based technology.' However, modern technology is not an end in itself for 3deluxe but is used instead to open up new fields of sensory and intellectual perception. Lauhoff stresses the importance of collaborating in multi-disciplinary groups to enable knowledge and technology transfer between the disciplines, which in turn leads to new design solutions.

In the initial phase of a project, 3deluxe offer design consultancy, incorporating graphic design, spatial design, business and corporate strategy, feasibility studies and cost/benefit calculations right up to advanced project development activities. They act as a general contractor to construction firms and specialist planners. They maintain close contacts with the research departments of leading companies and scientific institutions to make the best use of innovative technologies.

In the following stages of the design, 3deluxe handle overall management of the project, interfacing between the designers, the customer and any sub-contractors. In the case of temporary installations such as trade fair buildings or exhibitions, they supervise the building work and look after technical operations. They ensure that all the installations are tested in every detail.

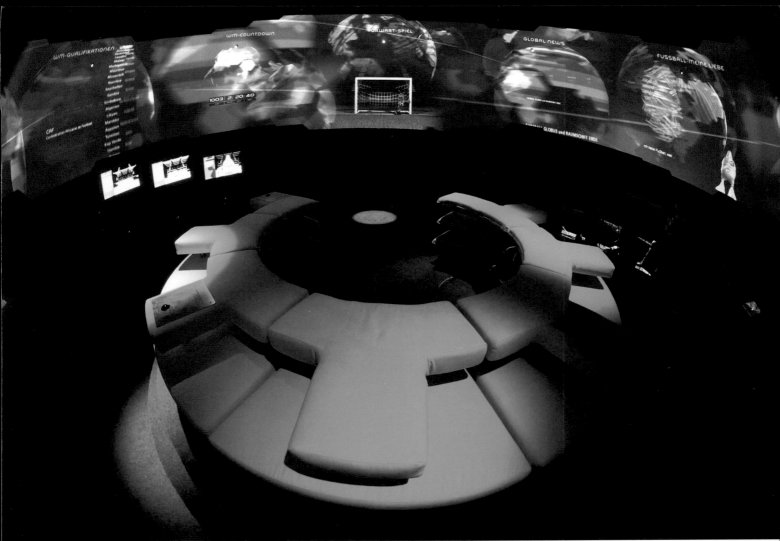

<table>
<tr><td colspan="2">1</td></tr>
<tr><td>4</td><td>3</td><td>2</td></tr>
</table>

The Football Globe, designed by 3deluxe in 2002, was part of the cultural programme accompanying the 2006 FIFA World Cup. Touring the 12 German cities that would host World Cup matches, the travelling pavilion encouraged visitors to engage emotionally and playfully with soccer culture. **1** The interior of the globe had a 360° projection to capture in real time the visitors' enthusiasm for soccer. **2** Two views of the Football Globe on location at night. **3** The installation had an interactive chronicle of all 634 World Cup games played since 1930. **4** Objects from the world of soccer were displayed in illuminated showcases.

▶ Speech recognition letterforms representing David Bowmann saying 'HAL' in an increasingly demanding tone in the film *2001: A Space Odyssey*. The same word uttered five times by the same speaker consecutively is never represented by exactly the same speech signal. *Project by Andreas Lauhoff*

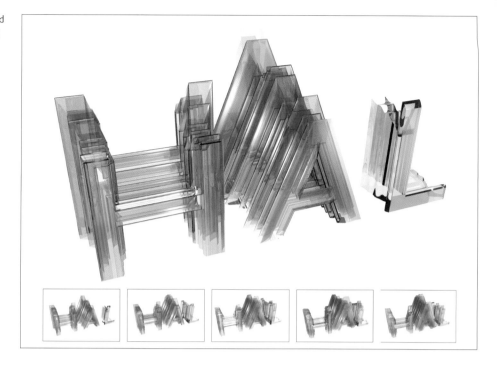

creative backbone of a thriving young industry. Small companies are the icing on the cake of the big international communications corporations, but they continually challenge the prevailing styles and conventions by coming up with new ideas and new ways of working. The excitement of being involved in such a creative, open environment attracts many people from disciplines other than art and design. A mixture of skills and backgrounds in a small collaborative group can be a great advantage. Programmers with degrees in computer science, graphic designers, musicians, artists, interior designers and architects can make up the teams or cooperatives in new-media design.

Freelancing in new-media design

Some designers may decide to work as freelance new-media designers, in which case they will need to make sure that they get their work constantly noticed. Networking is important for freelancers: they should keep in touch with college, university and work friends, as well as with people they have worked with – this often leads to commissions. Freelancers need to have their own websites and keep them up-to-date. Freelancers should remember that if they are taking their portfolio around to get work, they are not at their desk producing it. One option is to get representation from an agent who will do the footwork and advise on the designer's portfolio or book. The agent will take a cut of the fee, but they are likely to negotiate a better deal than the designer could on their own. Recruitment agencies are also good for placing freelancers with companies for short spells and for getting them permanent jobs. Entering work for special shows and festivals such as the Art Directors Club of New York or Design & Art Direction (D&AD) in the UK is also a good idea. If work is selected and shown, it will be noticed.

◀ Netdiver.net is an online digital-culture magazine and new-media portal, one of the best places on the Internet to see top international work.

▲ *Top:* Pixelsurgeon.com is a digest of creative work selected from the Internet. *Above:* heavy-backpack.com is a creative catalogue that showcases individuals, collectives and companies.

▶ Cubancouncil.com is a digital design agency based in San Francisco which also produces k10k.net, an online magazine and gallery.

Ross Cooper: Graphic and Interaction Designer

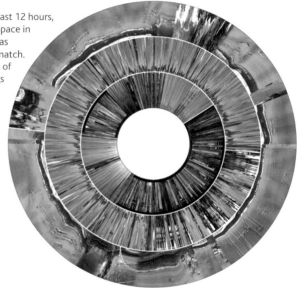

Ford VIOS concept car
Interactive digital dashboard & on board computer.
Interaction design in association with Bigaminal Design.
Premiered at the IAA Frankfurt motorshow September 2003.
Voted top 3 concept cars in show by the IAA.
Display uses ultra high resolution Sony display.
Launch Quicktime video >>

The dashboard.
Comfort Mode
The car has two modes 'Comfort' and 'Sport'. In 'Sport' spoilers extend from the front and back of the car, the engine settings change, driving position alters and seat bolsters inflate. The interface style changes to reflect the physical state of the car. The information on the dash also reflects the interests of the driver dependent on the mode that car is in.

Sport mode
Still from an animated sequence, like a trailer for the car, showing the features that change as the car switches to sport mode.

Comfort Mode
Vioos Car Exterior

◄ Ross worked with a team of Ford car designers on the dashboard interaction design for the Ford VIOS concept car. *Website images from Ford*

▲ Ross Cooper at his desk in the studio home in east London that he shares with four other designers.

Ross Cooper (www.rcstudios.com), a young British designer, chooses to freelance with different colaborators. Ross shares a large studio space in east London with four other designers. The studio has a positive, creative atmosphere and is cheap to run because everyone shares equipment – printers, digital cameras and video cameras – and there is more than one computer on which to work. The large, flexible space is big enough for a photoshoot.

Ross has been freelancing since completing his BA(Hons) at Central Saint Martins College of Art and Design in London. People expressed interest at his degree show and his work since has come by word-of-mouth recommendation. Ross is well known for his clock project, which he developed while he was a student at the Royal College of Art, in collaboration with the Finnish designer/programmer Jussi Ängeslevä. They initially generated ideas around the way that time is traditionally represented in seconds, minutes and hours. They then asked themselves a question: 'How would you incorporate into timekeeping a single video webcam that rotated every 12 hours?' Their answer was that you would be able to tell the time by

▶ The 'Last' clock captures the last 12 hours, last hour and last minute of the space in which it is situated. This image was captured at a World Cup soccer match. The outer ring recorded a minute of football action and the inner rings one and 12 hours.

seeing what the webcam was looking at in that particular moment. So, for example, if the video was set up outside your house, you might aim to get home by the garden fence rather than by 6 p.m. Their clock can be customized. Users can choose the webcam location: it might be anywhere in the world, in a different timezone, a place of natural beauty or on their own kitchen table. The clock has been shown in exhibitions in Slovenia, Taiwan, Boston and Dublin.

Ross's design thinking comes in part from an awareness of technology and in part from an understanding of the real world. He works by generating multiple possibilities, some of which are discarded. He discovers poetic resonance through experimenting with rough, scenario-driven, rapid prototyping.

▼ A 360° photograph of the studio living space Ross shares with his designer friends. Each person has a wooden garden shed for sleeping quarters. *Photograph © The Independent 2002*

Work is also published in art directors' 'source books', although in most cases there is a charge for entry. Source books are publications that act as showcases for professional design and illustration work, and are usually distributed free to commissioning editors and art directors, who often use these books when looking for new people to commission. Publishers of these books will often include or offer a number of 'tear sheets', single run-on pages of the designer's page, including their contact details, for the designer's own distribution. Subscribing to online portfolios is another possibility, and these can be linked to the designer's own website. Design resource websites also carry portfolio profiles and feature submissions from new designers; some also list job vacancies.

New-media designers find that their knowledge and skills are both portable and transferable, so they are able to collaborate with other specialists. It is a very rewarding experience to come together as part of a team to work on a project in which your contribution forms a part of a much larger whole. This kind of work is becoming more common.

Some designers also find they work particularly well with a friend or friends at college and decide to work together afterwards, forming a partnership. This has advantages in that collectively you may have a wider set of skills to offer than individually. Anyone going down this route must make a business plan. It may be necessary to borrow capital to set up a studio, buy equipment and pay yourselves. Drawing up a partnership agreement is also vital. Not all partnerships are successful, so if one member leaves or there is a dispute, the others are legally protected. Just like getting work in any other sphere of graphic design, starting up a studio and bringing in the jobs can be a slow process. Having the determination to succeed and the patience to target prospective clients and contacts are key. But the rewards for knowing you are making it can be fulfilling.

Workflow

It is very important for both large companies and independent designers to plan ahead so that they know they have work coming in to sustain their business. This means often working on several projects at once. Juggling time and being able to meet multiple deadlines are vital skills.

The pace of work in the graphic design and new-media communications industry is fast. Some jobs are turned around rapidly, so working long, unsociable hours to meet deadlines is not unusual. Regardless of whether a designer works as an in-house designer in a large company, runs his or her own studio or freelances, there are always tight deadlines. A print-based graphic designer preparing layouts for company publications would normally be expected to complete 30 or 40 pages in three days. Post-production designers working on television programmes or feature films would typically work on two six-second shots for three weeks, and might occasionally expect to work until three in the morning or not go home at all if the director or client changes his or her mind at the last moment. Speed is

▲ The musical-instrument display at the Horniman Museum in London allows visitors the ability to experiment with the sounds of rare and delicate instruments without handling them. *Rom and Son*

particularly important when making commercials. The client often sits in the post-production editing suite while the designer works, requesting changes that then have to be made on the spot – for example, type dissolving into smoke or removing an element from a shot. Designers creating television graphics may be given as little as a week to design, shoot and edit a station ident, teaser, sting or 'bumper' (the two-second company signature at the end of adverts or the five-second reminders of which television channel you are watching). Corporate websites can take a whole team several months to plan, develop, design and test, but a designer may be asked to turn around smaller jobs such as a website banner (a rectangular image box that flashes advertising at the top of a web page) in a few hours.

One-off jobs such as interactive exhibition graphics can be very complicated and take a long time to develop and test before visitors are allowed to use the exhibits. In the case of the display of musical instruments at the Horniman Museum in London by Rom and Son (www.romandson.com), a customized structure supporting a long, low horizontal touch screen needed to be designed to display information in front of objects in the collection. New software was developed and implemented over several months for the specific display functions. In all design commissions of this type, designers will need time to develop and construct prototypes, particularly if they are starting with an entirely new brief.

Clients often wrongly expect new-media design to be quicker and cheaper than design for print. There is an instantaneous feel about the medium in its completed form, which makes it seem fast, but developing the appropriate systems, making decisions and modifying the images, sequencing and user testing all take time.

Collaboration

Collaboration is essential in the field of new-media design. Good collaboration is based on trust so that a designer can feel they are getting an honest opinion about their ideas without feeling criticized. It is surprising how collaboration can lead designers to be less precious about their work and move their thinking forward. People work together so closely that sometimes it can be difficult to know precisely who has done which part of a job. Collaboration with other people means designers can share their successes and enjoy support in the hard times.

In larger design companies and studios, collaboration is one of the most important factors in new-media work of all kinds. They have the ability to form teams to scope out and understand a project through research, and set up planning and management responsibilities, possibly for several commissions at the same time. Teams of this kind depend on good communications and collaboration. The ability to turn to colleagues who are close by, to discuss aspects of the project design or technical issues, helps to ensure a smooth process throughout the commission.

Collaboration is also important in small two-person or three-person companies and for those who freelance independently as illustrators, animators or programmers, moving from company to company, client to client, as the jobs come up. Many of the freelancers and members of the small start-ups know each other and socialize together. They share experiences and form a network of friends. While they compete for the same jobs, they also recommend each other.

Andreas Lauhoff of 3deluxe says: 'Collaboration is not just an opportunity; it is a duty, part of the excitement of working in new media. For us, the link between 2D graphic design and 3D spatial design opens up new possibilities.' New-media graphics can be used with 3D design to come up with innovative hybrid solutions.

The two-person team Hyperkit (www.hyperkit.co.uk) – Tim Balaam and Kate Sclater – literally sit side by side while they develop, test and critique each other's work. They swap projects and work on each other's ideas. Nothing leaves the studio until they have both worked on it. As they say, it's not necessarily the most efficient modus operandi but it produces better work. 'It's not a job, it's who we are,' they

▲ Tim Balaam and Kate Sclater work closely on ideas and projects in their London studio, Hyperkit.

Airside

Airside (www.airside.co.uk), a London-based new-media company, was founded by Fred Deakin, a DJ and designer; Nat Hunter, a programmer; and Alex Maclean, an interior designer. The trio had freelanced for a while after leaving college before joining forces. The interdisciplinary Airside is founded on a willingness not only to share ideas but also to develop new ones together. 'As a good keyboard player you don't have to play the drums too,' says Deakin. His advice to would-be professional designers is to 'get in a team, get a vibe, get it going and be different from everyone else in the listings'. Airside design websites but also produce print and fashion items, playing with the boundaries between new and traditional media.

Deakin, Hunter and Maclean aim to combine sound business sense and enjoyment, with some notable successes. For example, they launched Airside with an enormous party and got a lot of work from the event. At the beginning of a job, all the members of the team sit round a large table in the studio and work out ideas together, often coming up with concepts as a group that they could not have developed individually. Hence the designers at Airside who specialize in building websites still have an input on illustration jobs and vice versa. When Anne Brassier, a photographer at Airside with a keen interest in knitting, came up with the idea of characters called Stitches, which looked a bit like stuffed socks with eyes sewn on, Airside developed a 'shop' section of their website and put the Stitches up for sale and adoption. People all over the world who acquire them are requested to send back documentary photos of their Stitches in their new lives to the Airside website. In this way, featuring online sales of other items such as T-shirts and key fob characters called 'Dot Com Refugees', their website has become fully interactive and the design group has created a cult following.

comment. They use their website to show their studio work as well as to advertise their personal interests. This combination, which they see as indivisible, has led to people contacting them about their work and interests from all over the world.

Collaboration is also an important factor between designers and clients. Frustratingly for designers, clients often tend to assume that they don't need as much of a production budget when commissioning new media as for print work. Because in new media there is usually no physical end product, such as a brochure or a book, as in printed work, it's often thought by clients that there must be fewer production costs. As such, they assume that they should pay less for new media than for printed work. In fact, the designer is going through very much the same process in both, managing design and production simultaneously. For example, a graphic designer may get 15 per cent of the total budget for a print commission, with the rest being paid to the printer and other specialists. The proportion of a design and production budget due to a new-media designer may well be greater than for print because more of the work can be studio-based. An added difficulty with new media is that because there is no printing involved, clients tend to continue to demand changes right up to the launch – reprinting a job to update it or correct mistakes is obviously very expensive and time-consuming. Designers have to learn how to be firm, explain the process and set realistic deadlines. A website must go live on a certain date or moving image work may need to go out to post-production before being released.

A client commissioned a logo for his film-processing business, and although delighted with the logo design, consisting of coloured dots, he challenged the designer by calculating how much each dot had cost him. The designer replied, 'It wasn't the dots that represented the fee, but the spaces in between!' The exchange was good humoured, but it highlights the more general problem about the perception of what is involved in the creative thinking process and how it is valued.

Getting your first job

So how do you, as an aspiring new-media designer, get your foot in the door of this fast-moving profession? Perhaps the easiest route is to take a college course in new-media design or an allied subject. In the UK, an HND (Higher National Diploma) course may not be as glamorous as a bachelor's degree (BA), but will be much more practically oriented, teaching specific software skills, and there is always the possibility of doing a BA or an MA (Master's) degree later. If you choose to study for an HND you will undertake design projects for real and imaginary clients. You will encounter part-time tutors and lecturers who also work in the real world, and may get a work-experience placement or internship at a company connected with the college. Above all, you will make friendships with other design students that may bear fruit in later life.

Some students establish useful links to the professional world by working as freelance designers while they are still studying or they get commissioned during their final-year show. After finishing college, one option may be to show your portfolio to large design and communications companies to secure a first job. It can be useful to work for a large company to get an understanding of professional practice and see the different roles needed to run a successful enterprise. As well as designers, all new-media companies need financial planners, managers and administrators to make sure that everything runs smoothly and that the company is paid properly for its work.

If you are clear that what you want to do is design websites, work with animation or in 3D graphics, for example, you can take specific courses at art school or university that will give you the skills and teach you to use the appropriate software to a very high level of proficiency. This will prepare you for a career in the industry at one level, but it may leave you without the flexibility to change direction if you need to at a later stage.

If you have just left college you will probably be looking for work at the same time as many other hopeful graduates. You may be exceptionally lucky and be offered a job or an internship at your final show or graduate exhibition. Otherwise you will need to go out looking for a job, starting by answering advertisements in the design press and researching for opportunities on design company websites. These often carry vacancies or guidelines for the kinds of people they employ. Or you may decide to go freelance straight away, either working for yourself or with other designers or groups of friends.

If you have had the opportunity to go on an internship or work placement during the college course and have enjoyed working with a particular company or design group, it is always worth keeping in contact; they should be invited to your college degree show and updated with the latest examples of your work. Even if there isn't a place for you at that moment, the company will keep your details on their books and may even recommend you to someone else. Look out for studios and advertising agencies that hold portfolio surgeries or review evenings; a designer who can attend one of these will learn a lot about their own work.

▲ Visit graduation shows to see what other young designers are thinking about and producing. You often see the next generation of big names in the industry.
Royal College of Art, London

If you are not working and still looking for a job you may be able to offer your services to a studio or company you would like to work for. Being in the work environment, running errands and generally making yourself indispensable is better than being dispirited at home, writing endless letters and waiting for the big job opportunity to come along. Even if they don't pay you a wage at the start, you will get invaluable experience that can be added to your CV. However, it is important to make sure you are not exploited – most firms will be fair – but you should move on if you feel a particular company is treating you unfairly. Sometimes a placement or internship can lead to full-time employment, but at the same time you can keep on looking for that dream job. Working in an area where there are other studios and companies, you can take the opportunity to drop off a CV, examples of work or a showreel.

Another route into the business is to start working for a company directly without any previous training in the area. This is often referred to as 'working up from the bottom'. You may start out in the post-room or making cups of tea, and will need dedication, patience and determination to watch and learn how other designers work and, of course, will need to show a talent for designing. There are many successful designers who have self-trained in this way. Adrian Shaughnessy is a self-taught graphic designer who co-founded the London-based design consultancy Intro and became its creative director for 15 years. Paul Elliman, also a self-trained graphic designer, now has an international reputation as a type designer and design commentator, teaching and lecturing around the world at universities and art schools in the USA, Europe and Australia. Rik Haslam took a temporary job in a small advertising agency, got a two-week trial as a creative and is now an associate creative director at Ogilvy & Mather, one of the world's largest marketing and communications companies.

Networking is vital. Keeping in contact with the friends you made at college and people you have worked with is important as they can often be a source of work. Going to events such as exhibition openings and lectures or discussions is another good way of making contacts. Joining special-interest groups centred on sharing skills and knowledge will help you keep up-to-date with the latest developments and provide a useful point of contact with other designers.

Telling the world about yourself and your work

To be noticed you will have to put yourself about a bit, either physically or virtually, and as a new-media designer you should be well placed to do this. A key way of doing this is to design or commission your own website so that you can advertise your expertise and services to clients and a wider audience. It can also include your portfolio online.

Christian Manz

Christian Manz has worked on a number of high-profile film and television projects at Framestore, London's largest post-production company, including *Brass Eye* and *The League of Gentlemen*. He trained as an illustrator but had to be shown how to switch on a computer when he realized that he would not get a job without knowing how to use one. He started work as a 'runner', making tea and literally running errands. As he walked around Soho, he posted his CV with photocopies of his drawings – now he would use DVD and video – through the letterboxes of all the firms he was interested in working for. He taught himself Photoshop and AfterEffects, and found the best thing about being a runner was the chance it provided to work on very expensive pieces of equipment, such as Flame, Inferno and Harry in the evenings or when they were not being used. Now he is a leading digital-effects artist and spends some time each week looking at videos sent in by new talent.

Mailing out self-publicity materials such as postcards or a CD or DVD showreel helps keep your name in front of art directors and commissioning editors. Once you have work to show or an interest you want to let people know about, producing your own publications, books and CDs, and selling them through bookshops or your website is another way of sharing your enthusiasms and can lead to commissions for work from unexpected sources.

Some magazines, both print and online, have gallery sections where they showcase examples of work submitted by designers. If your work is published or shown, email your contacts with the details. Also, enter your best work for design exhibitions and international festivals. If you are successful, the public exposure and press reviews will boost your chances of commissions in the areas of new-media design in which you really want to work.

▲ The front page of a website is used to promote the work of this two-person studio, combining design and technology capabilities. *Artificialtourism*

Your portfolio

When you have completed your training or education, or you feel that you want to be part of the exciting world of new media as a designer, the one most important thing that you will need to consider is your personal portfolio. If you have been at college you will have had to prepare your work for a final examination, so you will have started to edit your work into a coherent collection that represents your design thinking and practical capabilities.

Before you go looking for a job, there are a few really important things you need: a business card and a letterhead; a CD/DVD of your work; a 'style sheet' of printed examples of your work. This printed sheet should normally be a single page of reduced-size images, showing the range of your design work and giving your contact details, and is intended to act as a visual reminder of you. Everything that will represent you needs to be well designed and coordinated, including your CV, your website and your CD/DVD label and packaging. A portfolio for college projects is very different to a portfolio to get you work. A work portfolio should be smaller and more manageable in size with consistent printed examples, rather than original artwork, if it is for illustration. Never put into a portfolio the type of work that you wouldn't enjoy doing. There is nothing worse than being commissioned to do a job in a style you have moved on from and now dislike.

▲ A business card is recommended and a portfolio on CD is a good format for promoting new media work particularly images, movies and sound. *Graduate student portfolio on CD, Central Saint Martins, London*

There is no real substitute for getting your portfolio or book to a company and having it seen by the right person. An employer's decision to give you a job will be based on your personality as well as your work, so of course it's best if you are there in person to explain and enthuse. But often you will be asked to leave your portfolio for someone to look at in your absence. This may be common practice with some design firms and advertising agencies; you will be asked to an interview if they like what they see and whom they are hiring. Make sure that you leave your portfolio for only a short time and collect it yourself. You should give the impression that someone else wants to see your book. Before you approach a prospective employer, prepare yourself by finding out the name of the art director. If you want to work for a specific company or person, don't be frightened to send

▲ Portfolio cases come in several sizes and they usually contain transparent inserts to hold your work examples. A clean smart book makes for a good impression with potential employers.

Self-promotion

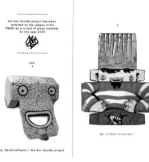

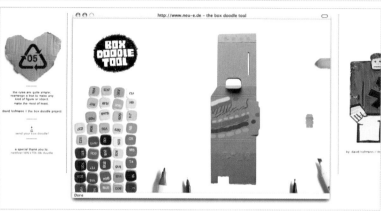

▲ The Box Doodle Project is the idea of David Hofmann. By combining web skills with a good idea, this site made a name for its designer, and won him awards and plaudits from designers around the world. In terms of self-promotion, the Box Doodle project is a winner. *www.boxdoodle.com*

▶ The DVD showreel, produced by graduating students of graphic design to accompany their final show, contains a wide range of still and moving image work.
Central Saint Martins, London

thea swayne online portfolio

◀ ▼ Online portfolio website by Thea Swayne, displaying books that were part of the work produced for her degree show. The site shows each of her books in detail with sample page spreads and sizes. Some of the books can be purchased from the website.
Thea Swayne, Royal College of Art, London

▲ Examples of postcards produced by graduating students and used for promoting their work.
Royal College of Art, London

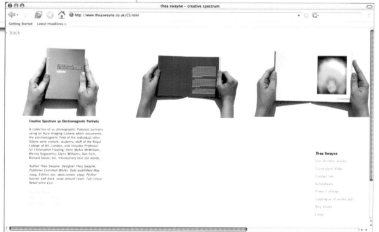

them a letter or email with some visuals of your work attached. You may need to follow this up with a telephone call. Even if they are not hiring at that moment, most companies and studios don't like to miss talent, so they may be persuaded to see you and, if they like you and your work, keep your name on file for future reference. Leave a sheet of printed examples and/or a DVD to remind them, and keep them informed if you move.

Designer's organizations – AIGA in the USA, D&AD in the UK, and AGDA in Australia – run events for young designers such as portfolio workshops and advice clinics. Hosted by professional designers, these have become popular meeting places and opportunities for talent spotting. It has already been mentioned how some design studios have portfolio review evenings, and these are also a good way of getting your work noticed. Ask about special events when you call for an interview and check websites for announcements.

One of the best ways to show both your design and practical skills is through your own website. Most importantly, make sure that it can be seen by almost anybody with a computer, whatever the platform, anywhere and at any time, via the World Wide Web. Your website is a perfect way of showing your expertise, and if it works the way you intend on any web browser at someone else's computer, you will have proved your technical abilities and you will have a truly global audience.

This demonstrates the fundamental change in the way designers have been working in recent years, certainly since the widespread adoption of computers in the profession. For one thing, where you work is no longer a restriction. Your client no longer has to be within physical reach of your studio. In fact, your studio can be anywhere you choose that has an Internet or communications connection.

In this book it is not our intention to tell you how to design and make your own website; there are plenty of instructional books that will guide you through the process and we have listed some on page 184. We suggest that you take a look at other designers' websites and gather ideas from the ones that you like the most. Then get a book or friends, to help you realize your ideas into a functioning website that shows off your work to its best advantage. One word of caution: people don't like to wait for complex pages made up of big graphic images or movies to download. So look at ways of reducing file sizes to speed up the accessibility of your website and keep the attention of your audience. Some designers add personality to their sites by including a 'blog' (web log) that allows them to publish their interests and invite feedback – and keep the website up-to-date. This is one way of keeping your site lively. Websites are hard work and demand dedication and time; avoid making an overly complex site; functionality is important if you are intent on selling your skills and knowledge as a new-media graphic designer in this way, and no one says you can't have more than one.

If you reply to an advertisement for a full-time job, make sure that your work is suitable for the post specified. Do your homework: find out about the company or studio. What is their work like? Do they offer other services? What is their profile?

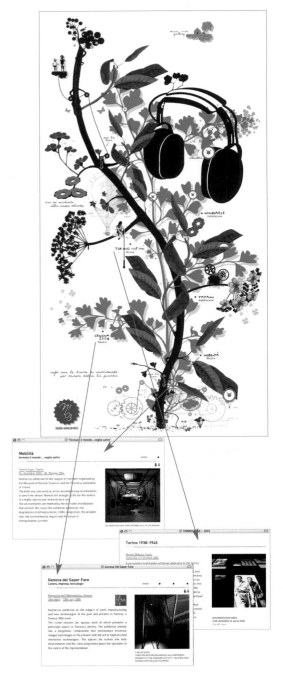

▲ N!O3 – Studio Ennezerotre in Milan, Italy. This unusual website grows like a plant from the bottom up in three stages. Movement and interaction indicate where to click to reveal floating windows that describe projects. www.ennezerotre.it

▲ Computer software skills are an essential part of any designer's portfolio. *Students and lecturer at Central Saint Martins, London*

◀ Going to college will give you a great opportunity to work within a design community of ambitious and like-minded people. *Project briefing at Central Saint Martins, London*

What are their key objectives, mission and culture? Who are their main competitors? Make sure that you are addressing the right person, and spell their name correctly! Check their website, read the design press, ask friends, ask yourself: 'Do I really want this job?' There is often an application procedure, so concentrate on making the paperwork look good; the aim is to get an interview, then it's up to you and your portfolio.

The image of job-seeking graduate designers with portfolio cases of varying sizes plying the streets of the design capitals of the world seems a little out-of-date in the age of electronic communication. However, once you have your foot in the door, the traditional portfolio or book still maintains its place as one of the most popular ways of showing work to a prospective employer.

The question for new-media graphic designers is how best to display work that is likely to be very diverse, from examples of print design to interactive displays and design for the Internet. But as we have shown in this chapter, there are now so many different ways of getting yourself noticed, especially for new-media graphic designers. For multimedia, the medium really is the message.

Preparing your CV

Your curriculum vitae, or résumé, is one of the most important personal documents that you will need to write as you prepare for professional life. You will continue to update it throughout your career, so getting it right at the start is vital. Since your CV will represent you as a designer, it should be a masterpiece of typographic design: unfussy, succinct and readable. Ideally it should occupy a single sheet of paper. Avoid embellishing it with decoration or visuals of your work. The latter belong in your portfolio or whatever you leave with a prospective employer or client to remind them of your talents and skills.

However your CV arrives on the desk of a potential employer, whether attached to a job application form, with an enquiry letter from you, or embedded in your website or demo CD/DVD showreel, always remember that it needs to make you stand out from the rest of the crowd.

What you need to know

The diversity of disciplines to which graphic and new-media designers now have access when interpreting projects means that they are increasingly called upon to find more exciting and original solutions to client briefs.

So, the more of an all-round designer you can be, the more employers and clients will appreciate your knowledge and skills. In recent years both computer hardware and software applications have developed to a very sophisticated level. In the past, computers were polarized around two platforms and operating systems. Apple, with its user-friendly MacOS interface, established its place in the creative, print and moving-image industries as the desktop system of choice, supported by some exceptional software. Manufacturers of PCs, computers running Microsoft Windows OS, have concentrated on the business market, developing computers mainly to run office applications, although they have now found favour with 3D designers. Both PC manufacturers and software developers were slower to see the potential for creative software. Now, however, you are likely to be required to work across both platforms.

The wide use of the Internet and the demands of new media are the main reasons why software giants, such as Adobe and Microsoft, have recently developed their software to work on both Macs and PCs. In most cases, the interface – that is, the way the software looks on screen and how it functions – is the same, so that moving files between computers is fairly straightforward, whether you are using a Mac or a PC.

Some software remains platform-specific, but this tends to be in 3D design or at the high end of film and video post-production. For the kind of software that you will be expected to know about, particularly as a recent graduate, most applications are now so well established that any new learning will involve becoming familiar with the changes and new features introduced with the latest versions or upgrades. If your work moves into a new or different discipline, you will find most skills are transferable, but you may also need to learn something new.

Here are some guidelines for what you should know in the main areas of graphic and new-media design.

Some Guidelines for writing your CV

- Write your CV on a computer. You can edit and update it easily. Two pages should be the maximum.
- Make it clear, concise and legible. Remember you are out to impress other designers.
- You don't need to use your full name, only the one that you use every day.
- Don't include your birth date or your marital status.
- Don't put a photograph of yourself on your CV.
- List your educational and employment details in reverse chronological order, most recent award and job first. Only list your relevant academic qualifications.
- List awards, honours, shows and exhibitions. Never lie about qualifications or experience.
- List computer skills, training and other languages. State if you hold a driving licence and passport.
- List positions of responsibility, but don't state previous earnings or salary expectations.
- Always ask someone to proofread your CV for spelling and other errors.
- Do make sure that you send your CV to the right contact in the organization.
- A page showing examples of your work or a postcard or business card can be attached.
- If relevant, a CD or DVD of your showreel or work, including a printable CV, is another way to present yourself.
- If you have a website, include the URL (but state if special plug-ins or software are required). Your CV can be included as a downloadable file.
- If you are applying to a studio or company who you would like to work for, or answering a particular job advertisement, tailor your CV and portfolio to that studio or job requirements.
- It is often better to say that references are available on request. However, if you do include referees, ask their permission first. Give their name, position, company or institution and work address. Also check that they are happy for you to give their email address or telephone number. Two referees are usually sufficient, one who can support your character, and one who knows you professionally. Normally you would update your CV to accompany a job application and this is where you may want to ask people relevant to the application.
- If you are represented by an agent, give their contact details and website.
- Always follow up your CV with a phone call and make an interview appointment.

Design for Moving Image

● *Design skills:*
Drawing, understanding of time-based media, film language and narrative.

Moving image is a fast, exciting and complex arena in which to work. From raw digital video (and film) footage, through editing and effects, to the final composite (what goes on television or to the cinema), it's about making something look convincing and real.

Moving image can include anything from very low-budget film festival entries, television documentaries, training films, and education films to high-spending advertising commercials, music promos and blockbuster films. High-quality work can be produced on a laptop computer, but the digital-effects and post-production industries are represented by a few large companies, mainly because of the huge investment needed to install specialist systems or equipment, such as Flame, Inferno and Harry, and to hire people to operate them.

'You need to be patient, conscientious and have an eye for detail, weight, movement, how images sit together, shadows, how light bounces – all knowledge gained from drawing.' Christian Manz, Framestore CFC, who trained as an illustrator and worked on the BBC *Living with Dinosaurs* series.

◀ Frames from the film *Turn the Tide* by Sophie Clements, winner of the Adobe Achievements Award 2005 in the Moving Image category. The film was made by shooting the players in the band on a digital video camera and printing the 5,700 individual frames onto sheets of paper. The sequence was then reconstructed by reshooting the individual frames onto video to create a smooth film. *Sophie Clements, Royal College of Art, London*

▶ A course assignment by Andreas Gaschka, from the media-design programme at the University of Applied Science, Mainz, Germany. Andreas created this broadcast design piece, based on the text of a radio traffic report. While the newscaster speaks, all the relevant information is displayed on a virtual map in 3D. An imaginary camera flies from one traffic report to another. This piece was the winner of the Adobe Achievements Award 2005, in the Broadcast Design category. It also won first place for TV design at Aninago and at Kurzundschöne, 2005.

Design for Animation

● *Design skills:*

Life drawing, character drawing, modelling, technical and architectural drawing, storytelling, scriptwriting and storyboarding.

For animation and 3D graphics it is very important that your showreel is outstanding. You will need to demonstrate that you understand the way that people, animals and objects move in everyday life and that you can translate this knowledge into a sequence of images that convey a number of emotions.

Try to become an expert with professional animation and 3D programs (you can download training or tryout versions of most software). It is important that you show your creative potential and that this is supported by your technical abilities. Sketches and ideas for characters and their environments should also form an important part of your portfolio, so include them on your showreel.

Get some professional advice by visiting computer-animation studios and post-production companies. Online computer-graphics and 3D communities are another good source of advice and support.

'The basic creative requirements of animation are to incite appeal, suspend reality and to be willing to stretch a point to bursting without losing your audience. Inspiration requires technique only as a means to serve an idea and there is no substitute for craft skills, imagination and an innate understanding of timing, performance, and both visual and aural design. It's all storytelling.' Philip Hunt, StudioAKA, London.

▲ Contemporary and historical fabric and garment forms modelled and animated entirely in 3D computer graphics by Jane Harris. Jane studied at Glasgow School of Art and the Royal College of Art, London. Her work with textiles, dress and computer graphics has earned her international recognition and has been widely exhibited. Above, *'Potential Beauty'*, *artist: Jane Harris, 3D CG: Mike Dawson, Performer: Ruth Gibson*

▼ *Top:* Television and cinema advertisement for Citroën cars. The animated 3D sequence shows the car becoming a transformer and performing a break dance before assuming its natural shape again. *The Embassy VFX, Vancouver, Euro RSCG, London*

▼ ▼ *Bottom: Arrow*, an animated sequence for Lugz Shoes, created by combining drawn backgrounds with realistic character action. *PSYOP, Avrett Free Ginsberg*

Design for the Internet

● *Design skills:*
User interface design, information architecture, accessibility awareness, usability testing.

As the Internet has grown in size and influence, designing websites has become a specialized discipline in its own right. The World Wide Web is now truly global and has altered the balance in the way in which consumers and providers use media of all types. The very nature of the Internet's diversity and reach demands much from website designers.

Being an expert in the use of a sophisticated web editor such as Dreamweaver is vitally important, but unless you are also able understand the underlying code (HTML, CSS, DHTML, XHTML), you may be seriously handicapped in implementing the design and functionality required by modern websites.

'The web is an amazing, abstract space; start with Google and you can go anywhere. Virtual worlds – painting, literature happen in your head, new media can do that very well,' says Tom Elsner, who trained as a graphic designer and now runs his own company, Bureau of Visual Affairs, in London.

▼ Co-produced by **moti**roti (London) and The Builders Association (New York), the Alladeen project has three forms, all sourced from the same material: the website (illustrated in the screens below), a music video and a cross-media stage performance. It explores how we all function as 'global souls' caught up in circuits of technology; how our voices and images travel from one culture to another; and the ways in which these cultures continually reinterpret each other's signs and stories.

Alladeen draws on the lives of people living in the global cities of New York, London and Bangalore – each of which is a place where many cultures collide, both in virtual and material reality. Aladdin's story is a perfect vehicle for this 'collision' since it is one that has been revised and retold many times. In Alladeen, Aladdin's fantasy of personal transformation is played out in the surreal world of Bangalore's 'call centres', telemarketing centres where Indian operators learn how to 'pass' as Americans. It explores the paradoxes of identity in an age of multiple realities.

www.alladeen.com: directed by Ali Zaidi; website concept, design and production by Petra Goebel, Axel Vogelsang and Stefan Zerwas.
*The Builders Association/**moti**roti's Alladeen*

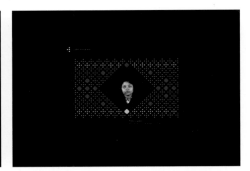

Design for Computer Games

- *Design skills:*

Drawing, spatial awareness, 2D and 3D animation and modelling, Artificial Intelligence (AI), writing and narrative skills, digital video.

Computer games are among the newest vehicles for telling stories and creating virtual worlds, but until quite recently becoming a games designer often seemed a difficult and uncertain career to pursue. Making digital games has long been the preserve of computer enthusiasts with great games ideas that have mostly become successful through being snapped-up by large development and marketing companies. However, with the emergence of educational opportunities in games design and production, and more accessible software, the pathways to becoming a professional in this area have created opportunities for new media graphic designers.

Getting started as a games designer may involve several stages after college – contributing significantly to a few games is where most people start. Being a designer who is inclined towards technical programming or a programmer who is artistic can also be good starting points. Two things you will need are a passion to create games and excellent written and communication skills.

'There is a growing realization that games need to diversify and become more creatively ambitious if they are to reach a wider demographic. The more forward-thinking developers are beginning to bring people with a broader creative experience (outside of games) into their games development teams.' Milan Prucha, Lionhead Studios

▾ Making use of the hoardings around the Royal Festival Hall's building site in London, *Gamelan Playtime* invited participation from commuters and visitors in an unexpected moment of collaboration and creativity. The tactile surface of the installation attracts the hands of pedestrians in Hungerford Terrace: their movements trigger sensors, which release recordings of a Gamelan workshop held in a local Lambeth primary school. The passers-by are surprised to hear the sounds of traditional Indonesian instruments mixed together with schoolchildren's voices in a startling musical collage.

The installation was created by students of the Creative Practice for Narrative Environments MA at Central Saint Martins, University of the Arts, London. *Arlete Castelo and Melissa Mongiat*

▶ Milan Prucha's Dreamcatcher project arose from his interest in multiplayer, online 3D gameworlds, including 'Second Life'. The paradox of interacting with people who are physically remote (indeed, they could be on the other side of the planet) and yet occupy a shared virtual space fascinated him.

There is a perceived dichotomy between virtual gameworlds and real life. The common opinion is that video games are merely a form of play, an escapist distraction; something entirely separate from the 'serious' business of real life. However, with the emergence of these new online worlds, the distinction between play and real life is becoming increasingly blurred. The merging of real and virtual economies, through the sale and exchange of virtual assets (avatars, objects, in-game currency, etc.), has resulted in these worlds providing, not only a medium for creative expression, but also the means of generating a 'real world' income. However, these virtual worlds have only recently begun to be utilized as a medium for 'serious' applications and commerce, taking them beyond previous definitions as merely arenas for 'play' or Internet chat. The obvious advantage of this new arena, however, is that it provides a design space with much unexplored creative potential. The unique challenges inherent in designing for a culturally diverse, globally distributed user 'community' make this an even more intriguing space to work with.
Milan Prucha, Royal College of Art, London

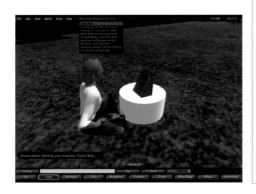

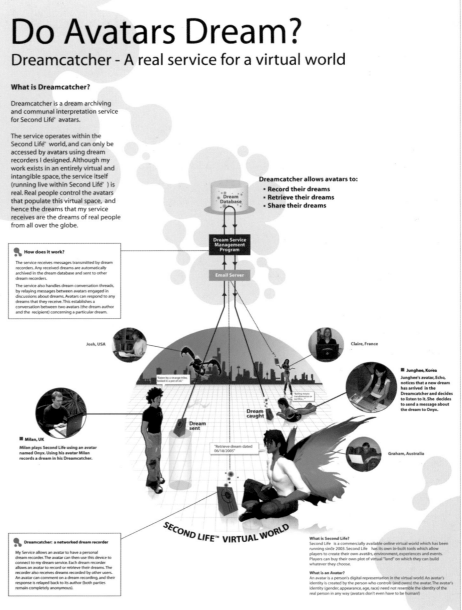

Do Avatars Dream?
Dreamcatcher - A real service for a virtual world

What is Dreamcatcher?

Dreamcatcher is a dream archiving and communal interpretation service for Second Life® avatars.

The service operates within the Second Life® world, and can only be accessed by avatars using dream recorders I designed. Although my work exists in an entirely virtual and intangible space, the service itself (running live within Second Life®) is real. Real people control the avatars that populate this virtual space, and hence the dreams that my service receives are the dreams of real people from all over the globe.

Dreamcatcher allows avatars to:
- Record their dreams
- Retrieve their dreams
- Share their dreams

How does it work?

The service receives messages transmitted by dream recorders. Any received dreams are automatically archived in the dream database and sent to other dream recorders.

The service also handles dream conversation threads, by relaying messages between avatars engaged in discussions about dreams. Avatars can respond to any dreams that they receive. This establishes a conversation between two avatars (the dream author and the recipient) concerning a particular dream.

Josh, USA

Claire, France

■ Junghee, Korea
Junghee's avatar, Echo, notices that a new dream has arrived in the Dreamcatcher and decides to listen to it. She decides to send a message about the dream to Onyx.

■ Milan, UK
Milan plays Second Life using an avatar named Onyx. Using his avatar Milan records a dream in his Dreamcatcher.

Graham, Australia

Dream sent

Dream caught

"Retrieve dream dated 06/18/2005"

SECOND LIFE™ VIRTUAL WORLD

Dreamcatcher: a networked dream recorder

My Service allows an avatar to have a personal dream recorder. The avatar can then use this device to connect to my dream service. Each dream recorder allows an avatar to record or retrieve their dreams. The recorder also receives dreams recorded by other users. An avatar can comment on a dream recording, and their response is relayed back to its author (both parties remain completely anonymous).

What is Second Life?
Second Life is a commercially available online virtual world which has been running since 2003. Second Life has its own in-built tools which allow players to create their own avatars, environment, experiences and events. Players can buy their own plot of virtual "land" on which they can build whatever they choose.

What is an Avatar?
An avatar is a person's digital representation in the virtual world. An avatar's identity is created by the person who controls (and owns) the avatar. The avatar's identity (gender, appearance, age, race) need not resemble the identity of the real person in any way (avatars don't even have to be human!)

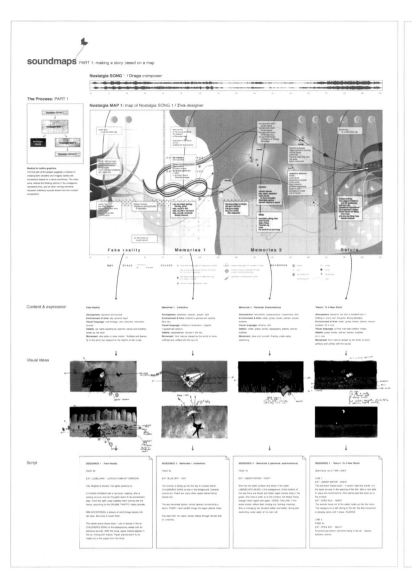

Nostalgia SONG 1 / Drago composer

The Process: PART 1

Nostalgia MAP 1 : map of Nostalgia SONG 1 / Ziva designer

Fake reality   Memories 1   Memories 2   Return

Content & expression

Visual Ideas

Script

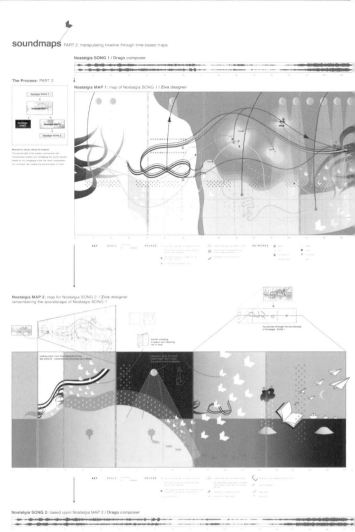

Nostalgia SONG 1 / Drago composer

The Process: PART 2

Nostalgia MAP 1 : map of Nostalgia SONG 1 / Ziva designer

Nostalgia MAP 2: map for Nostalgia SONG 2 / Ziva designer
remembering the soundscape of Nostalgia SONG 1

Nostalgia SONG 2: based upon Nostalgia MAP 2 / Drago composer

▲ Soundmaps are visual stills representing musical composition, where all individual sounds are drawn as icons and areas organized along space and time axes. Their shapes, colours, sizes, overall composition and meaning reflect the feelings evoked in the author of the map while listening. Initially developed as a tool to help conceptualize, direct and edit a music video based on original musical composition, soundmapping is a means to understand, interpret and express existing sound/music visually; and the reverse too – to 'visually compose' sound and hand over to a music composer to complete the process. *Ziva Moskric, Central Saint Martins, London*

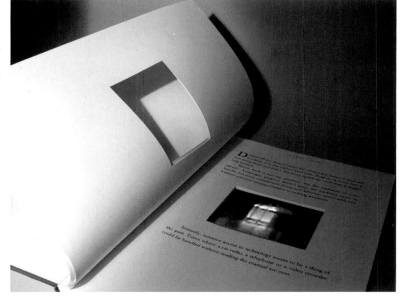

▶ The Memory Palace, a Master's degree project by Axel Vogelsang. The book has pages with a hole cut out, through which short video films are viewed. When a page is turned, the film changes and becomes relevant to the text printed on that page. When the book is removed, the visuals become a memory. *Axel Vogelsang, Central Saint Martins, London*

Design for Cross-Media, Graphics and Print

- *Design skills:*

Drawing, typography, photography, print production techniques, copywriting, accessibility issues.

Graphic designers should be interested in everything. You never know what sort of creative adventure the next job will take you on. More than ever, you must have all-round skills that will allow you to work in a variety of disciplines and across media, from design for print to multimedia and the web.

It is important that you take the opportunity to work in as many of the disciplines available as possible, both traditional and new, and gain as wide an experience of them as you can. You may become an expert in several, but you will need to understand how specialists work in other disciplines too in order to acquire the global overview that good graphic designers need.

'It is said that the world became smaller the moment it was first captured on film from space: our perspective changed. Similarly, as new media propose new ways of communicating, they impose new ways of seeing and thinking. Technological advances have changed not only the constraints and possibilities of individual media, but also the interplay between media, and our expectations. But while the technology may be impressive, its importance may be measured principally in terms of its ability to enable communication, which affects how we work, play, buy, sell and live.'

From *Dot Line Pixel: Thoughts on Cross-Media Design* by Michele Jannuzzi and Richard Smith.

▲ This example of cross-media shows the visually coordinated link between the information on a web page and in the printed prospectus for Central Saint Martins College of Art and Design, London.

Summary

Often as a graphic designer, especially in new media, you will find yourself art-directing or leading a project that will include design work by yourself and several other experts, such as illustrators, photographers, web designers, interactive designers, moving-image makers, animators, information designers, etc. In order to do this properly, you will need to understand something about the way these other specialists work.

There is no single pathway to becoming a new-media graphic designer, but whichever route you take you can be sure that you will have an exciting and rewarding time. All it takes is talent, enthusiasm, a willingness to learn and determination to succeed. Enjoy it and have fun! New-media designers see technology as an extension of the creative palette. As Christian Manz of Framestore says: 'The computer is just a different tool, equivalent to oil or watercolour.' New-media graphic designers are intrigued by what can be done with such tools. There is a kind of magic, for instance, in taking a still drawing and making it move, or in developing an idea that can ignite a trend and virtually following it around the world.

Glossary

Aliasing this term describes the jagged appearance of bitmapped images or fonts, and occurs when the resolution is insufficient or when they have been enlarged too much.

Animation a process of creating a moving image by moving rapidly from one still image to the next. Computer animations are created using specialist software that renders sequences in a variety of 2D and 3D formats.

Antialiasing the blurring of hard edges to create the appearance of smoothness. Most commonly used for graphics, and especially text. This is achieved by blending the edge of the object by adding pixels of a neutral colour between it and its background.

Application software programs that enable the user to carry out a specific task on a computer, such as writing, manipulating images or drawing.

ASCII (American Standard Code for Information Interchange), referred to generically as 'plain text' with no formatting, developed by the American National Standards Institute.

Aspect ratio width-to-height ratio of screen images or pixels.

Avatar a virtual representation of an individual human user in a VR (virtual reality) environment, videogame or a networked multi-user domain. Avatars are controlled directly by their human owners and act as vehicles for interacting with other people (via their own avatars).

Axis imaginary line that defines the centre of the 3D universe; x, y and z axes (width, height and depth) define each of the three dimensions of an object.

Bandwidth defines the capacity of a communications channel; the broader the bandwidth, the greater the speed and volume of information and data that can be transmitted.

Banner image on a webpage, usually at the top, which is deliberately designed to attract attention. Used generally for advertising purposes, banner advertisements are often animated.

Bit smallest unit (value 0 or 1) of computer data.

Bitmap graphic image made up of pixels, or dots, and usually created in 'paint' or manipulated in 'image-editing' applications, such as Painter and Photoshop, and saved in formats such as GIF, JPEG and PNG. Photographic and continuous tone images are best stored as bitmaps which are distinct from the 'vector' images created in 'object-oriented' drawing applications. See also **Vector graphics**.

Bitmap editors commonly called 'paint' applications, such software programs enable the user to manipulate the individual pixel of an image.

Blog (Weblog) an online journal, diary, or newsletter used to comment on a variety of topics depending on the interests of the blogger. It is updated frequently and intended for public consumption.

Brand physical and emotional concept by which a specific product or service is easily recognizable. Brands can be an organization's reputation, symbols, logos, names, trademarks (or a combination of all of these). Their purpose is to instigate or reinforce a relationship between customers and products or services.

Broadcast quality standard of video acceptable to broadcasting organizations.

Browser/web browser software that enables the viewing or 'browsing' of World Wide Web pages across the Internet. The most common browsers are Firefox, Safari, Opera and Microsoft's Internet Explorer. Version numbers indicate the level of HTML that the browser supports.

Button area or object, displayed on the screen, that reacts to some form of user input, such as the use of a pointer or the click of a mouse.

Byte a set of bits considered as an individually addressable unit in computer memory. In personal computers a byte normally equals eight bits and represents a single character, such as a letter of the alphabet, a number from 0 to 9, or a punctuation mark.

CAD (computer-aided design) any design carried out using a computer, generally used with reference to 3D design, such as product design or architecture, where a computer software application is used to construct and develop complex structures.

CD (compact disc) 120mm digital-optical disc used to carry or record audio, data or hypermedia programs (also referred to as CD-Rom).

Cel In non-digital animation this is a sheet of transparent acetate on which images for animation are drawn and painted. The traditional technique of cel animation is closely echoed in many digital animation applications, where animation is created on a number of different layers, and transparency is used to overlay the images.

CGI (common gateway interface) applications that administer interactions between web users (clients) and the HTML, and other webpage documents residing on a server. CGI programs can run programs on the server at the request of the user's browser, and return the results to that browser. This could be information accessed from a database on the server, or the results of a simulation or calculation performed on the server or other networked computer.

CMYK reflective 'full colour' model, used when working with print-based images that describes colours as mixtures of cyan, magenta, yellow, and black inks. CMYK (the letter K is used for black rather than B to avoid confusion with blue) contrasts with the RGB (red, green, blue), the transmitted colour model, used when working with images intended for computer monitors, televisions, data projectors and LCD screens. CMYK and RGB are also called 'colour spaces', because each defines its own colour gamut or the range of colours that it can represent,(RGB is capable of a wider colour range than CMYK).

Colour depth This is the number of bits required to define the colour of each pixel. Only one bit is required to display a black-and-white image, while an 8-bit image can display either 256 greys or 256 colours, and a 24-bit image can show 16.7 million.

Compression refers to a number of techniques for reducing the amount of data required to store and transmit information.

Copyright the right of a person who creates an original work to protect that work by controlling how and where it may be reproduced.

Cross platform a term applied to software or websites that may be run or viewed on different computer systems.

CSS (Cascading Style Sheets) allow multiple-style characteristics (font, size, colour, position, line spacing) to be applied to units of text, in a similar fashion to styles in word processors and page make-up applications.

Cursor the symbol that represents the screen position of a pointing device, such as a mouse. The shape of a cursor often changes to indicate its function at any particular moment.

Cyberspace coined by William Gibson to describe the interconnected web of databases, telecommunication links and computer networks that is a new space for human communication and action.

Data information stored in digital form.

Database Structured collection of data. The information can be stored, sorted, manipulated and retrieved through a computer system.

DHTML (Dynamic HTML) an enhancement to HTML that allows web pages to change dynamically with user interaction and over time.

Digital information represented by discrete units, usually binary numbers (0 and 1). The digitalizing of media elements, such as text, sound, image, animation and video, is the basis of hypermedia.

Digitize transform analogue to digital; convert anything – text, images or sound – into a binary form so that it can be digitally processed, manipulated, stored and reconstructed.

DNS (domain name system) a 'domain name' is given to each computer or network connected to the Internet, providing an alphanumeric address that is easier to remember than a numerical (or IP) address. This address is used by the protocols that control data exchange over the Internet.

Download process of transferring software or other digital information from one computer to another over a network.

DPI dots per inch; the closer the dots the sharper and clearer the image. see also **PPI** and **Resolution**.

DVD (digital video disc) a standard for digital-optical discs. A standard DVD is the same diameter as a CD-Rom (l20mm) but stores 4.7 gigabytes of information. Other versions are double-sided and give a capacity of up to 17 gigabytes per disc, capable of storing a feature-length movie at broadcast quality.

DVD-Rom a version of the DVD format that can store a blend of digital video and mixed data. While DVD is primarily a linear medium, DVD-Rom provides more interactive programs.

e-commerce business transactions conducted across the web. This area of web design is very specialized and requires in-depth understanding of secure protocols and financial transactions technology.

Email messages sent over a computer network. One of the most popular uses of the Internet.

EPS (Encapsulated PostScript) a format that includes all the PostScript data necessary to display and reproduce images in many graphics and layout programs.

Extranet an intranet accessible from outside an organization's internal network.

FAQ frequently asked questions.

Firewall security against external, sometimes malicious attacks on a network.

Flash software for creating vector graphics and animations for web presentations. Flash generates files that are small and can be scaled to any dimension, which are quick to download.

Flowchart schematic diagram of a hypermedia program, or a work schedule.

Font a set of characters or 'glyphs', normally alphanumeric, sharing the same typeface and size. See also **Typeface**.

FPSs (frames per second) units in which frame-rate is most often specified.

Frame rate the speed at which the individual frames of an animation are substituted for one another and the animation is played. This rate is usually specified as a number of frames per second, e.g., 15, 24, 30 fps.

GIF (Graphics Interchange Format) one of the bitmapped image formats used on the Internet. GIF is a 256-colour format including features such as the use of transparent backgrounds. GIF is suitable for line images and other graphics, and usually makes small file sizes.

Gigabyte one thousand megabytes.

Greyscale rendering of an image, in a range of greys from white to black. On a computer monitor, this usually means a maximum of 256 levels of grey in a digital image.

GUI (Graphical User Interface) a human computer interface that uses screen graphics to display – Windows, Icons, Menus and a Pointing device (WIMP). GUIs were pioneered at Xerox PARC and commercialized by Apple Computer with the Macintosh. Prior to GUIs, most user interfaces used a 'command line'.

Home page the main, introductory page on a website, usually with a title and tools to navigate through the rest of the site. Also known as the index page and sometimes the portal page.

HTML (Hypertext Markup Language) the code that websites are built with. HTML is a set of 'tags' that specify type styles and sizes, the location of graphics, and other information required to construct a webpage. To provide for increasingly complex presentations such as animation, sound and video, the basic form of HTML is seeded with miniature computer programs, or applets.

HTTP (Hypertext Transfer Protocol) set of communication standards that together enable different kinds of computer to communicate with one another over the World Wide Web.

Hypermedia computer-based multiple media (text, image, sound, animation and video) with user interaction and the capability to link items of information with other items within the system.

Hypertext a term originally coined by Ted Nelson to describe a form of non-sequential writing. Now generally refers to computer-based text that is linked in a variety of linear and non-linear ways. The World Wide Web was devised as a hypertext-based system.

Icon graphical representation of an object (such as a disk, file, folder or tool) or a concept or message used to make identification and selection easier.

Interactive the dialogue between a computer and its user that involves an immediate and reciprocal action between a person and a machine.

interface is used to describe the screen design that links the user with the computer program or website. The quality of the user interface often determines how well users will be able to navigate their way around the pages within a website.

Internet the entire collection of connected worldwide networks, including those used for the World Wide Web.

Interpolation a computer calculation used to estimate unknown pixel values that fall between known ones. One use of this process is to redefine pixels in bitmapped images after they have been modified in some way – for instance, when an image is resized (called 'resampling'). The program makes estimates from the known values of other pixels lying in the same or similar ranges.

Intranet an internal or private network of webpages. Large companies often maintain a private web presence on their intranet.

IT (information technology) computer and telecommunications technologies that have been developed for handling information.

ITV (interactive television) services delivered via a television set, connected to a network by a combination of phone line, cable, ADSL and satellite links.

Java a programming language created by Sun Microsystems that can be used to create applications.

JavaScript a 'scripting' language that provides a simplified method of applying dynamic effects to webpages.

JPEG, JPG (The Joint Photographic Experts Group) an ISO (International Standards Organization) group that defines compression standards for bitmapped colour images. A compressed file format in which the degree of compression from high compression/low quality to low compression/high quality that can be defined by the user.

Key frames in traditional animation the drawings that show the position of characters, etc., at the start and finish of a movement or action. The in-between drawings are then created to complete the illusion of a smooth or effective movement. This concept has been transferred to digital animation and motion graphics in the form of key frames as opposed to those frames that are interpolated or 'tweened' – by computation. See also **Tweening**.

Kilobyte 1,024 bytes.

LPI (lines per inch) the dot ruling on an image to be printed. See also **Resolution**.

Logo words, letters and/or symbols that together make up the physical brand of a product. Most logos are pictorial representations of the brand's product or service. Some logos will also feature a motto or phrase.

Megabyte 1,048,576 bytes or 1,024 kilobytes.

Memory this can be either 'dynamic RAM', the volatile 'random access' memory that is emptied when a computer is switched off, or ROM, the stable 'read only' memory that contains unchanging data – for example, the basic startup and initialization functions of most computers.

Menu display on a computer screen showing the list of choices available to a user.

Metadata provides a summary of the information contained within webpages. Search engines often use metadata information as a way of categorizing and providing search references for websites.

MPEG A standard defined by the Motion Pictures Expert Group for the compression and decompression of motion video images.

Multimedia (multiple media) combination of digital media – sound, video, animation, graphics and text – incorporated into a product or presentation.

Navigation the process of guiding the user around the contents of a hypermedia program or website.

Network System that links computers and other information/telecommunications technologies by any means.

Online Any activity taking place on a computer or device while it is connected to a network such as the Internet. The reverse of offline.

Operating System (OS) Operating Systems define how a computer works. Common personal computer Operating Systems include: Microsoft's Windows, and Apple Computer's MacOS.

PDF (Portable Document Format) a cross-platform format that allows complex documents to be created with multiple features, retaining all text and picture formatting, then viewed and printed on any computer that has an appropriate 'reader' installed.

Pixel (Picture Element) smallest component of any digitally generated image, including text, such as a single dot of light on a computer screen. One pixel corresponds to a single bit: 0 = off, or white, and 1 = on, or black. In colour or greyscale images or monitors, one pixel may correspond to up to several bits. An 8-bit pixel, for example, can be displayed in any of 256 colours (the total number of different configurations that can be achieved by eight zeros).

Plug-in a small program that 'plugs-in' a loan application to extend its features or add support for a particular file format.

PostScript Adobe Systems' proprietary page description language for image output to laser printers and high-resolution imagesetters/filmwriters.

PPI pixels per inch. See also **DPI** and **Resolution**.

Program a set of statements and instructions designed to enable a computer to perform a specific task or series of tasks.

Programming the process of preparing a set of instructions for a computer in order to make it perform a particular activity.

QuickTime a set of standards developed by Apple for dynamic (time-based) data handling, including image and audio compression/decompression. Computers running QuickTime software can play audio, animation and video without additional software or hardware.

QuickTime VR a format and software developed by Apple. QuickTime VR enables developers to create 'virtual' worlds, either as panoramic movies that enable a user to look at and move around a 360° scene, or as objects that can be viewed from a variety of angles. These virtual worlds can be created by taking images from the real world, using photographic or digital cameras, or by using computer-generated images.

RAM (Random Access Memory) the memory 'space' made available by the computer into which some or all of an application's code is loaded and remembered while you work with it. Generally speaking, the more, the better. Imaging software such as Photoshop needs up to five times the size of the files you are working on to process images.

Rasterize electronically convert a vector graphics into a bitmapped image. This is often necessary when preparing images for the web; without a plug-in, some browsers cannot display certain image files.

Raytracing rendering algorithm that simulates the physical and optical properties of light rays as they reflect off a 3D model, producing realistic shadows and reflections.

Real-time an operation where the computer calculates and displays the results as the user watches. Real-time rendering, for example, enables the user to move around a 3D scene or remodel objects on the screen without having to wait for the display to update.

Rendering The process of creating a 2D image from 3D geometry to which lighting effects and surface textures have been applied.

Resolution refers to the number of dots per inch (dpi) or pixels per inch (ppi). The degree of quality, definition or clarity with which an image is reproduced or displayed, for example in a photograph, or via a scanner, monitor screen, printer or other output device – the higher the resolution, the sharper the image appears.

RGB (red green blue) the primary colours of the 'additive' colour model, used in video technology, computer monitors and for graphics, such as for the web and multimedia that will not ultimately be printed by the four-colour (CMYK) process. See also **CMYK**.

Scanning an electronic process that converts a hard copy of an image into digital form by sequential exposure to a moving light beam. The scanned image can then be manipulated in the computer or output for use on a webpage or as separate film for printing.

Second Life an Internet-based virtual world and virtual reality community. Developed by Linden Lab, a downloadable client program enables its users, called 'residents', to interact through animated avatars, providing an advanced network service.

Simulation the process of modelling and representing an activity, environment or system on a computer. Used to train airline pilots.

Software the programming code or data components of a computer system. It is now broadly used to cover the content of media (such as music, film, animation and hypermedia programs) as opposed to the physical medium that carries them.

Streaming video/audio a method of transmitting video or audio that allows it to be played continuously and apparently in real time. Segments of the received data are buffered while the user's software plays the previous buffered section.

Surfing the act of searching for material on the World Wide Web.

Telecommunications the transmission and reception of information from point to point, via wire, radio, microwave or satellite.

3D three dimensional - an effect that gives the illusion of depth on a monitor screen or flat page.

Thumbnail a small representation of an image used mainly for identification. Thumbnails are also produced to accompany PictureCDs, PhotoCDs and most APS and 35 mm films submitted for processing.

TIFF, TIF (Tagged Image File Format) a standard and popular graphics file format used for scanned, high-resolution, bitmapped images and for colour separations. The TIFF format can be used for black-and-white, greyscale and colour images, which have been generated on different computer platforms.

Tweening an animator's term for the process of creating 'in-between' frames to fill in-between key frames in an animation.

Typeface the term (based on 'face' or the printing surface of a metal type character) describes a type design of any size, including weight variations on that design, such as light and bold, but not other related designs such as italic and condensed. As distinct from 'type family', which includes all related designs, and 'font', which is one design of a single size, weight and style. Thus 'Baskerville' is a type family, while 'Baskerville Bold' is a typeface and '9 pt Baskerville Bold Italic' is a font.

URL (Uniform Resource Locator) the unique address of every webpage on the World Wide Web. Every resource on the Internet has a unique URL.

Vector graphics images made up of mathematically defined shapes, such as circles and rectangles, or complex paths built out of mathematically defined curves. Vector graphics images can be displayed at any size or resolution without loss of quality, and are easy to edit because the shapes retain their identity, but they lack the tonal subtlety of bitmapped images. Because vector graphics files are typically small, they are well suited to web animation.

Viral marketing an Internet advertising campaign, the success of which relies on individuals sending material associated with the product, either a game, animation or video, to a number of friends, who in turn send it on to more friends, usually by email.

VoiP (Voice over Internet Protocol) is a technology that allows you to make telephone calls using a broadband Internet connection instead of a regular (or analogue) phone line.

VR (virtual reality) simulations in which the user is immersed within a computer-generated environment. VR usually involves real-time 3D animation, position tracking and stereo audio and video techniques.

VRML (Virtual Reality Modelling Language) a set of specifications and standards for creating and viewing 3D multimedia and shared virtual worlds on the World Wide Web.

Weblog see **Blog**

Webpage a published HTML document on the World Wide Web, which forms part of a website.

Web server a computer ('host') that is dedicated to web services.

Website the address, location (on a server) and collection of documents and resources for any particular interlinked set of webpages.

Window part of the 'Graphical User Interface' (GUI) of a computer, a window is an area of a computer screen that displays the contents of disk, folder or document. A window can be resized and is scrollable if the contents are too large to fit within it.

Wireframe a skeletal view of a computer-generated 3D object before the surface rendering has been applied. Also used to describe the working drawings and designs for webpages.

Workflow describes the working process and schedule of a job.

Workstation describes very powerful, single-user, computers with very high-resolution graphics, mainly used for engineering and scientific applications.

World Wide Web (WWW) the term used to describe the entire collection of web servers all over the world that are connected to the Internet. The term also describes the particular type of Internet access architecture that uses a combination of HTML and various graphic formats, such as GIF and JPEG, to publish formatted text and images that can be read by web browsers.

World Wide Web Consortium (W3C) the global organization that is largely responsible for maintaining and managing standards on the web.

Further Reading

Emile Aarts and Stefano Marzano, *The New Everyday: Views on Ambient Intelligence*, Amsterdam: 010 Publishers, 2003

Michael Bierut, William Drenttel and Steven Heller (eds), *Looking Closer 4*, New York: Allworth, 2002

Max Bruinsma, *Deep Sites: Intelligent Innovation in Contemporary Web Design*, London and New York: Thames and Hudson, 2003

Bob Cotton and Richard Oliver, *Understanding Hypermedia: From Multimedia to Virtual Reality*, London: Phaidon Press and New York: Chronicle, 1993; revised edition as *Understanding Hypermedia 2.000: Multimedia Origins, Internet Futures,* London: Phaidon Press, 1997

Hillman Curtis, *MTIV: Process, Inspiration and Practice for the New Media Designer*, Indianapolis, Indiana: New Riders Press, 2002

Maia Engeli, *Digital Stories: The Poetics of Communication*, Basel: Birkhauser, 2000

Paul Farrington, *Interactive: The Internet for Graphic Designers,* Hove, East Sussex: RotoVision, 2002

Roger Fawcett-Tang (ed.), *Mapping: An illustrated Guide to Graphic Navigational Systems,* Hove, East Sussex: RotoVision, 2002

Flips 5 Music Vs Motion, Hong Kong: Systems Design Limited, 2001

Jorge Frascara, *User-Centred Graphic Design: Mass Communications and Social Change*, London: Taylor and Francis, 1997

Gordon Graham, *The Internet: A Philosophical Inquiry*, London and New York: Routledge, 1999

Bob Hughes, *Dust or Magic: Secrets of Successful Multimedia Design,* Harlow, Essex: Addison-Wesley, 2000

Michele Jannuzzi and Richard Smith, *Thoughts on Cross-Media Design*, Mendresio, Switzerland: Gabriele Capelli Editore, 2000

Steven Johnson, *Interface Culture: How New Technology Transforms the Way We Create and Communicate*, San Francisco: HarperEdge, 1997

Robert Klanten (ed.), *3 Deluxe: Projects, Interior and Graphic Design*, Berlin: Die-Gestalten Verlag, 2002

Margot Lovejoy, *Digital Currents: Art in the Electronic Age*, London and New York: Routledge, 2004

Nico Macdonald, *What is Web Design?* Hove, East Sussex: RotoVision, 2002

Lev Manovich, *The Language of New Media*, Cambridge, Massachussetts: MIT Press, 2001

Scott McCloud, *Understanding Comics: The Invisible Art*, New York: HarperPerennial, 1994

David Muggleton and Rupert Weinzierl, *The Post-Subcultures Reader*, Oxford: Berg, 2003

Donald A. Norman, *The Design of Everyday Things*, Cambridge, Massachusetts: MIT Press, 1998

Donald A. Norman, *Emotional Design: Why We Love (or Hate) Everyday Things*, New York: Basic Books, 2004

Howard Rheingold, *Smart Mobs: The Next Social Revolution: Transforming Cultures and Communities in the Age of Instant Access*, Cambridge, Massachusetts: Perseus, 2002

Michael Rush, *New Media in Late 20th-Century Art,* London: Thames and Hudson, 1999; revised edition as *New Media in Art*, London: Thames and Hudson, 2005

Julian Stallabrass, *Internet Art: The Online Clash of Culture and Commerce*, London: Tate Publishing, 2003

Gerfried Stocker and Christine Schöpf (eds), *Timeshift: The World in Twenty-Five Years*, Ostfildern Ruit, Germany: Ars Electronica/Hatje Cantz, 2004

Edward R. Tufte, *Visual Explanations: Images and Quantities, Evidence and Narrative*, Cheshire, Connecticut: Graphics Press, 1997

Peter Wildbur and Michael Burke, *Information Graphics*, London: Thames and Hudson, 1998

Benjamin Woolley, *Virtual Worlds: A Journey in Hype and Hyperreality,* Harmondsworth and New York: Penguin Books, 1992

Matt Woolman, *Digital Information Graphics*, London: Thames and Hudson, 2002

Magazines are an invaluable resource for looking at interesting work and following creative industry trends. Those listed below often have useful illustrated tutorials with trial software on CD. They are available in the UK and Europe, the US and Australia (usually monthly)

Computer Arts
Computer Arts Projects
MacWorld
MacUser
MacFormat
Digit
3DWorld
WebDesigner
MacAdict
Communication Arts
Print
Layers
NET Magazine
Wired
iCreate
IdN Magazine (bi-monthly)
Eye (quarterly)

Websites

This list of websites is a guide to some of the services on the Internet and sites that we found interesting while researching this book. All websites are a platform for other discoveries. The websites listed were all active in spring 2007.

Computers and software

http://www.adobe.com
Adobe is one of the largest software manufacturers to the creative industries. They introduced PostScript, the page description computer language that, with the Apple Macintosh, launched desktop publishing. Their best-known applications are Adobe Photoshop, Illustrator, InDesign, Premier and more recently, Dreamweaver and Flash have joined the line-up. Fully functional 'try-out' versions of software can be downloaded from this website and used for 30 days. Adobe also develops and distributes classic and original typefaces. The annual Adobe Design Achievement Awards are open to students from art and design institutions in countries around the world.

http://www.apple.com
Apple Macintosh computers have long been the choice for many creatives. Innovative product design and operating systems have created a loyal user base. Apple also produces software such as Final Cut Pro for digital film and a suite of other software for professional and home users. Integration between the range of Macintosh computers and Apple products such as the iPod, continues to make these the favoured tools for designers and artists.

http://www.microsoft.com
Famous for its operating system Windows, which runs on most business machines, and the web browser Internet Explorer. Microsoft dominates the PC world and in recent years other software manufacturers, such as Adobe, have migrated creative applications to run on PCs as well as Macs.

General interest

http://www.nasa.gov
National Aeronautics and Space Administration

http://www.jpl.nasa.gov
Jet Propulsion Laboratory, California Institute of Technology

http://www.parc.xerox.com/about/history/default.html
XeroxPARC (Palo Alto Research Center), California

http://www.aec.at
Prix Ars Electronica Annual conference and international competition for CyberArts

http://www.siggraph.org
Annual conference for computer graphics and interactive techniques

http://www.howconference.com
Annual conference for graphic designers on creativity, business and technology

http://www.gdconf.com
Annual week-long conference for developers of computer, console, mobile, arcade and online games

http://www.publiclettering.org.uk
This site is based on a walk through central London, developed by Phil Baines for graphic design students at Central Saint Martins to observe examples of interesting public lettering.

Useful reference websites

http://www.furl.net
Furl is a free service that saves a personal copy of any page you find on the Web, and lets you find it again instantly by searching your archive of pages. You can share your archive with others.

http://www.flickr.com
Flickr is a website for storing your photographs; you can choose to make your photographs either public or private, annotate and add captions to them. You can add 'tags' and share your pictures with other users.

http://del.icio.us
Driven by personal interests and creative organization del.icio.us lets you store and bookmark your favourite webpages. By using 'tags', you can build a collaborative repository of related information to share with other users. To view everybody's bookmarks on design, visit del.icio.us/tag/design.

Design organizations

http://www.aiga.com
AIGA (American Institute of Graphic Arts)

http://www.icograda.com
The International Council of Graphic Design Associations (ICOGRADA)

http://www.agda.com.au
Australian Graphic Design Association (AGDA)

http://www.dandad.co.uk
D&AD (Design and Art Direction)

http://www.thersa.org
RSA (Royal Society of Arts)

http://www.csd.org.uk
Chartered Society of Designers

http://www.theaoi.com
Association of Illustrators, London

http://www.a-g-i.org/
Alliance Graphique Internationale

http://www.societyillustrators.org/
Society of Illustrators (New York)

http://www.typocircle.co.uk
The Typographic Circle

http://www.tdc.org
Type Directors Club (New York)

Online design resource websites

http://www.newstoday.com
http://www.netdiver.net
http://www.pixelsurgeon.com
http://www.heavy-backpack.com
http://www.k10k.net
http://www.graphicdesigngate.com
http://www.mediainspiration.com
http://www.rhizome.org
http://www.futurefarmers.com
http://www.designtalkboard.com
http://underconsideration.com

Online picture libraries

http://www.getty-images.com
Getty Images include some of the biggest collections and archives: Photodisc, Tony Stone, Hulton Archive, and more; creative, sport, archival, etc.

http://www.stockbyte.com
http://pro.corbis.com
http://www.sciencephotolibrary.co.uk
http://www.bridgeman.co.uk
http://www.maryevans.com

Reference websites and search engines

http://www.wikipedia.org
http://www.amazon.com
http://www.ebay.com
http://vivisimo.com
http://www.google.com
http://www.altavista.com
http://www.yahoo.com
http://www.hotbot.com
http://www.alltheweb.com
http://search.msn.com
http://www.baidu.cn

Design discussion websites and weblogs

http://www.designobserver.com
http://www.designers-network.com
http://www.thedesignencyclopedia.org
http://www.adbusters.org

Weblog publishing platforms

(most 'blogging' services are free but some also have 'paid for' or 'premium' upgrades)

http://www.blogger.com
http://www.sixapart.com/movabletype
http://www.wordpress.com
http://www.typepad.com
http://www.livejournal.com
http://www.xanga.com
http://noahgrey.com/greysoft

Art schools, colleges and universities

There are too many art and design schools, colleges and universities to list them all here. However, we have listed below those we have had some contact with or know of by reputation. There are two websites that list schools, one mainly for North America and the other for Europe. These may help you locate a college and a course.

http://www.artschools.com
Worldwide listing of art schools and colleges

http://www.elia.org
European art schools and colleges

http://www.arts.ac.uk
University of the Arts (UAL), London

http://www.rca.ac.uk
Royal College of Art, London (postgraduate Master's degrees only)

http://www.csm.arts.ac.uk
Central Saint Martins (UAL), London

http://www.calarts.edu
California Institute for Design (CalArts), Los Angeles

http://www.usc.edu
University of Southern California, Los Angeles

http://www.sva.edu
School of Visual Arts, New York

http://parsons.newschool.edu
Parsons The New School for Design, New York

http://www.pratt.edu
Pratt Institute, New York

http://www.saic.edu
The Art Institute of Chicago

http://www.academyart.edu
Academy of Art University, San Francisco

http://www.artcenter.edu
Art Center College of Design, Pasadena

http://www.scad.edu
Savannah College of Art and Design, Georgia

http://www1.sheridaninstitute.ca
Sheridan School of Animation, Arts and Design, Toronto

http://www.uiah.fi
University of Art and Design, Helsinki, Finland

http://www.ensad.fr
L'École Nationale Supérieure des Arts Décoratifs, Paris

http://www.cafa.edu.cn
Central Academy of Fine Arts, Beijing

http://www.artdes.monash.edu.au
Monash University, Melbourne

http://www.cofa.unsw.edu.au
College of Fine Arts, University of New South Wales, Sydney

http://www.dab.uts.edu.au
University of Technology Sydney, Faculty of Design, Sydney

http://www.rmit.edu.au/creativemedia
RMIT University, Melbourne

http://www.hed.swinburne.edu.au/design/
Swinburne University of Technology, Faculty of Design, Melbourne

http://www.anu.edu.au/ITA/CSA/
Australian National University, School of Art, Canberra

Museums

http://www.computerhistory.org
Mountain View, California

http://www.sfmoma.org
San Francisco Museum of Modern Art

http://www.moma.org
Museum of Modern Art, New York

http://www.designmuseum.org
Design Museum, London

http://www.tate.org.uk
Tate, London, Liverpool and St Ives

http://www.ica.org.uk
Institute of Contemporary Arts, London

http://www.nationalgallery.org.uk
National Gallery, London

Index

Page numbers in **bold** are for glossary definitions

A

accessibility 79–80, 100–2, 167
accountants 83
Adbusters 106
Addictive TV 57, 60
additive colour 68–9
Adobe Systems 33, 126, 128
Advanced Computing Center for the Arts and Design 123
advertising films 45–6, 137, 159–60
AGDA 153, 167
agents 156
AIGA 52, 153, 167
Airside 33, 58–60, 81, 86, 141–2, 161–2
Aldus 33, 126
aliasing **180**
All Of Us 53
Alladeen project 173
Alto 31
Amazon.com 83
analogue (meaning of) 10
Anamorph (Anderson) 46
Ananova 145
Anderson, Matt 46
Andreessen, Marc 33
animatics 69
animation, digital 44–5, 120–3, 172, **180**
Antenna Design 13, 62
antialiasing **180**
Antirom 58
Apple Macs 31–2, 33, 34, 126, 169
application **180**
ARC 29
arcade machines 138
Art+Com 55, 107
art, different from design 63
Artificialtourism 115, 165
artists, use of digital technology 106, 122–3
ASCII **180**
aspect ratio **180**
association and interpretation 76–8
attachments 112
audience research 80
    see also users
Australian Broadcasting Corporation 112
automated search engines 100–2
avatars 145, **180**
axis **180**

B

Babel 101
back-end technologist 83
Baines, Phil 13
Balaam, Tim 161
bandwidth **180**
banner **180**
Bass, Saul 28, 45, 128
Batman (film) 44
BBC, Domesday laserdisc 131

BBC website 97–9, 112
Berners-Lee, Tim 29, 32, 96, 97
binary system 14–17
bit **180**
bitmap/bitmap editors **180**
Black & White (computer game) 140
blended learning 108, 110
Blinkenlights 94, 95
Blinn, James 120
blogs (or weblogs) 30, 102–3, 167, **180**
Brainerd, Paul 126
brand(s) 83, **180**
Brassier, Anne 161
'Breadcrumbs' 67
Brell, Dieter 154
brief 63, 81–2
Brin, Sergey 102
British Film Institute 57
broadband 116
broadcast media 97–9, 104, 137, **180**
    digital broadcasting 112–13, 144
browser 30, **180**
Brucker-Cohen, Jonah 105–6
Brüllmann, Boris 58
Buch/Le Livre (Verdoux) 43
Bunnies Studio Soi 24
Bush, Vannevar 28–9
button **180**
byte **180**

C

CAD **180**
cameras, digital 50
careers in new media design 149–59
Carson, David 65–6
CD/CD-Rom 131–2, **180**
CD/DVD, of designer's work 165
cel **180**
Central Saint Martins College, website 38, 92, 177
CGI **180**
CGRG (Computer Graphics Research Group) 123
'chat bobs' 145
'chroma key' 132, 134, 135
CIG (computer-image-generation) 123
Cinefeel 57
cinema, digital effects in 134–7
'Civic Exchange' (Antenna Design) 52
classification 96
client server, definition of 30
clients 80–2, 125–6, 160, 161
clock project 158
CMYK (cyan, magenta, yellow and key) 68–9, **180**
coding 88–9
Cold War 119–20
collaboration 160–2
collective action 106
colour 68–9
colour depth **180**
Comella, Alicia 115
comics 69
commerce online 83, 113–16

commercial interests 100–2, 137–44
commercial web design 82–90
communication, new media 13–14, 99–100
communication skills 150
companies, design 151–6, 161, 163–4
company brands 83
compression **180**
CompuServe 100
computer games 39–42, 75, 137–44, 174
computer graphics 29–30
    and imaginary worlds 118–23, 145–6
    and multimedia 128–32
    and music promotion 60
    and simulation 123–5
computer-imaging: for simulation 123–5
    for visualization 120–2
computer modelling 125
computer revolution 14, 28–9
computer screens 19–20
    as page 33–4
    scale, and onscreen display 66
    as virtual physical space 35
computer-imaging 120–5
computers: in design process 92, 169
    first portable PC 31–2
concept stage 85
consumers 113–14, 116
content, and layout 66
content management system 87
content strategist 83
continuity 71
Cooper, Kyle 45
Cooper, Ross 158
cooperative web-based activity 102–7
copyright **180**
costs of production 69–71, 85, 162
creative director 83
creative process, of web design 85–9
cross platform **180**
cross-media design 127, 144, 177
Cross-Media Publishing System 127
CSD 153
CSS 30, 66, **180**
Csuri, Charles 122–3
Cuban Missile Crisis 119–20
'culture jamming' 106
cursor **180**
Curtis, Hillman, *MTIV (Making the Invisible Visible)* 82
customer-led sites 114
customers 113–14, 116
CVs 168–9
cyber-personalities 137, 145
cyberspace 93, 97, **180**

D

D&AD 167
Dadaism 28
data **180**
    collection of 102
    searches 97, 99

visualization 47–9
   see also information; Internet
databases 18, **180**
DataCloud 115
Davis, Don 121, 122
deadlines 159–60
Deakin, Fred 58, 161
design: different from art 63
   education and training in 41–2, 142, 162–3
   interactive 115, 141–2
   see also graphic design; new-media graphic design
design brief 63, 81–2
design process 80–5, 125–8, 150
desktop publishing 32, 126–8
DHTML **181**
digital **181**
digital broadcasting 112–13, 144
digital effects industry 132–7
digital photography 50–2
digital technologies 14–18, 126–8
   see also print-based and digital technologies
digital tools, drawing 42
digital TV 13
digitize/digitization 27, **181**
distance learning 108–10
DNS **181**
Domesday laserdisc (BBC) 131
Donkey Kong 41, 137
Dorling Kindersley 33
dotcom boom 114
download **181**
DPI **181**
drawing skills 42, 67
Dreamcatcher project 175
DVD/DVD-Rom 132, 165, **181**
Dwiggins, William Addison 2

E
Eames, Charles and Ray 128, 130
eBay 24, 114
e-commerce 83, 113–16, **181**
e-learning 108–10
education: in design 41–2, 142, 162–3
   e-learning 108–10
   Internet access to 98–9, 107
   multimedia applications for 131–2
electronic artefacts 1
Elliman, Paul 164
Elsner, Tom 37, 38, 173
email 111–12, **181**
embedded networks 96
'emotioneering' tools 145
Englebart, Douglas 29
entertainment 132
Entropia Universe 40
environment, physical 95–6
EPS **181**
Evans, David 123
Evans & Sutherland 123–5
Exceeda 58
exhibition spaces 56, 107, 141–2, 145–6, 160

exhibitions, of designers' work 156, 165
experience design 52–6
experimental graphic work 154
extranet 111, **181**
eye-tracking system 55

F
FAQ **181**
'feeds' 134
Fetter, William A. 29
File Transfer Protocol *see* FTP
films 107, 134–7, 144
   advertising films 45–6, 137, 159–60
financial transactions, online 83
firewall **181**
flash **181**
flashlight, for interactive navigation 53
Flickr 105
flight simulators 123–5
floatingnumbers (2003) 55
flowchart **181**
'fly-through' experiences 107
focus groups 88, 89
font 26, **181**
4Corners 112
FPSs **181**
frame rate **181**
freelancing 156–9, 162
Friendster 105
front-end technologist 83, 88–9
FTP 30, 112

G
galleries 56, 107, 141–2, 145–6
games 39–42, 75, 137–44, 174
games designers 141–2, 144, 174
games machines 13
gaming genres 142, 144
Garcia-Perate, Gonzalo 115
gateways (or 'portals') 100
genre definition, of games 142, 144
Gibson, William, *Neuromancer* 93
GIF **181**
gigabyte **181**
'God' games 138, 140
Google 100, 102
Google Earth 95
Grand Theft Auto 41, 75
graphic design 9, 28, 33–5, 78, 93
   see also design; new-media graphic design
Greiman, April 20
greyscale **181**
grids 64, 65
GUI 31, 99, **181**
guidelines: for writing CVs 169
   style guidelines 76–8

H
Harris, Jane 172
Haslam, Rik 164
HCI 34, 79, 99

Heartfield, John 28
Hellboy 44
hinting 27
hoax interventions 106
Holzman, Bob 120
homepage(s) 87, 102, **181**
Horniman Museum 160
'hotspots' 95
HTML **181**
HTTP **181**
human-motion capture 145
Hummingbird (film) (Csuri) 122
Hunter, Nat 161
Hyperkit 76, 161
hyperlinks 19, 79
hypermedia 29, 31, **181**
hypertext 29, **181**

I
IBM 47, 48
ICOGRADA 153
'icon' 67, 68, **181**
identity, personal 102
illustration, digital 42–4, 67–8
images 35, 68–9, 171
   picture searches 52
imagination 76
imaginary worlds *see* virtual worlds
'in-betweening' 122
independent learning 108, 110
information: online 95–100
   traditional collections of 96
   and use of multimedia 128–32
   and visual sensation 78
information architect 83, 99, 110
information design 67
information storage 18–19
information visualization 47–9
inputting 48
inspiration 76
installations 56, 141–2, 145–6
interactive: computer games 141–2, 142–3
   design 115, 141–2, 154
   websites 161–2
Interactive Institute, Stockholm 53
interactivity/interactive 11–14, 48, 52–6, 128–31, **181**
interface **181**
Internet 28–9, 35
   definitions of 30, 93, **181**
   design skills for 173
   educational uses of 98–9, 107, 108–10
   history of 93–100
   multimedia applications for 132
   picture searches on 52
   as platform for self-publicity 153
   routes into 100–2
   social space of 102–7
   virtual worlds in 76, 100, 107
   see also web design; websites
Internet 2.0 (or Web 2.0) 30

Internet banking 114
internships 163
interpolation **181**
interpretation and association 76–8
intranet 110–11, **181**
Invisible Shape of Things Past (Art+Com) 107
IT **181**
ITV **181**
Iwai, Toshio 35

J
'Jam: Tokyo/London' exhibition 141–2
Jannuzzi Smith (consultants) 38–9, 177
Java **181**
JavaScript **181**
The Jew of Malta (opera) 55
jobs *see* work
JPEG/JPG **182**
JPL Computer Graphics Lab 120

K
ka-chew! 71, 72
Karlén, Per José 74
Kay, Alan 31
kerning 27
key concept 86
key frames **182**
kilobyte **182**
King Arthur 44
Kitching, Alan 24
Kurzweil, Ray (aka Ramona) 145

L
Land Design Studio 92
Landor 153
LANS 110
Lara Croft 137, 138, 144, 145
laserdiscs 131
LaserWriter 33, 126
Lauhoff, Andreas and Stephan 154, 161
layout 64, 65–6, 87
learning *see* education
Levin, Brian 36
libraries 96
Licko, Zuzana 33
'lifelong learning' 110
Light Surgeons 24, 59, 60, 118
linear narrative 75
links 19, 79, 102
Lionhead Studios 140, 174
'live' information 48
location-based graphic interventions 95
location-based information systems 95
location-based mobile communities 102–7
logo **182**
Lord of the Rings trilogy (film) 44, 135
LPI **182**
Lüsebrink, Dirk 55

M
McCloud, Scott, *Understanding Comics* 69

Macintosh computers 31–2, 33, 34, 126, 169
McKean, Dave 42
Maclean, Alex 161
Maeda, John 36
'Mailing lists' 112
The Man with the Golden Arm (film) 45
Manz, Christian 164, 171, 178
maps/mapping 47–8
  of cyberspace 97
  printed maps 95
  site maps 87
market research 82, 144
marketing 113–16, 156–9, 163
Mario 41, 137
Martin, Andy 42
The Matrix (film) 44, 135
'matte' 135
measurement, typographic 26
megabyte **182**
Mellowtrons 58
memory **182**
menu **182**
metadata **182**
meta-tags 100, 102
Meta.L.Hyttan project 53
Mies typeface 38
MMOG 75
MMORPG 40
'mobile Internet' 95
mobile phones 138, 142
modelling, computer 125
modernism 28
Molyneux, Peter 140
Moriwaki, Katherine 106
Mosaic 33, 132
motion capture 135, 145
motion graphic 45–7
movement, new-media techniques 73–5
moving images 171
MPEG **182**
MTIV (Making the Invisible Visible) (Curtis) 82
multi-disciplinary groups 154
multimedia 128–32, **182**
  cross-media design 144, 177
multiplayer games 40
museums *see*, exhibition spaces
music, and motion graphics 45–6
music graphics 57–60

N
Nakamura, Yugo 36, 141
narrative 74–6
NASA missions 120–2
Nelson, Ted 29
network visualization 48
network(s) **182**
  embedded 96
  social 102–7, 156, 164
  wireless 95
Neurath, Otto 130

Neuromancer (Gibson) 93
new media, characteristics of 11–20
new-media design companies 153–6, 161
new-media graphic design 21
  careers in 149–59, 171–8
  vocabularies and techniques 63–80
  see also design; graphic design
Nielsen, Jakob 37, 78
Nike 84
Nintendo 138
NoDNA 145
Norman, Donald A. 19, 78

O
old media 10–11
  see also print-based and digital technologies
online **182**
online communities 104–5
online financial transactions 83
online information 99–100
online marketing 113–16, 159
online portfolios 159, 164, 167
'open content' 105
open-source software 104–5
operating system (OS) **182**
optical-storage media 131

P
Page, Larry 102
page(s): computer screens as 33–4
  data collection from 102
  design guidelines for 78
  homepage 87
partnerships 159
PayPal 114
PDF **182**
Pentagram 151
performance art 55, 63
personal computer *see* computers; Macintosh
  computers
personal identity 102
photography 50–2, 95
photo libraries 52
photomontage 28
physical environment 95–6
picture searches 52
pitch 80, 81
pixel **182**
players: of computer games 142–3, 144
  see also users
plug-in **182**
podcasts 30, 112
political use of Internet 106
Pong 41, 73, 137
pornography, internet 106
portable games consoles 138
portable media players 13
'portals' (or gateways) 100
portfolios 159, 164, 165–8, 167
post-production 44, 153
PostScript 26, 33, 126, **182**

PowerPoint presentations 85–6
PPI **182**
pre-digital films 45
presentations, commercial 85–6
print-based and digital technologies: compared 35, 89–90, 92, 95, 99, 118
computerization of print-based 126
old media 10–11
production costs 160, 162
use of scale 66
printing, historical overview of 25–8
product design 63
production constraints 69–71, 85, 159–60, 162
professional associations 153, 167
program/programming **182**
prototyping 76
Prucha, Milan 175
publishing: desktop 32, 126–8
personal 102–4

Q
qualities, of designers 148–51, 171–8
QuarkXPress 128
QuickTime/QuickTime VR **182**

R
radio, BBC website 98, 112
RAM **182**
Ramona (*aka* Ray Kurzweil) 145
Rand, Paul 24
rasterize **182**
raytracing **182**
real time 48, **182**
Renard, Nathalie 72
rendering **182**
resolution **182**
RGB (red, green and blue) 68–9, 78, **182**
Rheingold, Howard, *Smart Mobs* 95
Rhizome 101
rich media content 30
robots 145
role-playing games 75
Rom and Son 48, 58, 160
RSS 112
Rules of Play (Salen and Zimmerman) 141
Russell, Steve 138

S
Salen, Katie 141
'sandbox' games 75
satellite photography 95
Sauter, Joachim 55
scanning **182**
Scient 87
Schweiger, Nikolaus 154
Sclater, Kate 161
Scott, Ridley 137
screens *see* computer screens
screensavers, corporate 48
Seal, David 121
search engine(s) 30, 100–2

search sites 102
searches: information searches 97, 99
picture searches 52
Second Life 76, **182**
Sega Megadrive 138
self-publicity 153, 164–9
self-training 164
sequence 69–71
Se7en (film), title sequence 45
'shareware' 105
Shaughnessy, Adrian 164
Shirky, Clay 106
The Sims 41, 75, 143
simulation 123–5, **182**
site map 87
site-specific communication 95
'sketches', screen-based 85
skills, of designers 150–1, 171–8
drawing skills 42, 67
Smart Mobs (Rheingold) 95
social space 102–7
software 46, 66, 122, 141, 169, **183**
'web crawlers' 100
Sonic the Hedgehog 137, 138
Sony PlayStation 138
sound: BBC radio website 98, 112
and image 35
motion graphics 45–6
and new-media graphic design 63, 73
text-to-speech 145
soundmaps 176
'source books' 159
space race 120–2
SPACE software 122
space/time concepts 107
Spacewars 138
spoken word, text-to-speech 145
sponsored links 102
Star Wars: Attack of the Clones (film) 135
Star Wars Galaxies 40, 137, 143
static media 10–11
Sternbach, Rick 122
stories (narrative) 74–6
storyboards 69
streaming video/audio **183**
Studio AKA 69, 172
studios *see* work and working environments
style guides 76–8
'style sheet' 165
surfing **183**
suntractive colour 68–9
Sutherland, Ivan 29, 120, 123–5
Swiss Style 28

T
tables 66
Tankard, Jeremy 27
teams 83, 160–1
'tear sheets' 159
telecommunications **183**
television 98, 112–13

digital 132, 134, 144
template(s) 87, 122
testing 27, 88–9
text-based communication 93
text-to-speech 145
theatre 55, 63
Theban Mapping Project 107
theme parks 145–6
3D **183**
3deluxe 154–5
thumbnail 68, **183**
TIFF/TIF **183**
time: and production 71, 159–60
'real time' information 48
Titanic (film) 135
Tomb Raider games 137, 138, 144
traditional print technologies *see* print-based and digital technologies
training *see* education
Tschichold, Jan, *Die Neue Typographie* 28
Tufte, Edward, *Visual Explanations* 47
Turing, Alan 29
Turkle, Sherry 102
tweening **183**
typeface 26, 35, 38, **183**
typography 25–8

U
'ubiquitous' computing 96
Umbrella.net 106
Understanding Comics (McCloud) 69
URBIS visitor centre 56, 146
URL **183**
Usability 78–80, 88–9
usage 27
user-centred design 80
user-interface designer 83
users: of computer games 142–3, 144
of computer-generated animation 122, 125
consumers as 113–14, 116
and experience design 52
and the HCI 34, 79
of Intranets 111
of new media 19
and usability 78–80, 88–9
see also interactivity

V
vector graphics **183**
Verdoux, Jeanne 9, 43
vidcasts 113
video-sharing networks 112
viral marketing **183**
virtual characters 145
Virtual graphic design studio 125–8, 167
virtual learning environments 108, 110
virtual worlds 76, 100, 107, 143, 175
and computer graphics 118–23, 145–6
visual flair 150
visual flight simulators 123–5
visual music systems 35

visual sensation, and information 78
visualization: computer-imaging 120–2
    of information 47–9
VJing (video jockeying) 58
VLEs (virtual learning environments) 108, 110
VoiP **183**
Voyager space missions 120–2
VR **183**
VRML **183**

W
weather mapping 115
'web crawlers' ('web spiders') 100
web design 37–9, 66, 82–90, 99–100, 16
    see also Internet; websites
web page **183**
web server **183**
webcams 158
webcasts 112
websites: designers' own 156, 164, 167
    and digital broadcasting 112
    for discovery and learning 97–9, 107, 109
    example of good design 38
    guidelines for effective 78
    of online communities 104–6
    strategy for 90
    see also Internet; web design
Why Not Associates 129
Wieden + Kennedy 151
Wikipedia 104
wikis 104
window **183**
wireframe 87, 122, **183**
wireless networks 95
Wolff Olins 153
work and working 151–9, 162–4
    virtual graphic design studio 125–8, 167
workflow 159–60, **183**
World Wide Web (WWW) 97
World Wide Web Consortium (W3C) **183**
WPP Group 151–3
WWW (World Wide Web) 30, 32–3, 97, **183**
WYSIWYG 31, 128

X
Xerox Corporation 30–1
Xerox Parc 31

Y
Yeast 59
Yesmen 106

Z
Zajac, Edward 30
Zerseher (De Viewer) (Sauter and Lüsebrink) 55
Zimmerman, Eric 141

Picture Sources and Credits

Every effort has been made to contact all copyright holders, but should there be any errors or omissions, Laurence King Publishing Ltd would be pleased to insert the appropriate acknowledgement in any subsequent printing of this publication.

Acknowledgements

Thanks to Jo Lightfoot and Robert Shore at Laurence King who commissioned and edited this book, to Dani Salvadori, Thembi Morris-Hale, Ishbel Neat and Sabine Gottfried at Central Saint Martins for their help and support in preparing this book.

Thanks too to all those we consulted and to our colleagues at Central Saint Martins, University of the Arts London and the Royal College of Art for their forbearance and understanding. Also to the students at both colleges for their inspiration. To the numerous companies and individuals in the design and new media industries who helped us assemble the contents of this book.

Special thanks are due to our collaborators; Charles Hayes, Steve Radmall, Amelia Noble, Andreas Lauhoff, Marc Silver, Peter Higgins, Michaele Januzzi, Richard Smith, Joe Stephenson, Ross Cooper, Gonzalo Garcia-Perate and Alicia Comelia, Axel Vogelsang, Golan Levin, Tobi Schneidler, Fred Deakin, Joachim Sauter, Christain Manz, Anthony Burrell, Kip Parker, Tom Elsner, Lev Manovich, Max Bruinsma, Tim Balaam and Kate Sclater, Andy Altmann, Alan Kitching, Tyrone Messiah, Jonathan Warner, Avril Hodges, Nathalie Rennard, Jeanne Verdoux, Sophie Clemments, Andreas Gaschka, Ziva Moskric, Peter Molineux, Milan Prucha, Philip Hunt, Catlin Smail, Lewis Blackwell, Hugh Rickard, Jeremy Tankard, Toby Glover, César Harada, Per Karlén, Thea Swayne, Julian House, Mat Cook, Rufus Kahler, Robert Charlton, Tobi Schneidler, Leon Williams, Sam Doust, Christopher Neve, Russell Lowe, and to the contributors and designers whose work appears in the book. We apologise to anyone we have omitted. If we have missed you, let us know and we will put things right in the future.

Finally, thanks to our closest friends and families who put up with our long hours at our computers and on the phone, and are somehow still smiling!

Dedication
Our partners, Alan and Sally.